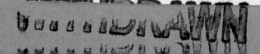

A Primer of Ignorance

The Lion and the Honeycomb
Language as Gesture
The Expense of Greatness
The Double Agent
Form and Value in Modern Poetry
Eleven Essays in the European Novel

The Good European, *and other poems*
The Second World
From Jordan's Delight

R. P. BLACKMUR

A PRIMER
OF IGNORANCE

Edited by Joseph Frank

Harcourt, Brace & World, Inc., New York

The essays in Part Two and Part Three first appeared separately in *The
Kenyon Review, The Sewanee Review,* and *The Yale Review.*

Excerpts from *The Letters of Henry James,* edited by Percy Lubbock
(copyright 1920 by Charles Scribner's Sons; renewal copyright 1948 by
William James and Margaret James Porter), are reprinted with the permission of Charles Scribner's Sons; excerpts from *Letters of Henry Adams,*
edited by Worthington C. Ford, are reprinted by permission of Houghton
Mifflin Company; the poem "Medallion" by Ezra Pound, from *Personae*
(copyright 1926, 1954 by Ezra Pound) is reprinted by permission of the
publishers, New Directions Publishing Corporation and Faber and Faber
Ltd; excerpts from T. S. Eliot's "East Coker," in *Four Quartets* (copyright,
1943, by T. S. Eliot), and "The Waste Land," in *Collected Poems 1909–1962*
(copyright 1936 by Harcourt, Brace & World, Inc., copyright © 1963, 1964
by T. S. Eliot) are reprinted by permission of Harcourt, Brace & World,
Inc. and Faber and Faber Ltd; excerpts from William Butler Yeats's "A
Deep-Sworn Vow," from *The Wild Swans at Coole* (copyright 1919 by The
Macmillan Company; renewed 1946 by Bertha Georgie Yeats), and "Leda
and the Swan," from *The Tower* (copyright 1928 by The Macmillan Com-
pany; renewed 1956 by Georgie Yeats) are reprinted with the permission of
The Macmillan Company; the same excerpts, from *Collected Poems of
W. B. Yeats,* are used by permission of Mr. M. B. Yeats and Macmillan &
Co. Ltd.

Preface

Before his death in February 1965, R. P. Blackmur had often mentioned the title of a volume of essays which was to follow his *Eleven Essays in the European Novel*. This succeeding volume was to be called *A Primer of Ignorance*—a title that went back to a long-nourished plan of Blackmur to write a book about the American cultural situation vis-à-vis Europe.

In a letter to his old friend John Marshall of the Rockefeller Foundation (June 27, 1955), Blackmur outlines the idea for this proposed volume as being a response to such questions as: "What does America look like abroad to American eyes sharpened by European spectacles? How does Europe affect the form—the knowledge of the form—in which America declares her identity and the possibilities of her action? I take it that form is the limiting principle by which a thing is itself."

The letter continues: "You will remember that it struck me at the Columbia conference on The Unity of Knowledge last fall that the Europeans present showed vastly superior force of mind to the Americans and you will remember I quoted Robert Oppenheimer's response to my comment on this that it was Rome and Greece all over again. The more I reflect, the more forcible this statement seems. If America does not display force of mind she certainly exhibits great momentum. How is it possible to relate the force of momentum with the force of mind? How do these forces transform one into the other—in education, professional life and in politics taken as culture?" After some further paragraphs outlining the travel plans necessary to gather material for such a book, Blackmur says that he regards the work "—and here is my title—as *A Primer of Ignorance* with the *Primer* pronounced either way—yours as well as mine and everyone's who will read."

This work was never written in the form suggested here, but the stimulus of these questions continued to preoccupy Blackmur and to dominate many of his later essays. Hence, some years later, the title shifted to become that of a volume of essays which are described in some notes by William B. Goodman, Blackmur's editor at Harcourt, Brace. On April 2, 1963, Mr. Goodman transcribed the following results of a conversation with Blackmur at the latter's home in Princeton.

"A book to be called *A Primer of Ignorance*," Mr. Goodman writes. "The book would begin with his four 1956 Library of Congress lectures: 'Anni Mirabiles, 1921-1925: Reason in the Madness of Letters' and would include 'The Swan in Zurich' (Yale Review, 1958), a piece on the Roman catacombs, another on Allen Tate, and a final piece, 'The Lovely American Princess, Sub-Category Bitch, and Her Homely Husband.' The last three to be written for the book. All these pieces respond to themes and pathologies in American culture."

The present volume of essays remains substantially faithful to this plan outlined by R. P. Blackmur himself. The essay on the Roman catacombs was never written, nor, alas! was the savory project of an essay on "The Lovely American Princess,

Sub-Category Bitch" ever carried to completion. All the other works that Blackmur mentions as destined for *A Primer of Ignorance*, however, are included. To round out the volume, I have taken the liberty of including other essays by Blackmur— printed in magazines but never before collected for a book— which clearly deal with "themes and pathologies in American culture," or which center on the same complex of issues that inspired the original idea for *A Primer of Ignorance*.

JOSEPH FRANK

July, 1966

Contents

CONTENTS

Part Three
AMERICAN WITNESSES

Part One

ANNI MIRABILES
1921-1925

REASON IN THE
MADNESS OF LETTERS

(Library of Congress Lectures, 1956)

1

The Great Grasp of Unreason

δικαίων ἀδίκους φρένας

The unjust minds of the just

IT IS ALWAYS a help to speak from a text, and it seems even necessary—in looking at twentieth-century literature, so huge and amorphous a mass it is—to use two, or even three texts in order to limit our approach to the literature and to suggest a governing theme in our response to it. With our texts in mind, we can then set about further limitations—I will not say screening or testing—as to what examples of the literature we can best use to illustrate the theme. Other texts would suggest other themes and other limitations in example, and I expect our own would be much modified in their presence. I hope our own will be interesting enough to complement the order and significance of what lurks in the minds of others—or indeed in your own. This is, I think, an application in the field of literary criticism of the principle of indeterminacy, the principle of complementary variable relations; but I do not look for so much advantage from it here in criticism as it has shown in physics and mathematics. I hope only that the principle will seem vivid with possibility. Indeterminacy is life.

Here are my texts, and as it does not matter in what order they come, the most familiar shall be first. It is from *King Lear* and is an aside interjected by Edgar into a long speech by Lear to serve as dramatic punctuation—like a rest in music—while the King is gathering breath in the long late rush of his being.

> O! Matter and impertinency mix'd;
> Reason in madness.

It is a curious thing that we might not ourselves see any madness in Lear's words were it not for Edgar's aside. We might rather see the poetic mind at its ancient task of coping with, responding to, and acknowledging all the irrational horror and injustice and disorder of human behavior. We would see reason at work: we would see what Sophocles calls in the *Antigone* "the unjust minds of the just." Still, it is reason in madness. The scholar who edits my copy of *King Lear* (Kenneth Muir, Arden Edition, London, 1952, p. LX) complains of another scholar (Schücking) with regard to our text that he "seems to be only partly aware of the paradox that Lear when ostensibly sane cannot distinguish between Cordelia and her wicked sisters: he acquires wisdom by going mad, and his wildest speeches are a mixture of matter and impertinency— 'reason in madness.'" I would complain against both my scholars only this far, and chiefly in the interest of looking at the literature of our own times—of which, of course, we want to make *King Lear* a part. Was it not by releasing himself from the bonds of both institutional and personal reason that Lear renewed in himself the task of reason? Reason is in substance all the living memory of the mind; in action (or, if you like, in essence) reason is the recognition and creation of order where disorder was. It is Edgar's aside that sees that this is what Lear was doing. Reason in madness.

4

Our second text is only less familiar than the first, and is like unto it because it enlightens it in terms of our own interest by setting us in our own time—or in a kind of minus version of our own time where we see where we are not as well as where we are. This is from part five of Eliot's "East Coker" Quartet:

So here I am, in the middle way, having had twenty years—
Twenty years largely wasted, the years of l'entre deux guerres—
Trying to learn to use words, and every attempt
Is a wholly new start, and a different kind of failure
Because one has only learnt to get the better of words
For the thing one no longer has to say, or the way in which
One is no longer disposed to say it. And so each venture
Is a new beginning, a raid on the inarticulate
With shabby equipment always deteriorating
In the general mess of imprecision of feeling,
Undisciplined squads of emotion. And what there is to conquer
By strength and submission, has already been discovered
Once or twice, or several times, by men whom one cannot hope
To emulate—but there is no competition—
There is only the fight to recover what has been lost
And found and lost again and again: and now, under conditions
That seem unpropitious. But perhaps neither gain nor loss.
For us, there is only the trying. The rest is not our business.

This is Eliot mixing, like Lear in Edgar's ears, matter and impertinence, and finding reason in the madness that grasps him all about. This the very last lines of the poem make plain in the way that the flushing movement of breath makes plain there is life.

Through the dark cold and the empty desolation,
The wave cry, the wind cry, the vast waters
Of the petrel and the porpoise. In my end is my beginning.

In the long part of these quotations Eliot generalizes the pursuit of reason in madness; in the last lines—where he puts together the incarnation of reason and the beautiful and dreadful partial and always changing incarnation of behavior, the petrel and the porpoise—he exemplifies it. Matter and impertinence.

The third text has a kind of official familiarity, which we would redeem out of natural piety and because it both generalizes and exemplifies our theme; thus it needs to be quoted in two English versions. Here is a recent version of the *Antigone* 610-614: "Through the future and distant time to come, as through the past, this law will prevail, working not without calamity for the lives of men throughout this citied world." (Goheen, *The Imagery of Sophocles' Antigone*, Princeton, 1951.) The earlier version of Jebb and Pearson gives for the sense of the last phrase: "Nothing that is vast enters the life of men without a curse" (cited *idem*, p. 143). Jebb died in 1905 and his version reflects Victorian predilections about fate and says nothing about the *hyperbasia* or transgression, and therefore involvement by man in his fate which is present in the later version. This is one of the differences between the age before 1914 and our own; if our age does not understand the difference, our writers have understood it very well. Human behavior has gotten conspicuously into the second version in much the same way it had gotten into *King Lear* and *The Four Quartets*. It is the unreason of behavior that grasps reason to the quick: reason in madness.

So much for our three texts. I should like to think that the ode from the *Antigone* sang the praises—the precious belief—of the literature of our own citied world.

The great advantage of these texts is that they come after the literature they are intended to illuminate and yet also link them to the past, and they both illuminate and link by their power as images set side by side with our literature and our lives. A later time will perhaps want different texts and will see a different literature from the point of view of a different mind —which will make a judgment more nearly right from their point of view but could not correct what we see and what we respond to; we can only look at what is in front of us, with the aid of our own sense of the past and with our own lives, towards a particular future. Who knows, it may be the next age will not express itself in words (in the sense that words are poetry, that art is poetry) at all, for the next age may not be literate in any sense we understand or that the last three thousand years understood. Poetry may yet become an even more secret craft than it was during the dream of the dark ages; and indeed there is a promise of this in the very struggle towards difficulty our poetry shows, and in the very refusal it makes to come to terms with the leading features of the actual mind of the society which confronts it. This is the struggle between the old literacy and the new illiteracy, which is not ignorance but fragmented and specialized knowledge.

Toynbee has a passage of reason and madness in *A Study of History* which bears on this.

The bread of Universal Education is no sooner cast upon the waters of social life than a shoal of sharks rises from the depths and devours the children's bread under the philanthropists' eyes. In the educational history of England, for example, the dates speak for themselves. Universal compulsory gratuitous education was inaugurated in this country in A.D. 1870; the Yellow Press was invented some twenty years later—as soon as the first generation of children from the national schools had come into the labour market and acquired some purchasing power—by a stroke of irresponsible genius which had divined that the educational philanthropists' labour of love could be made to yield the newspaper king a royal profit.

The effects of free education and the Yellow Press in our field —at any rate their concomitants—were Art for Art's sake and the *Yellow Book* and the long series of increasingly intransigent declarations of independence on the part of the arts which have lasted, with diminishing intellectual force, and an increasing lack of that coherence of images which we call verisimilitude, even after the Second World War. But Toynbee has something else to say about another aspect of our society, which perhaps explains the relaxation of our educational policy, and which is also pertinent to our poetry.

Our Western scientific knowledge of which we boast, and even our Western technique for turning this knowledge to practical account —a technique upon which we depend for our wealth and strength—

is perilously esoteric. The great new social forces of Democracy and Industrialism, which our Western Civilization has thrown up in the course of its growth, have been evoked from the depths by a tiny creative minority. Even this minority is wondering today whether it will be able to control and guide much longer these forces which it has let loose. . . . And the main reason why this would-be Western Salt of the Earth is in fear, today, of losing its savour is because the great mass of the Western body social has remained unsalted. . . . In the latter-day perversion of our Western Press, we see the "drive" of Western Industrialism and Democracy being employed to keep the mass of Western Humanity culturally depressed at, or perhaps even below, its pre-industrial and pre-democratic spiritual level; and the same new "drive" has been put, with similar evil consequences, into the old institutions of War and Tribalism and Slavery and Property. [III, 241]

First, I would remind you that this passage, like the other, was written in the thirties at the safest possible distance between the two wars, and has in no wise lost its applicability. Second, so that it may apply the more closely, I would suggest that we substitute the word "poetic" for the word "scientific" in the first sentence quoted above. "Our Western *poetic* knowledge of which we boast, and even our Western technique for turning this knowledge to practical account . . . is perilously esoteric." Does it not read well enough for Toynbee, and, to the present purpose, much better for ourselves? For we have not only an enormous increase in potential or required audience but also a diminution, relatively if not absolutely, in the means of reaching, let alone controlling, that audience. So put, we see at once how the new knowledges, so managed, so esoteric, have been reflected in the habit and superficial character of poetry and the poet himself. He has found himself speaking a private language and has grown proud of it.

What else could the writer do but invent a vital dogma of self-sufficiency?—and I do not say he was not right in doing so. Faced with the dissolution of thought and the isolation of the artist, faced with the new industrialization of intellect, what else could he do but declare his independence and self-sufficient supremacy both as intellectual and as artist? Let us admit the new independence came partly out of the old claims for and defenses of poetry from Aristotle through Shelley, partly from the nineteenth-century claims made by Ruskin and Arnold, all of which allied art deeply to society, but partly —and this is the biggest emotional part—from the blow of the First World War and what seemed the alienation of the artist from a society increasingly less aesthetically-minded—less interested in the vivid apprehension of the values of the individual. It is when you have lost, or think you are about to lose, the objective recognition of your values, that you assert them most violently and in their most extreme form—as every unrequited lover knows. You either go into the desert, kill yourself, pull your shell over your head, or set up in a new business: in any case, whether lover or artist, being as conspicuous as possible about it. To be either a dandy or dirty, and especially where out of keeping, is always a good role; and to be an anchorite or an oracle combines the advantages of both. You are in any case among enemies.

A Russian socialist, Georgi Plekhanov, thought this sort of attitude develops when artists feel a "hopeless contradiction between their aims and the aims of the society to which they belong. Artists must be very hostile to their society and they must see no hope of changing it." But let us put it one more way—as near neutral as possible. It has always been difficult to pay for art out of the running expenses of any form of society, and it has become unusually difficult under finance-capitalism (or any current money-based form of democracy) to find a means to go beyond the economy or find a special privy-purse. Also, it has always been difficult to find a sure or satisfactory audience for the living artist; and this has become increasingly difficult in societies like our own where education has become both universal and largely technical—at any rate less generalizably literate—and which has at the same time enormously multiplied the number of its artists. So, too, it has always been difficult for the artist to find the means of expressing his own direct apprehension of life in conventions which were, or could

9

be made, part of the conventions of society in general; and this, also—this problem of communication—has become excessively difficult in a society which tends to reject the kind of faithful conventions under which the artist has usually worked, and a society in which, under the urban process, and under the weight of the new knowledges, so much of thought has been given over to mechanism which had formerly operated under faith. These are the conditions under which the artist has felt, in his exaggeration of them, isolated and has asserted himself under the general state of mind that runs from art for art's sake through surrealism to *Existenz*—It is no wonder. Yet it was Coleridge who, as reported in *Table Talk*, put the matter most succinctly—there were, he said, three silent revolutions in the history of England: "When the professions fell off from the Church; when literature fell off from the professions; and when the press fell off from literature." I will not say what the fourth silent revolution is: it is ours, and now going on.

But if we cannot name the fourth revolution we can discern some of its features in a sketch of some of the materials that go to make up our immediate intellectual history. We can touch on some of the conditions and forces of our minds. We can look into our fictions to see what gave them idiom. Idiom is the twist of truth, the twist, like that of the strands of a rope, which keeps its component fictions together. History is old and twisted beyond our reach in time. But the sense of moving background which we call history began to grow with Gibbon and we began to feel it imperative in the last ninety years—or since the war of 1870. We now take into account the extremes of several forms of time as part of our history which had not got much into history before that date—time outside the chronicle and the chronometer alike. We have time in anthropology, ethnology, mythology, psychology, physics, and mathematics, and as a response to these times we have changed our heroes.

Politics began to pretend a century and a half ago that the good society had no hero but itself, and did so on the conviction that the old heroes were malevolent. As the old Chinese believed, a great man was a national calamity. About 1870 two opposed heroic shapes were thrown up by society: the artist as hero and the heroic proletariat. Mussolini, Hitler, Stalin came to represent the hero (by dictatorship) of the scum of the earth. The scum on the pond is the reimagined primeval slime, and we are nothing if we are not primeval. In psychoanalysis we regurgitate the scum, only to discover it inexhaustible. Taboos become totems. St. Francis of Assisi becomes Vicar of our scummiest behavior. Society takes on the aspect of uniform motion. The artist is the hero who struggles against uniform motion, a struggle in marmalade.

For the artist regards uniform motion as the last torpor of life. Torpor is the spread of momentum, but we prefer to believe it is the running down of things. For three generations we have heroized the second law of thermodynamics, which is the law of the dissipation or gradual unavailability of energy within any system—which is the law of entropy or the incapacity for fresh idiom, time and perception going backwards. Entropy, from the point of view of the rational imagination, is disorder and is indeed its field. Actually, we have been as busy, as violent, and as concentrated as the ant-heap. We are torpid only because we are glutted with energy and feel it only as trouble. The strains are out of phase with each other and we have techniques only for the troubles.

If we say this sort of thing as example—and we could say so much more—are we not the first age which is self-conscious of its own fictions; and hence the first age of true Pyrrhonism: doubting the value as well as the fact? We believe only in the techniques of manipulating and counting. Not in choice, not in the imperative, chiefly in opinion. Thus we believe in the analysis of conduct as a means of discounting behavior, in the drum-majorette of fourteen as a means of showing sex as force without having to take account of it.

Our age is full of great hymns to the puerile, what in medicine and art are called images of fundamental frustration. If you look in the Oxford dictionary, all the early meanings of frustration were positive. You frustrated villainy, which was desirable. Now we frustrate our own good, and we lend Hamlet our own frustrations. In the history of the word there is part of the history of our psyche. When we recognize frustration as a *fundamental* condition of life, it ought no longer to be frustration, but fate, tragedy, damnation, the Cross, the other side of every infatuation. But we would not think we expressed ourselves if we said so.

Here one does not exactly ask if we are to have a deliberate resurrection of the dark ages, one only looks in the closet and under the bed and remembers how Freud said that our dreams make it possible for us to sleep. If the dark ages had had a mind, it would have been both cyclical and on sale to the devil. We migrate from one to the other, from hope without longing to longing without hope, and on the whole we prefer instruments to speculation, method to madness, as if we would obliterate the *daring* part of consciousness, which looks into the glass to see. We prefer, even in our art, poetry, and religion, confused alarms on lonely shores.

It is considerations like these which make us reflect that there may actually be a new phase of culture at hand: mass culture. But it may be only that too much of our research leads us into the mass-part of man's soul: into the anonymous and communal saga in which the actions of the individual are construed as sinister and somehow less than his own. Thus the superman or hero tends to be either the mass-man or the arch-criminal or the pure heel. It is the glory of James Joyce that in the figures of Bloom and H. C. Earwicker he worked against all these in a valiant attempt to create a new kingdom of man: an independent, individual morality against the society that made it necessary. Yet he deflected the common mode of research very little. He was a proper author and redeemed the validity of experience in the theorems he called his art. Besides Joyce, there are the others, to whom we shall come if we hold out.

What holds us, what keeps us, what moves us, must be a combination of our under-momentum and our bourgeois hu-

12

manism. These are the correctives as they are the aching sources, the true enliveners, of our great men. Bourgeois humanism (the treasure of residual reason in live relation to the madness of the senses) is the only conscious art of the mind designed to deal with our megalopolitan mass society: it alone knows what to *do with* momentum in its new guise; and it alone knows it must be more than itself without losing itself in order to succeed.

The decay of the prestige of bourgeois humanism was perhaps necessary, but only as an interim, a condition of interregnum, when new forces overran us. In order to restore the humanism we have to overcome the forces. We have to take stock, too, of the multiplication in the number of the artists and to remember their insistent disrelatedness. It was never to have been expected that society—especially a centralized state like our own—would be willing to pay for the cost of the artists who as a class, and often individually, raised the severest problems of that society: images of the deep anarchies out of which the order of the state must be remade if that order is to be vital. But it ought to have been expected that the incentive of the artists themselves should have remained fixed on that living relation between anarchy and order. Instead, we have the apparition of the arts asserting their authority in a combination of the spontaneous and the arbitrary, in pure poetry and pure expression and pure trouble. Instead of creation in honesty, we have assertion in desperation; we have a fanaticism of the accidental instead of a growth of will. The true anarchy of spirit should always show (or always *has* showed) a tory flavor. It is the artist above all who *realizes* that revolutions—however fresh, violent and destructive, however aspiring, or groping, or contagious—have always *already* taken place; as private murder represents a relation already at crisis or already sundered. Revolution and murder are only the gross cost, assessed too late: the usury of dead institutions.

The anarchy of our artists is in response to facts as well as in evasion of facts. The two great external facts of our time are the explosion of populations and the explosions of the new energies. The two great internal facts of our time are the recreation of the devil (or pure behavior) in a place of authority and the development of techniques for finding destructive troubles in the psyche of individuals. With neither of these pairs of facts, without a vital order in society, can the individual keep up except as corrosion may be said to keep up with the salts that cause it—to the point of incoherence in purpose and collapse of structure. The two pairs of facts are I think related. The devil and the techniques are the slow form of population and energy explosions. But if we let this relation transpire in the mind we see we have the power to cope with the facts themselves; for we then behold the nature of our troubles in what used to be called the unity of apperception. To say this is to involve bourgeois humanism once again. It may not be the right force, or the right muse, but they are the only ones we know, and the only ones which we know have within themselves the capacity to generate by absorbing disorder into order. We can remember in the past it was the artists who taught society this skill.

The latter end of our time—1920-1950—is an age of critique: critique as a means of criticism and critique as a means of creation. Critique as criticism we see in the expanding omnivorous techniques for the examination of poetry. Critique as creation we see in Proust, Mann, Joyce, and Kafka. Critique is the wiggling extreme articulation of vital elements into an order of vision: especially the elements of the new powers and the new troubles.

With critique as creation we shall have much to do. Here I want a passing emphasis on criticism in its widest sense. Some of the criticism merely extends along new lines the malicious criticism of knowledge (the attack on the validity of perception) which is the net practical result of the current of philosophy beginning with Berkeley and running into the sands of the Existentialists. Epistemology was taught to prevent knowledge or at least to gravel it with doubts; so most criticism of poetry. All the apprehensive powers of the mind have been put at such a discount that they are felt to be irrational, when actually they are the fountainhead and fountain reach of reason herself. It strikes me here that in result upon our general mind, modern physics and mathematics make a parallel extension of the same malicious criticism of knowledge: as refinement of critical abstraction, good for manipulation, rotten for apprehension—that is, for the sensual knowledge that is the immediate rock of physics and the thing indexed by mathematics. As compared to literary criticism, the critique supplied by physics is both more malice and more knowledge and is also more remote from the apprehending reason. The effect of these malicious critiques is profound: almost they dissolve our sense of the texture of moral experience. It is the writhing of actual knowledge under these malicious techniques that makes choice and purpose and taste so difficult, uncertain, and fractious. We tend to relapse from all human creation back into almost pure momentum (in analogy to pure sensation), with all our activity becoming mere sports on the movement of inertia. Thus it is we seem to manipulate for manipulation's sake and find the *acte gratuite* a liberation when it ought to be a warning, an explosion when it ought to be a play, a gesture, a feint. It is thus that we *become* our problem when we ought to exemplify some effort at the solution of it. We become, in Dante's language, the War of the Journey without active knowledge of the War of the Pity. It is the two Wars that need the Muses; either, taken solely, puerilizes man.

The malicious criticism of knowledge is reflected also in the unmoored diabolism that makes so many mansions in the modern sensibility, and makes them uninhabitable sink-holes of terror and dismay, full of the uncleanly and aborted approximations of the unseemly. Hysteria, which ought to be the clue to reality, becomes its creator. This we see in Freud, who began his studies with the etiology of hysteria and proceeded with its deification: as if all the gross responses unconformable with conduct could ordain conduct. The sequence is interesting: hypnotism, psychical research, hysteria, neurosis, psychosis, psychoanalysis. The very title, *Psychopathology of Everyday Life,* in itself a lie, told that we might mistake the conditions of our struggle for its object; in short, a malicious criticism of knowledge. It is a queer thing that we should desire to make experience itself suicidal to its own impulses: queer but actual. The devil always takes the form of the actual, most conspicuously in an expressionistic age. But only the bourgeois humanist would know this.

But it must be the bourgeois humanist in his role as artist who knows—for it is he who is nearest the expressionism of our times, the artist thrown up as a heroic type and a heroic image. And indeed it has been that class which has known most, or expressed the most—especially in that explosion of talent that took place in the twenties, crystallizing between 1922 and 1925 in *Ulysses, The Waste Land, The Magic Mountain, The Tower, The Counterfeiters,* and a great deal more. It is a version of the general *artistic* problem which gave condition to this explosion that I have been leading up to. All these books came deeply from the bourgeois humanistic tradition and come as near masterpieces as our age provides. They were a part of the great expressionistic period between the wars, not only in literature but in all the arts. Older talents crystallized and reached pinnacles and took on new dimensions; new talents were flung off like sparks from a Catharine wheel or the blobs of light from a roman candle. Expressionism—what I say is both myself in truth and creates a new world—tends to pyrotechnics; the fireworks are within us and are all around us and are their own meaning—subject to the least possible external control or common predictable forms of understanding. In expressionistic art we see what the forces are which we have to control by other means: the actual forces of human nature, of nonrational behavior, and of the industriously rational machinations of the devil—the diabolic, the demonic, and the chthonic—the life that is in our soil. Expressionism compacts the Faustian spirit and the adventures of our conduct. This is a new claim for the arts, and perhaps the most ambitious yet in the long series since Aristotle. It is precisely the opposite from Shelley's claim that poets are the unacknowledged legislators of the world. It constitutes for itself rather the claim to undermine, to readjust, to put into fresh order the frames or forms in which we make the adventure of conduct tangible to our minds, and it therefore denies validity to pre-existent legislation on human relations.

No wonder all that we mean by the state and most of what we mean by public morals turn stony against expressionistic art. No wonder, too, that for all its talent and all its novelty, expressionistic art has never been popular with the new mass society that threw it off as a new turn—a new force—of the mind. It has been popular rather with the human fragments which the mass society also threw off—with the remainder of the old élites and with the new professional and intellectual proletariats: all those of us who, in Toynbee's phrase, are *in* but not *of* the great mass society. All art is in a sense the daydream arrested and compacted in form. Most people like their daydreams to conform to their normal expectations and their immediate ambitions and to do so in familiar forms. Most of us like either happy endings or a lonely glory in our affairs. We dream to get rid of our reality and to charm the lights of love. Here popular art helps us out. More serious art—high-brow art—is also daydream, but it insists on responding to the pressures that make our dreams so strange and so full of prophecy: nightmare or revelation. Instead of rationalizing our experience we give our experience what form we can and set reason new and almost impossible tasks to perform. We recreate reality in rivalry with our own wishes. I think of Thomas Hardy who tried to write popular melodramatic novels for money out of ordinary melodramatic daydreams but, in what we call his better novels, found himself responding to and shaping dark forces. I think also of Henry James who wanted to write the best possible popular novels, but never knew what the deep moral troubles in his psyche were that prevented him (the very troubles which as he expressed them give him stature) until, in August 1914, he saw that *this* is what we have been leading up to all along.

We have had another war since then, and the enclosure of the two wars suggests certain things about the talent that lay between them—or at least puts certain things in a violent murky light. We lived in a time of troubles, when the very torpor of our momentum let us see what monsters and what heroes we could make of ourselves in imagination—the monsters of our behavior newly seen, and the heroes of our struggle with that conduct newly construed. Newly seen and newly construed: for not only did we live in a time of troubles, we lived also in a time when we were learning a whole set of techniques for finding—even creating—trouble: new ways of undermining personality and conviction and belief and human relation. I myself can remember when the Oedipus complex was a shattering shock and a neurosis was a ravening worm. It was not till later that we had the law of uncertainty in mathematical physics, which broke the last healthy remnants of moral determinism. But we had psychology which dissolved the personality into bad behavior, we had anthropology which dissolved religion into a competition, world- and history-wide, of monsters, and we had psychiatry which cured the disease by making a monument of it and sociology which flattened us into the average of the lonely crowd. We had thus the tools with which to construct the age of anxiety out of the older debris. Almost, the tools guided the hands and predicted the work. As if that were not enough, the same monsters, and more intolerable heroes (those who accepted the monsters) began their work in the world of managers. It was in 1922 that Mussolini made his march on Rome; and by 1939 the Faustian spirit within had come very near succumbing to the dictatorship of the scum of the earth without.

It need not have happened that way, but the risk of its happening that way was very great, and is still with us; and the arts have more than ever the job of enforcing new tasks upon reason: to show poetry as the wisdom of our violent knowledge—which is what Giambattisto Vico said, in 1744, that poetry could do in his great work, *Principi di una Scienza Nuova*, the new way of looking at knowledge. It was also, I think, how he came to say that justice was an emanation of the human conscience, and therefore changed as times and forces changed.

In the darkness and hope of these remarks something else we have long known shows the more clearly: the shifting contour and widening focus, not of one or two generations, but of three or four centuries, in the burdening and the possible scope of literature as it is a development in history. It is not the atheists and agnostics but the committed men like Reinhold Niebuhr and Arnold Toynbee who habitually say that we live in a post-Christian world; and the history of literature bears them out. In Shakespeare justice is the endless jar of right and wrong as it strikes upon the conscience. We feel in Shakespeare what troubled Joyce's Stephen Dedalus so much: the agenbite of inwit, or remorse of conscience. In Shakespeare, as in Montaigne, and not again going backwards till Dante, nor going forward till Pascal, you feel the constant explosions of violently irrational forces upon the conscience. These explosions were of their talent. From the First World War onward the explosions are commonplace, though the talent may be less or at least less acceptable. Except Dante, who I think prophesied it, we are all heirs to a realignment of the usurping and abdicating institutions which manage our relations to our irrational experience. There are many ways of putting this. Here is Marcel Raymond, who is trying to explain the apparition of nonrational French poetry from 1870 onwards: "An explosion of the irrational elements in the human personality had occurred in the era of the Counter-Reformation and Baroque art, but at that time the Church had determined the course of the mystical upsurge without much difficulty. Two centuries later, after the critique of the 'philosophers,' she was no longer in the same commanding position. It was the task of art (but not of art alone) to gratify some of the human demands that religion had thus far been able to exercise.

"From then on poetry tended to become an ethic or some sort of irregular instrument of metaphysical knowledge. Poets were obsessed by the need to 'change' life, as Rimbaud puts it, to change man and to bring him into direct contact with existence. The novelty lies less in the fact than in the intention, which gradually emerges from the realm of the unconscious, of reconquering man's irrational powers and of transcending the dualism of the self and the universe." (Raymond goes on to remark that modern civilization and Romanticism crystallized at the same moment.)

An irregular metaphysic for the control of man's irrational powers, if I may so condense M. Raymond, these words on the sequence of these remarks seem to me to enlighten the motive-power, the *moving* power, of the extraordinary outburst of creative talent in the twenties. No wonder it is sometimes called a rival creation.

Let me list a few in literature. Pirandello wrote *Six Characters in Search of an Author* in 1921, *Henry IV* in 1922: or how it is we struggle for identity. Ortega y Gasset wrote *Invertebrate Spain* in 1922, *Revolt of the Masses,* in 1930. Valéry published *Charmes* in 1922: the identity of the spirit with its senses. For that year Proust had *Sodome et Gomorrhe:* the beast which springs and is sprung of spirit. Ezra Pound had finished *Hugh Selwyn Mauberly* and some of his most characteristic *Cantos* in 1921: the artist as hero *manqué.* Wallace Stevens' *Harmonium* appeared in 1923: a dandy finding an old chaos in the sun. Mann's *Magic Mountain* came in 1924: the intellect entered literature at a new level to meet and merge with the sick and the unseemly. Two years later, 1926, Gide produced his *Counterfeiters:* the migratory black devil in Puritanism. And so on.

For our purposes, we have only to remember that Eliot's *Waste Land* and Joyce's *Ulysses* appeared in 1922, and that around that year hovers Yeats' most powerful work. Do not these works, as we lump them in one image which we cannot swallow and of which we cannot free ourselves, constitute a deep plea for the wisdom of our violent knowledge? Is not the poetry in them precisely the wisdom with which we respond to the great grasp of unreason?

2

The Techniques of Trouble

ONE OF THE themes that inhabited my last lecture was that all our new knowledges—or all the new forms into which our knowledge has segregated and incriminated itself—have come out as techniques for finding trouble in ourselves and in the world. It is almost as if to make trouble had become the creative habit of the general mind. We made new violences where there had been order and as a result have been living in a combination of turbulence and apathy, of novelty and isolation, immersed in the new failures of human relationships. If Tolstoi could begin a great novel by saying that all happy marriages were the same, all unhappy ones different, we can say that every age has a new way of finding human relations difficult or impossible: the very hardship and the very joy of life we cannot and would not escape and with which we must deal. These are our techniques of trouble, and if there were no troubles we would invent them or would find new ways of looking at old troubles. In life we do what we can and what we must; in literature and the arts (and sometimes in our day-dreams and what we call our thought) we make a kind of rival creation always, one way or another, in response to the actual life itself; and in our great creations we alter that actual life in the sense that we alter what we think about it, what we acknowledge about it, what we see in it, and what we do about it in our private selves where most of our time is spent. Hence our need for making desperate and preposterous cries: the form of expression in which we are best understood and where we feel most intimate with others. But hence also we cling to what we can of the cumulative memory of our past which we call reason, and of our cumulative hopes for the future which we call our aspiration or imagination; and indeed these are the substance in us which cries out: which explores and shapes and expresses the life which besets us in terms of the life which is our own. Great literature—great art of any kind—finds techniques for dealing with the trouble otherwise provided. It is with these techniques that we are now concerned as they apply to the great burst of creative talent in the twenties.

But there is nothing new about any of this. Here is Stephen Dedalus speaking of Shakespeare in the Library chapter (which may also be called Scylla and Charybdis) in *Ulysses* (p. 210): "He found in the world without as actual what was in his world within as possible. Maeterlinck says: *If Socrates leave his house today he will find the sage seated on his doorsteps. If Judas go forth tonight it is to Judas his steps will tend.* Every life is many days, day after day. We walk through ourselves, meeting robbers, ghosts, giants, old men, young men, wives, widows, brothers-in-love. But always meeting ourselves." This is Joyce's aesthetics; it is also one statement of the whole theme of *Ulysses.* But for our immediate purposes we can find in these words a motto or text for the violence of great talent in its task of meeting great trouble.

As text or motto Joyce's words given to Stephen need to be joined to others more topical to the situation at the end of the First World War. Here are some sentences from Marcel Raymond's *From Baudelaire to Surrealism* (p. 270). He is speaking of the dadaists as characteristic of "the moral crisis of the 1920's and the current of anarchistic individualism, the refusal to be useful, that upset so many slogans and age-old beliefs." Then, speaking of the contributors to the dadaists' magazine *Littérature,* he goes on: "Life itself undertook to destroy whatever illusions they might have had about the 'real' world—: the regimentation of morals, the distortion of religious feelings, a science that celebrated its greatest triumphs in the calculations of ballistics, the greatest 'trahison des clercs' (betrayal of the intellectuals) that mankind had ever seen—there was ample ground for disillusionment." In the eyes of these men "everything had already been torn down; dadaism could be only an inventory of the ruins, and a declaration of the failure, or more accurately, the death of a civilization." Later (p. 272), M. Raymond speaks of the dadaists' "sense of bitter joy, almost indistinguishable from despair—the joy of flaying a society that crushes man" and reminds us that we "must not ignore the tragic anguish they reflect. Even if all dadaist poetry were to sink into oblivion, a few sentences would still deserve to be rescued—sentences which are among the most striking ever written to express the precariousness of man's fate and the sorrow of him who is lost and cannot resign himself to his destiny." He quotes, among others, Aragon, Reverdy, and Soupault.

The sharp difference between the situation of the dadaists and that of Joyce is that where the one prevented masterpieces at all costs the other is the theme of one of the greatly ordered masterpieces of all literature. The one has forgotten its ancestry and feels itself wholly bastardized, the other springs from a full bourgeois humanism of which it has lost nothing still alive and to which it adds its own innermost life. Shakespeare, the Bible, and Aristotle are all at work here, as is also all the working of June 16, 1904, in the city of Dublin, all working to-

23

gether into an order of the rational imagination. Indeed, there is a sense in which we can say that *Ulysses* is the book that *made* an order out of the substance of the dadaist imagination. Perhaps we say this because Joyce's book has power to make order out of anything.

To join in our minds the sense of Joyce and the sense of dadaism, there is a little scene in Mann's *Magic Mountain* where after Settembrini the humanist and Naphtha the Jesuit have broken off one of their inconclusive debates, Hans Castorp, that young and plastic soul, turns to his friend Joachim Ziemssen. Just as always, says Hans, first an anecdote, then an abstraction; that's his humanism. Anecdote and abstraction, abstraction *and* anecdote. Otherwise, as Hans sees in his dreams of Settembrini, the humanist is only an organ-grinder, with a monkey not a man at the end of his string.

A good deal of literature is always organ grinding, and some of it can be very good, as it reminds us or extends the sense of our common predicament, and there is perhaps no more than usual in the literature of our times; only since it is ours we see it too plainly. In Virginia Woolf human relations disappear in the very technique of sensibility in which they were supposed to be lodged and understood, and I think this is true of writers like Rebecca West, Frances Snow Compton, and most of Elizabeth Bowen (though with Miss Bowen, not at heart). In Virginia Woolf's world there is no possible society or daily life, which I suppose is its beauty; both the voices and the flesh are separated from us, and staled, by the intermission of woolen curtains through which nothing is touched; and Mrs. Woolf in her diary could not understand what all the bother over *Ulysses* was about. In D. H. Lawrence the hysteria of direct sensual experience destroys every structure of sensibility, and there is only as much human relation as there is possible in the swoon of the blood, which is a very powerful and very destructive relation indeed. André Malraux as a novelist (not as an art critic, or even as a politician, and certainly not as a public figure, but as a novelist) seems to me in much the same situation; the flashes of his violence on his adventures are quite

24

as vivid and exhibit as great a turbulence as the violence of the
world itself between 1920 and 1950; and there is a part of us
for which his novels cry out.

All these writers of whom I have expressed such exaggerated
sentiments belong in our time not only by date but also by the
nature of their talents (for Lawrence, genius besides: he is an
obstacle that cannot be gotten round); but I do not think they
ever overcame the techniques of trouble in our society with
techniques of their own. Thus they are nearer the dadaist situation than to that of Joyce.

Of other writers, other discriminations. Let us think of
Faulkner (also a man of talent and of genius) and ask of him
why it is that he has deliberately surrendered the advantages of
syntax without establishing any comparable control over the
movements of his beautiful prose. Why has he left the harmony out at the level of notation, at the level where the reader
is instructed how to read? It is precisely what the reader cannot
be trusted to put in. In his books, the words if not the people
fall out of relation; indeed the words heap round the people
and obscure them—quite as if Faulkner used the words for
which he has in fact an overwhelming gift only because on the
printed page he could not do without them. As with Mallarmé
deliberately, one sometimes thinks it is in the white spaces between that the thought goes on. And why, too, in Faulkner, is
there a deliberate denial or abnegation or blurring of the intelligence? Why is so much of *The Sound and the Fury* told
deliberately through the putative mind of the idiot Benjy?
One remembers Henry James' precept, made in commenting
on *The Turn of the Screw,* that what you want in fiction, at
least if you want veracity, is the abnormal or evil or unusual as
seen by *normal* intelligence. I am not here making a moral criticism, nor would I touch on Faulkner's metaphysics; Faulkner
has a powerful moral imagination and has a kind of black
Christianity of his own (a Christianity without either the gos-
pels or the Greeks) which I do not much admire as a religious
experiment but which I feel as a special revealing force in his
work. I merely inquire why he blurs the operation of intelli-

25

gence, and I can only suggest as an answer that he has the kind of sophistication which will accept only a low degree of order, the order of actions whether of the psyche or of the conflict of interests and loyalties before they have been understood and so have lost some intimacy.

The question about Faulkner sharpens itself if we think also about Proust. It must be a common experience, in reading the history of Proust's enormous rival creation of the world, to come with the relief of a change of weather upon those scenes where men and women burst out of analysis and the deployment of narrative into the excitement of action upon each other and into fresh voice. Many years ago Ramon Fernandez, who was a very good critic indeed, observed out of some crotchet in his mind that there was no moral progress in Proust. Fernandez was wrong, as wrong as a professional bourgeois humanist can be, which is when he regards what *ought* to be there, to the disadvantage of what is there. In Proust there is a continuous approximation of moral progress—among other places in the continuous quarrel of jealousy with the vitality and the intermittences of the heart. His whole book is morals in action, and if Fernandez did not at the moment see it, it was, I like to think, because there were so few scenes where the morals were released into actions of the whole person. Thus he is pretty much the opposite of Faulkner. His syntax is complete and is only as difficult as it needed to be, and his intelligence is used to the utmost—a kind of incalculable constant showing in approximation after approximation. Though Proust thought of himself as anti-intellectual, it was only so that he could keep himself from the fixed intellect and the formalized point of view; he maintained intelligence at the pitch where it refuses action; he preferred transmutations to action, the shifting of the phases of the heart to the phases of the reason, both somehow attached to the deep viscous memory, of which the heart and the reason are two decimations. May we not say, then, that Proust and Faulkner at bottom both suffer from absence of syntax, the power of composing or arranging things, giving them ordinance, so that their parts are in living relation to the intelligence? Faulkner runs to the syntax of analogous action; Proust runs rather to the syntax of words and intelligence and only seldom engages them in the autonomy of dramatic action.

Very similar discriminations beseech us when we think of such authors as Pirandello and Kafka. Here, in both, there is the question of human identity. In almost all Pirandello's later work the theme is that in the title of his best known play: *Six Characters in Search of An Author.* Who am I? And who can recreate me as I change? How can I *be,* both with myself and with others, and in spite of others? *Right You Are, If You Think You Are* and *As You Desire Me*—two other titles—suggest the kind of movement and the kind of withdrawal the psyche makes in its craving for that form which determines identity. It is almost a biological form and is rather like an amoeba (a figure which for this context I borrow from Francis Fergusson speaking of the psyche in Dante)—an amoeba which takes form and color and shifting contour—indeed takes its detours—from the forces which attract it or which touch it. In Pirandello the self is adaptable by contagion and by desire and by thought, and both to itself and to others. The self is dramatically creative in all the roles it assumes, but remains— whence its sufferings and its joys—through all its phases vitally itself, its own identity, something as diaphanous, as individual, and as humorous as an ever-fresh voice. This, if you like, is the *play* of modern psychology by which the personality achieves itself. To read the novels and stories, to read or to see the plays of Pirandello leads all the amoeba in oneself to take on the successive adventures of being. In Pirandello, the principle within fastens itself onto all the possibilities from without.

In Kafka, what happens cuts down everything but the indestructible principle of the self, and what is left alive is all that might have been become excruciating, intolerable, proud, impossible: an inner shriek of the deracinated quick of spirit: as if Pascal had become a novelist on the theme of how the monstrous world attacks the guilty self. I think of Gregor in "The Metamorphosis" who becomes a cockroach and is squashed by his family, and I think of the prisoner in the penal colony whose crime, whose identity is gradually written upon him with needles and knives; and when the writing is done he dies, or perhaps before—for it is possible that the crime of identity can only be achieved posthumously. In Kafka you find your identity in your guilt, you find it in an alien and official world, which is yet most desirable, and you find it only when you have been excluded and turn yourself in absolute isolation. In Kafka you have religious novels of rebirth where only the agony, not the birth, takes place. Kafka is a master of all that in us which craves to the point of absolute jealousy the condition of frustration: the vision of which has been one of the crimes of modern society taken from modern psychology. The jealous god excruciates the jealous soul. It is what happens when the Jewish part (some say the Calvinistic part) of Christianity forgets all practical wisdom and replaces it with the terror of logic, the nightmare from which we cannot wake up. The logic of Kafka—and no imaginative writer was ever more logical, more sharp in syntax—is like that. It is a world where to achieve identity there is a logical reduction of possibility and where, as Gide says in another context and with the opposite response, God loves us only by the calamities he imposes on us. It is no wonder Kafka never finished any of his major works; his own death had first to supervene. He had a terrible vision of all within us that is against ourselves; he did not destroy, but he inverted his bourgeois humanism; precisely as Pirandello, as all but the worst Italians do, began afresh with what made humanism worth while.

In all these writers whom we have mentioned human conduct flourishes and literature finds its life. In them all—and in so many others not mentioned—we saw fragments of the troubles that are, forms from the techniques of new troubles our age has discovered, and attempts, greater or less, to encompass and to cope with these troubles with the technical resources of the humane imagination; with whatever had survived in the gift of each author of bourgeois humanism. For another name, we could perhaps call it charity of understanding or passion of perception or the everlasting need to cry out, to cry up or to

cry down, the sweetness and the torture of the human in relation to human. But to them all, I think, we had primarily to
bring something which was our own and not specifically called
for; we had to bring what was not there and needed. Like
ourselves, the work of these writers was incomplete. Let us turn
now to three writers who require us to bring a great deal, and
more than our other writers, but who specify in the very nature
of their work what it is that we must bring; and precisely because they are writers whose work is more nearly complete and
cannot easily be exhausted; work which because of its formal
superiority, supplied with tact and skill by the authors, goes on
if not to new life at least to new and different uses, and which
as much as any of the rival creations of the mere mind has a
life of its own, a life which consists precisely in having given
shape and theoretic form to our troubles.

We shall speak a little of Thomas Mann, a little more of
André Gide, and as much as there may be room for on James
Joyce. This order and these brevities do not represent an esti-
mate of stature or importance. I have said a good deal elsewhere on Thomas Mann and if I quoted myself at all would
have to do so at great length; I myself have gotten more out of
him than from any prose writer alive and working in my time,
and I will say that his last book, *Felix Krull,* is in effect a mar-
velous and heightened version of my own autobiography, and
it is with great personal regret that I remember that he died
before he could carry the story beyond the hero's twentieth
year. I regret that I shall never know what was in store for me
in the unwritten years of my life. As for Gide, I have loved him
with aversion, and have fought him with delight, for above a
quarter century; he is another twist to my own Protestant New
England heritage with a Mediterranean addition which is both
his and mine. He looked at the world with his own need for
revolt and demeaned himself with an excess of honesty, just as
with an excess of economy he very often nearly threw himself
away. He seems to me to have created a rival world for all
those not myself, but to have used part of myself in doing so.
As for Joyce, he is a part of my bloodstream since my sixteenth

year, and as my blood changed so he changed within it. I knew he was a great writer, and a writer who would be great for me, before I had finished reading the Christmas dinner scene in the *Portrait of the Artist as A Young Man.* As for the rest, I give no precedence in honoring Bloomsday.

But these writers are all familiar to you; indeed they mean a great deal even to those of you who have never read them. They are a part of our conscience, and in the change of our conscience, towards the world, they are part of how we see the world. They ask for a judgment beyond the literary judgment precisely because they are masters of literature. They made great forms, and it was by their forms that they aroused antagonism and commanded assent; and they demanded attention, which they often got, beyond the habits of the amused part of the mind at this or in any other time. Let us see how this was done.

I would ask you to observe of Thomas Mann that almost all his heroes are bourgeois humanists tainted by art. Sometimes they are artists themselves like Aschenbach in "Death in Venice." Sometimes plastic imaginations like Hans Castorp in *The Magic Mountain,* sometimes poets within themselves like Joseph, and sometimes artistic scoundrels like the lamented Felix Krull. It is the taint of the artist in them that raises them to heroic proportions; for it is that which compels them to take stock of the sick and ailing, to seize on the unseemly, to expect the equivocal, and to rejoice in the problematic. These heroes are the outsiders within and participating in their society. They are all demonic people redeemed from the diabolic by the human, but they would not have been daemonic had they not gone in for all the upsetting, all the low-grade relations we have in human nature. This is what Mann does with the humanistic; sometimes in action as with Hans Castorp, sometimes in the refusal of action as with Joseph tearing himself loose from the clutches of the magnificently infatuated Potiphar's wife. So it is, too, with that portrait of the greatness of Goethe in *Lotte in Weimar,* where the very greatness consists in the conceit with which the hero tampers with human souls and aggrandizes his own very humanistic soul at every human expense. Almost one says that these heroes are all great, in their different ways, by reason of their infatuation. Almost, but not quite; for they all are gifted and skilled with the other lust which is the humanistic lust for knowledge, till knowledge itself seems a degradation of being or another taint in the soul, and truth becomes a kind of fiction—a kind of vital fraud practiced by the artist on his humane knowledge out of his total irresponsibility. It is by our frauds that we incriminate ourselves into the truth. "Now," says Felix Krull to himself as a boy, "Now you look plain and unpromising, but one day you will rise to the upper world magnificently adorned, to take your place at feasts, at weddings, to send your corks popping to the ceilings of private dining-rooms and evoke intoxication, irresponsibility, and desire in the hearts of men." And again, when he was living a double life as a waiter and man of the world, he says of himself: "Thus I masqueraded in both capacities, and the undisguised reality behind the two appearances, the real I, could not be identified because it actually did not exist." Thus it is that Mann does something with his bourgeois humanism; he adds the equivocalness of behavior explored.

André Gide had a lighter touch, though he, too, is aware of the heaping of knowledge, and knows how it must be made frivolous to be kept tolerable; which is a very humane sort of insight indeed, and is the way in which he knows that humility opens the gates of heaven, and humiliation those of hell. The taint in his heroes is not of the artist pure, but as the artist full of curiosity; he is aware of the sense in which even the purest artist is somehow artist *manqué,* the artist in spite at and of himself. He is the French puritan who nurses the devil within him, not as a poor relation as in Mann and Dostoevsky, but in his older and prouder role as the Prince of Darkness in whose service we must perform most of our acts, since he is our feudal self.

This I think can be illustrated in *The Counterfeiters.* You will remember that at the end of the book the young Boris kills himself for no good reason and every bad reason, the victim of the counterfeiters' plot. Just after the death Edouard, the novelist who is both a character in the book and who is writing a book of the same name, makes this entry in his journal: "I shall not make use of little Boris' suicide for my Counterfeiters . . . I accept reality coming as a proof in support of my thought, but not as preceding it. . . . Boris' suicide seems to me an indecency." The rest of the chapter explains the indecency: how the suicide was the only act not counterfeit that Gide records, how, in effect, Edouard is the greatest counterfeiter of them all. The last sentence in the book is Edouard's. He looks at his young nephew Caloub, brother to the other nephew whom he has seduced triumphantly but from whom he is now separated. "I shall be very curious to know Caloub," says Edouard, and you feel the whole thing is to do over again, and there will be other suicides, other counterfeits. It is old La Pérouse, the dying music-teacher who makes us understand the sadness of this last sentence. La Pérouse tells us our blood makes a continual noise which drowns harmonies. (" 'In this world God always keeps silent. It's only the devil who speaks. . . . No, no!' he cried confusedly, 'the devil and God are one and the same; they work together. We try to believe that everything bad on earth comes from the devil, but it's because, if we didn't, we should never find strength to forgive God.' ") It is thus, to use La Pérouse's earlier words, that God's love for us becomes our calamity. He sacrifices his son and he gives us the devil's voice in our blood through or under which to hear the silence of his own. This is Edouard—or Gide—as the black puritan. "I feel very curious to know Caloub." As a man in the wrench of sincerity will achieve perfidy and slap our own face.

Sometimes it seems to me that Gide belongs in the tradition of Orpheus and that this work—*The Counterfeiters*—is his account of Orpheus' life between two deaths. Ovid gives it this way in the Loeb translation (*Metamorphoses*, X 79-85): "Orpheus had shunned all love of womankind, whether because of his ill success in love, or whether he had given his troth once for all. Still, many women felt a passion for the bard; many grieved for their love repulsed. He set the example for the people of Thrace of giving his love to tender boys, and enjoying the springtime and first flower of their youth (aetatis breve ver et primus)." It was a false life for Orpheus, full of true music, pure desperation, and compulsive debauchery; he had the job of finding himself, or re-creating the motive of which he had been deprived; and if Ovid is right he tried many times. I think the interest here is considerably more than anthropological. It is one of those things, this legend of Orpheus, into which the uncertain and ambivalent heroes of Gide and Proust may be made most naturally to fit, and where, once fitted, they will gain significance and an authenticated place in the order of nature. Gide could not have written this for himself; writing it himself he would I think have undermined himself—again excruciated himself as he did, it seems to me, in his *Theseus*. It is not every man who can understand *in himself* his classical matrix. I am the more sure of this when I reflect—not only on Proust and his obeisance to Mme. de Sévigné and the duc de Saint Simon—but also on George Santayana thinking he had tried twice to explain the dilemma of moral form, in *Lucifer* when he was young and in *The Last Puritan* when he was already old. The frames, not the content or the insights but the frames of the older societies were nearer to actual behavior than the Christian. But this is something to feel rather than to insist on, lest inadvertently another false frame be produced.

In any case, Gide never settled the moral question ahead of time—not the experience of morals, but the question of them. He and his books led a shady life in which the shadows exacerbated as often as they comforted, and I mean the same shadows. And this is our warrant for raising the matter substantively. It explains, I think, his need in *The Counterfeiters* for the multiple positive critique—the journals and the journals of the journals with which the book is furnished—each element of which criticizes and corrects the others constantly and with instant hind-thought. Each snaps at the tender heels of the others. But the multiple critique does not stop there, as it could not, for Gide, have arisen there. It needs as source and object the mimesis of reality, not realism, but a mimesis made

33

out of a belief in the spontaneous, and a love of the final, and recurrent mimetic reminiscence of society itself. Gide "knows," as in the book Profitendieu "knows" with the aid of his spies. He has the secret police of a lifetime's devoted observation of the half instinctive, half deep-patterned secret societies of the heart. He knows the equivocal talismans that bind flesh and spirit. He knows, too, not at all equivocally but as directly as possible the shame of motives late-revealed, intermittent and shifting as the revelation may be. He knows the poverty of the body in relation to the poverty of the spirit. He knows that phase of Christian insight down to the marrow's chill and into the chill vertigo of the spirit, and how these may have joined in the swimming of blood and of silence in little Boris' head when he drew the fatal lot. He knows the devil almost better than anybody, and that, as scripture says, he has but a short time to live, and must needs change his form and place and latch on to a new start. Hence in his *Journal* his note that the devil is circulating incognito throughout the book. Circulating is the word; but there is a better word.

If you think the devil brings God at his heels (as he cannot help doing) and that he exists until he is recognized—just as God does not exist until He is recognized—at least in the conscious soul—if you believe this, then you will see the advantages of saying that in Gide's novel the devil is migratory and that his migrations are desperate and rashly resolute. The devil migrates from character to character. In some he seizes the form of *dépit*—chagrin mixed with anger, rancor, and grudge as motivation: the source of what people do against their own good in relation to others. In some he floods woe and anguish, as in Laura and in La Pérouse: the source of what people do to their own ill for the good of others or the service of truth. In some he encourages instinct when thwarted or released by wealth or frustration, as in Passavant or Armand or Lillian. This devil always comes intending to stay; he is the prince of others' means. He has great strength of personality, great capacity for taking advantage of the situation, whatever turns up, or might turn up, and he cheats nobody so much as those who would woo him. Sometimes he is a mere spectre prodding energies that already exist, or precipitating a fall that was already in nature, as in Olivier the nephew whom Edouard seduces. Sometimes he is the flesh itself, as in Lillian and Vincent. Again he is *every thing but* the soul, as in Pauline who will sell her children to the devil for the sake of affection. In Boris, the boy who killed himself, this cannot be done: the disease was part of his soul. Boris is the little God who comes at the heels of the devil and the devil can only contaminate his *understanding* of God. The same thing may possibly be true of old La Pérouse: it is his understanding rather than his soul that was degraded: the mere depths of his nature. Possibly the mysterious artifact of Strouvilhou (who runs the counterfeit gang) is by *tour-de-force* one whom the devil actually makes the soul. We do not know him: in him the devil exists.

The devil, then, is what we do in our poverty to our poverty. Poverty, chastity, obedience. When the monk vows these he vows himself to accept three temptations of the devil and to meet him on his own ground, as if he could thereby be nearer to God: or to the understanding of God.

With such a bias, however described, how could Gide have been otherwise than, as a novelist, anti-mechanical, anti-James too, at every surface level. It was for him, in his obstinate black protestant puritanism, at the mechanical level that the devil could most creep in unseen; in consistencies of surface and consistencies of character . . . Like the monk, Gide wanted his novel to meet the devil face to face; wanted to find him whenever he took a fresh start. "I feel very curious to know Caloub." God too seemed possessed of a migratory habit, permanent only in transit and metamorphosis.

Gide was the most naked of all our novelists. If that is so then Joyce was the most protected. No book of our time exhibits so many deliberate and varied and compacted structures as *Ulysses,* unless it is perhaps *Finnegans Wake;* and for something comparable we have to look back to Dante. Think of Dante who read the soul of man, his double history pagan and

Christian, through every mode of understanding from an *apex mentis,* a peak of thought, of the Christian world, just after it had begun to lose its balance. In order to read Dante we have to read his reading of the world as he himself read scripture: with *longo studio* and *grande amore* and so as not to offend the spirit of truth. It seems to me that we have to read Joyce much as we read Dante—only a little less so—with certain reservations and certain characterizations inappropriate to Dante. Our real interest is in what is there instead. It is what is underneath: the bubbling up, from under: what comes into creation, the cause and destruction of what is already created: the image of Molly-Penelope, the idea of Vico, the image of the circular cycle, the Homeric pattern, and all the various psychological and physiological and rhetorical patterns. This is the "characteristic" (not virtue, not defect) feature of the mind benefiting and suffering under the romantic impulse. To Dante there was experience which we must explore and understand. To Joyce there is unlimited experience which we must master and create, but which, in the end, reaches not into the heaven of truth but back into its sources. Nevertheless, Joyce went at his work as Dante did and tried to read his experience through every form or mode of knowledge available to him. The interesting thing is that he did so against the general will and custom of his time and without the aid of recognized modes for the creation and interpretation of such a reading. He had no four-fold pattern. He had to revolt against himself as well as his time and he had to use both himself and his time. He was compelled to create, as if singlehanded, symbolic modes in which he could dramatize the city of man he knew. Whatever success he had came from his fundamental mastery of actual experience and his equally fundamental mastery of actual language, where each mastery was a foil and counterpart to the other. His failures, I suggest, came about insofar as he had hallucinations about either mastery: that omniscience is equal to total record, or that neologism is creation. But here I have no intention of judging either success or failure, only to indicate what it means to try to read Joyce as we read Dante—which is of course not at all the same as saying you would get the effect of Dante out of Joyce.

Among so many possible choices, we can perhaps do as well as not with a simple schematic comparison of the two heroes of *Ulysses:* of Stephen who moves under the sign of the Ashplant or Augur's rod, and Bloom who walks with a potato in his back pocket, the moly which is the black root with the white flower of safety in identity and conscience. Stephen is the image of Lucifer, an outcast by his own will, and intransigent to the last bite on the nail. Bloom is Christ (or, as the book says, "another"), is an alien by definition, and is supremely transigent in response to every twist of experience. Stephen is the son Telemachus, Bloom the father Odysseus, and in either image are both Christian and Greek. In Stephen there is the spirit of pride and warfare, in Bloom humility and persecution. Stephen is the artist, Bloom is No-man. Stephen mocks, Bloom accepts. Stephen would destroy, Bloom would discover what is there. Stephen is in isolation, Bloom is lonely. Stephen scars himself with hatred, Bloom has falling qualms of fear. Stephen would woo lust, Bloom love. In Stephen there is a sequence of attributes which confront breakdown and lead to extinction; in Bloom there is a sequence which confronts the momentum of things and leads to revelation. In Stephen there is the kingdom of the son, which is gone; in Bloom there are intimations of the Third Kingdom, which is to come. Stephen is stricken by the agenbite of inwit; Bloom brims with full conscience. Stephen blasphemes what inhabits him and is lacerated with the farce of things. Bloom grasps what he does not understand and is in full accommodation to it. Thus Stephen represents what lives but must be transformed. Thus Bloom represents what has been transformed and what must be reformed. Between the two is criticism and prophecy. Here is the trouble of the two exiles, the exile of him who cannot inherit and the exile of him who cannot transmit his inheritance. Joyce has made a rival creation in which we can become lost and can find ourselves, but which we cannot imitate except in him.

3

Irregular Metaphysics

For THE PURPOSE of this lecture it is almost enough to begin by saying that where the great novelists of our times have dealt with the troubles caused by the new knowledges (and the erosion of some of the old ones) in a kind of broad and irregular psychology, so the poets have been led to deal with them (or to repel them, or rival them) in a kind of irregular and spasmodic, but vitalized metaphysics. Both have done so in terms of the charge of maintaining the health and the possibilities of language under the conditions of our knowledge. One of those conditions is the relative disappearance of generally accepted (if only for argument) systematic metaphysics that bears on daily life, the life of our own adventure, in which we have by no means lost our interest. Thus the poet and the literary man generally find themselves in the very irregular task of doing what they can by literary means to adjust the new and old relations of our knowledges to life. This is, I think, why Eliot began his early critical work by remarking on the dissociation of ideas which marks our times almost with stigmata. Thus it is that Paul Valéry could ask: "Whenever you think do you not feel you are disarranging something?" And thus, in writing about Valéry, Elizabeth Sewell could observe that "Words are the only defense of the mind against being possessed by thought or dream." Surely Housman had this in mind here:

> But men at whiles are sober
> And think by fits and starts,
> And if they think, they fasten
> Their hands upon their hearts.

Only poets have the incentive of the anti-poetic and anti-verbal. It is their material. This is an ancient condition seen in a contemporary form, and we have only to look back a little to Shakespeare to see how different our own form is, and would have seemed to him. If we think of the sonnets we see that they are instances of as near as possible straight statement, garnished with the version he used of the sonnet form; and we notice that there is the echo running through them of almost logical thought, gained from verbal syntax and retained from the medieval syllogism and the theory of destructive argument. Besides this there was at work the long history of gallant love that sprang from Toulouse and Bologna. All these surround, and feed, and it may be even create, by reasonable means, the intuition and the attitude—the procession of things attended to *in form*—which, in their procession, in *that* order, constitute the poem. In the sonnets, as elsewhere in Shakespeare, reason is often queried—as the adventure of the unreasonable is often seized—but the query is always made from the point of view of Reason herself.

This is almost the opposite to Rimbaud's famous declaration in *Une Saison en Enfer,* the section called Alchemy of the Word: "I invented the color of vowels:—A black, E white, I red, O blue, U green.—I regulated the form and the movement

of every consonant, and with instinctive rhythms I prided myself on inventing a poetic language accessible some day to all
the senses. I reserved all rights of translation. At first it was an
experiment. I wrote silences. I wrote the night. I recorded the
inexpressible. I fixed frenzies in their flight."

Here, and it has been the ambition of many great writers
since, the policy is taken up from *inside* the experience and
outside the point of view of reason. Rimbaud would conquer
fate by making one of his own. He is the permanent adolescent
in us all—what lasts of adolescence—turned into, and fixed, as
an eternal essence; hence his enormous and continuing appeal.
He uses the trappings not the substance of his tradition—and
is in his very freedom from it the more victim of its manipulations. One must be (in all prudence) as intimate with one's
order as with one's disorder; else they become confused, and in
a sense lose the power of existence—the experience of the love
of men the Greeks called *philia*. There is no patience in Rimbaud; it is everywhere in Shakespeare.

If you do not like to think of Rimbaud in line with Shakespeare, it may be more agreeable to think of Shelley in one of
those sentences struck off late at night, which yet last in the
day by their own light. I have nothing to do here with the
unacknowledged legislators of mankind, which was mere special pleading, but with one of those passionate insights into the
nature of one's own work at its best—one's work if it really
worked. It is like a Rimbaud who was not *only* adolescent.
"All the authors of revolutions of opinion are not only necessarily poets as they are inventors, nor even as their words unveil the permanent analogy of things by images which participate in the life of truth; but as their periods are harmonious
and rhythmical, and contain in themselves the elements of
verse; being the echo of the eternal music." Here is the whole
program of modern poetry and the gist of half its achievement.
One would repeat, as text for everything wanted here to be
said: The poets' words "unveil the permanent analogy of
things by images which participate in the life of truth." The
rest would be important if we were talking about prosody, but

we are talking only about irregular metaphysics. The permanent analogy of things in images which participate in the life
of truth, will do us very well. Shelley was only saying ahead of
time, and abstractly, what Rimbaud was saying in the *élan* of
ambition. Possibly this is what Maritain is saying, in the course
of an examination of just the metaphysics of all modern poetry, as an afterthought about a process still going on. "Art
bitten by poetry longs to be freed from reason." *This* is the
disassociation of ideas, it is the fusion of senses and the exercise
of their interchangeability in words and thereby thoughts and
ideas, and it *is* the representative notion behind the enormous
stride of sensuality in the last century of poetry—for however
metaphysical or symbolical we may have become in our poetry
we have also acquired for it a sensuality no modern language
has hitherto known. If Rilke had his angels, Lorca had his gyp-
sies. It is these we have put side by side, and in them seen our
permanent analogies.

Analogy is exactly the putting of things side by side. In
poetry they are bound together by rhythm, sped by meter,
united by vision, experienced by music, said in voice. In analogy we get the relation of attributes, not substances; we get the
form of reality as if form were itself a kind of action. If we
think of the Greeks, we would say that the Oedipus of Sophocles is the more nearly logical, and that the Heracles of Euripides is the more nearly analogical; and it is for this reason that
we have only lately begun to grasp the form of Euripides.
Analogy is also the deep form of reminding that there is always
something *else* going on: the identity which is usually a mystery apprehended in analogy; what is lost in "mere" logic, but is
carried along in the story.

Analogy is like the old notion of under-plot, or second plot
in Elizabethan drama. Sometimes these under-plots were only
two logics, sometimes one and sometimes another; but sometimes they were a multiplying process. One times one equals
one, but a one which is also a third thing, which is fused in the
mind, in the looking of one working on the other. Emotions
can be like plot and under-plot. If we put two emotions of the

41

established sorts in association (like love and hate) we get an artistic emotion differing from either but with attributes common to both. In association, emotions are fruitful, and we get a sense of living action where there had been sets of abstraction: as in the Mass. Feelings are even more fruitful than emotions. When Robert Frost comes to the end of his poem "Stopping by Woods on a Snowy Evening"—

> The woods are lovely, dark and deep,
> But I have promises to keep,
> And miles to go before I sleep,
> And miles to go before I sleep.

When he has got to the end, he has made a revelation in feelings; what you cannot otherwise touch; only *so;* and the analogies multiply and deepen into surds of feeling.

Analogy is indeed the very name for our characteristic poetic logics. No doubt the attraction of analogy for us is in the fragmentation of faith and the diversity of logics and the divisiveness of our minds generally. These fragments, says Eliot, I have shored against my ruins. For two gross of broken statues, says Pound, for a few thousand battered books. What shall I do for pretty girls, says Yeats, now my old bawd is dead? And so on. One should remember that the attraction of analogy for the medieval mind (to which we so much and so diversely resort) was just the opposite. To the medieval mind the unity of things was insistently present, and had to be interpreted; to us unity is what we only seek by all the machineries of desperation and longing, sometimes longing without hope; and the means of our search is by analogy or collateral form.

The reason why "Prufrock" is *now* a popular poem (though it was a very difficult poem for most people for its first twenty years of life) is that the analogies with which it is composed have had time to sink in. This, too, is how poems change and grow and even sometimes disappear: in relation to our apprehension of what is in analogy, where the elements go on working. The obscurity is like that of the womb. Collateral or analogical form is as near as we are likely to come to the organic. Dialectic (in the modern sense) only excites the passion for analogy in the creative sense. We can say for poetry that only in analogy are the opposites identical; and it was a similar perception that led St. Augustine to say that in every poem there is some of the substance of God.

My point had perhaps better be pushed a little further and by an analogy taken from mathematics and physics thought of beside poetry and morals. In mathematics it is not necessary to know what one is talking about; in physics it is, since the test is in knowledge. Yet the mathematics (creating out of the rigor of formal relations) generates the physics, and often does so without being itself understood. Mathematics is theoretic form for the *feeling* of the relation of things.

Poetry is like mathematics, morals like physics; and it is sometimes "true" that poetry creates the morals in the sense that poetry creates the felt relations of things which unite the substance and the problems of morals. Poetry is the rebelliousness and the pang of what is alive; poetry gives, as Dante says, the war of the journey and of the pity: creates the story of them. Poetry takes action in morals as mathematics does in physics.

There is a sense in which knowledge, when we have given it form, is creation—all knowledge, including revelation. Mathematics created the physics of the modern world, created the terms and released the powers of all our troubles. It is only an exaggeration, then, to say that poetry created the morals of the modern world, and sets in action the modes of human love and all the other heroic or rebellious modes of human behavior.

In this analogy, mathematics confronted the old physics; poetry confronted the old morals. Out of each confrontation comes the response either of a rival creation or an increment to creation, and in each case the relations between the two are likely to be irregular. The old physics and the old morals still tyrannize those parts of us and of the universe which do not conform—and because of truth or vitality—to the new powers and pangs. A firm rational view is possible in either field, but the poetic impulse is rather towards creation just as our behavior springs from the "enormous lap of the actual," and just because we believe in most, and find most precious, what of the actual we ourselves create. I do not say that this is what modern poetry "really" does, but that this is sometimes its operative ambition and its saving illusion. It is a course in which we have not—and cannot—reach the extreme. Even as our minds create new knowledge, we are still God's spies. Every new form of knowledge, or of the human, is monstrous until it is made a part of the acknowledgment of reason. Reason likes the finished job; poetry *likes* the new job—the living process rather than the vital purpose.

It is not surprising that an enterprise of this order—combining as it does, in intention, all the reach of the senses and all the norms of the mind—should have produced the first learned poetry in England since Milton, with the singular difference that it is also and deliberately irrational in its processes—is indeed an effort to erode the rational for metaphysical purposes. This is because the metaphysics was itself expressionistic, arising out of personal warrant and with a distrust of existing forms, whether intellectual or aesthetic. Many of these metaphysical poets rejected much of their traditional craft and syntax and quivered with horror at all statements not drawn from dreams. Expressionistic metaphysics has often paraded in a masquerade of painful unlearning, and a special kind of illiteracy goes with the learnedness where it remains. It knows its own fragmentariness and must reject every system as a deceit, and must therefore erect systems known to be inadequate.

Of all that has been said so far of the contours of this ambitious form of the poetic mind, there is no livelier illustration than *The Waste Land.* I say nothing here of what I hope to exemplify at the end of these remarks: the dramatic sensuality of the thought in the poem. Here I am concerned with the structures of the poem as they can be easily separated, the structures with which Eliot protects his poem from the ravages of its subject. Like the *Ulysses* of James Joyce, only less so, *The Waste Land* affords and requires a maximum of structures, and requires it in the effort to do the job of reason in the absence of effective predictive form. Reason had above all to do the labor of making the form all over again, for it had the labor of associating the elements of a sensibility believed to be dissociated empirically. This, if you like, was reason in madness, operating and drawing from madness; it was reason controlling madness. Let us list a few of the elements of this structure, and let us begin with the epigraph about the Cumean Sibyl hanging forever in a cage because she had forgotten the need for regeneration in the mere lust to endure. When, when, *when,* WHEN will the sands run out? She is perhaps the heroine of the poem, and the boys, acolytes, choirboys, scamps can only help her by jeering at her, and she can answer them only in Greek: I wish to die. She is the heroine of all that is stupid and clutching in life, if you like of all that survives, and is a little outside the poem, suspended over it in a cage. Against her, within the poem, is Tiresias, the hero of all that is numinous and comes from the godhead, but in the poem bored as well as tragic; he is the perspective and fate, of all that was created and made. He is the blind foreseer, the man who was woman. He is the hero of all our meanings that are beyond safety, the very peril of vision. Between the Sibyl and Tiresias —between the two forms of prophecy and their enactments— comes the up and down and all around the town of the poem; everything that goes with the actions of this poem and its frames, all that has to do with the Tarot pack of cards, with Christ, the Holy Grail, and Buddha. Through all these, in the walls and ceilings and floors as stringers and uprights, run various other structural elements. There is the liberating force of "literary" religion and the liberating force of "literary" anthropology (what comes from Jessie Weston and Frazer), and the preserving force of "allegorical" understanding. I do not know which of these has been more misinterpreted, and I would for myself only suggest that we accept them as part of Eliot's means of giving the weight of various intellectual orders to his poem, much as we have done with the merely "literary" references in the details of the text—all the better when we have not recognized them.

Here are two sentences that bear, taken from Basil Willey's *The Seventeenth Century Background* (Anchor edition, p. 72). "It is hard to say which is the more misleading—the 'fundamentalist' reading which mistakes mythology for history, or the Alexandrian, which sees allegory where none was intended. In both there is a lack of capacity to distinguish between what is 'statement' and what is emotive speech, a deficiency which not only affected scriptural interpretation, but rendered impossible any satisfactory theory of poetry for very many centuries." So with the interpretation of Eliot and Yeats. In these various orders which Eliot has used there is no recognizable principle of composition. Even the Sibyl and Tiresias are not enough. The reason would not have been able to take up her task of poetic thought had not the psyche (one's private share of the Numen) brought in the compulsive force of images, of the obsessions of dreams, and of the force of dramatic mimesis to set up and reveal the hidden analogies of things. Thus it was that those of us who knew the least in the intellectual sense, in the first instance understood the poem best.

To reveal the hidden analogies of things; Shelley's insight was Eliot's task as poet; he has in his images to remind reason of its material, to remind order of its disorder, in order to create a sane art almost insane in its predicament. He had to make a confrontation of the rational with the irrational: a deliberate reversal of roles.

Here is part IV of *The Waste Land*, "Death by Water":

> Phlebas the Phoenician, a fortnight dead,
> Forgot the cry of gulls, and the deep sea swell
> And the profit and loss.
>   A current under sea
> Picked his bones in whispers. As he rose and fell
> He passed the stages of his age and youth
> Entering the whirlpool.
>   Gentile or Jew
> O you who turn the wheel and look to windward,
> Consider Phlebas, who was once handsome and tall as you.

This, as you will remember, is all there is to this section of the poem; it is a lyric interlude put in to remind you what the rest of the poem is about. Here the Reason and the Psyche together make a *poetic* rival creation, and make it in analogous symbolism, not logical allegory. The analogy moves wherever you wish it and wherever it wishes to move you. Here again are Valéry's question and Miss Sewell's comment. "Whenever you think do you not feel you are disarranging something?"— "Words are the only defense of the mind against being possessed by thought or dream." It is the words working on each other that make the life and the identity in the analogy.

We could as well speak only of Eliot and Yeats, letting all others go, and still have a good image of the poetry that crystallized in the middle twenties; but that would be to regularize that poetry too much, when what we want is the sense of the rich irregularity of the time. The ripe fruit is still falling all about us in various tang, if all fed from the same soil yet variable in exposure to the weather. So let us try a handful, but returning to Eliot and Yeats at the end, with a better sense of their variety and their irregularity and, I should hope, our own practicing metaphysics, regular and irregular.

There is Hart Crane and Wallace Stevens, from whom I must beg off except to say that their stature is incontestable. The one represents every ignorance possible to talent when it has genius, every willfulness tolerable because of expressive intention; Crane, of all American poets, could deprive words of almost all their meaning but yet could so wall them about with his poetry that they had the effect of actually inexhaustible meaning. Stevens could play with every nuance of thought and yet, because he had no generalizing or organizing power, give the effect of wayward impromptu music possible to a Harmonium. Crane you understand best if you try for nothing beyond the senses, Stevens is for relishing as the longest repetition of sweet things in the world. Crane had no manner, but a kind of style. Crane was the vice of our time, and the strength of it never left him. Stevens was more the excess of our time, part of it only because deliberate, and the weakness of that was never quite made up for. Both men are saved by their sensuality, by "the dry sound of bees stretching across lucid space" in Crane, or, in Stevens, "the dark encroachment of that old catastrophe, as a calm darkens among water-lights."

But this is to say nothing. And there are others, like Marianne Moore, of whom there is no doubt as to stature but of whom nothing at all can be said here. It seems simpler therefore to skip over men like Allen Tate with his passionate grasp after insight, and John Ransom who makes lyric incantations in light forms of all that can be made durable through the close caressing observation of the fleeting. (Besides, I speak of friends.)

Let us look rather at the obstinate figure of Ezra Pound, and to force the point of our irregular metaphysics, let us look at him together with Whitman. Each is a barbarian, and neither ever found a subject that compelled him to composition; each remained spontaneous all his life. In Whitman you find the sprawl of repetition, in Pound the heap of ideographs; in either case we ourselves make the thought emerge. In Whitman there is the catalogue which is not catalogued. In Pound there is the catalogue, these jewels of conversation. In both you have to know your way around and who the people are.

Nobody ever learned anything but attitude or incentive from Whitman. His example liberates the vatic weakness in others—that easiest of all reservoirs, spontaneity. Everybody has learned from Pound how to go about his own work; he liberates the compulsion to knowledge of his craft—at least in those who do not look merely to express themselves for themselves. So far as influence on aspects other than craft, Whitman is a better influence than Pound because of the great general blobs in which he uses the language. Whitman could have been an influence on Melville; but Melville must have been a threatening example to Whitman. Whitman wrote *Leaves of Grass*, Melville *Moby Dick; or The Whale*. One is the rush, the other the mighty effort to organize the rush. Pound's *Cantos* are less than a rush.

The barbarians are those outside us whom we are tempted to follow when we would escape ourselves. We imitate Whitman to get emotion; we imitate Pound to strike an attitude which might destroy the emotion we already have, or at least render it harmless. There is never, except in fragments, any shape given to the emotion itself, nor any organization of the feelings into an emotion. Both are good poets when we ourselves wish to be fragmentary. This is the sort of judgment we reach if we apply Coleridge's notion that poetry should show a state of more than usual emotion in more than usual order.

Pound is a crackerbarrel Mencken proceeding by crotchets and *idées fixes;* but he is also *Il miglior fabbro* and at that level knows everything, and knows besides all that his ears and eyes could tell. Here is "Medallion":

> Luini in porcelain.
> The grand piano
> Utters a profane
> Protest with her clear soprano.
>
> The sleek head emerges
> From the gold-yellow frock
> As Anadyomene in the opening
> Pages of Reinach.
>
> Honey-red, closing the face-oval,
> A basket-work of braids which seem as if they were
> Spun in King Minos' hall
> From metal, or intractable amber;
>
> The face-oval beneath the glaze,
> Bright in its suave bounding-line, as,
> Beneath half-watt rays,
> The eyes turn topaz.

Whitman is a crackerbarrel *Song of Solomon* proceeding by seizures. But he is also the Bard of everything in us that wants to be let alone so that we can be together, and he knows how to get rid of all the futility of mere meaning and the horror of mere society. When we read him in another language, as French, all our riches are there. When we read Pound in another language, as Italian, all our poverty is there. In neither is our *miseria* or our passion.

If when we think of Pound we think of Whitman, then in thinking of E. E. Cummings let us think of Dryden. In Dryden there is the effort to find the harmony of things, in spite of any obstacle, and with echoes from everywhere present. There is the tension of the classical and the Christian, the allegory of the will of God clothed in good sense, but spangled with another will, that of poetic harmony. But there is never a serious question of what is the will of God. The created world reflects the harmony, and the will is the light shining in the darkness. There was never a serious trouble in the head or in the heart—though the heart might have occasionally to change its beat. Dryden was one of those men who could always make up his mind—and, at an easier level, could always change his mind as one changes clothes with the weather—to maintain a durable state within. But there was little balance of perilous things, no heart of silence, in his great syntax.

Cummings has no syntax, and I do not mean merely the syntax of grammar; he lays out his fragments typographically, almost topographically. His reason is in his point of view—from which he sees, argues, arranges the simplest of all conformities, that of the salutation and the insult, of assent and rejection. He marshals nothing, but wants things his own way. This is why he deprives many of his words of as much as possible of *their own* meaning: so that they may take on *his* meaning. This is also why he rids himself of the pointing power of punctuation: so that the current of *his* meaning will not aim at, or flow, against his will. I suspect that he is afraid of the music of poetry (of which his early poems show that he is a master, and of which his later poems show that he never lost the memory) for similar reasons; he is afraid that the music would communicate another enthusiasm than his. It is not so much that Cummings is a poet of the anti-intelligence; he wants rather to transform intelligence into a kind of instinct: as if instinct could be one's own creation. Hence his simplicity and his sentimentality. Hence too his use of connectives as substances, pronouns as nouns, prepositions as verbs. His unity is in the substantial unity of emotion in experience. Dryden's unity is in the achieved unity of intellect taken as conviction.

For another sort of adventure, let us think of W. H. Auden along with Tennyson. In Tennyson the verse and the sensibility have contour (as different from fingering or phrasing) and plastic competence (as different from substance of thought). The wild within him is held in. By comparison, we have in Auden the roughness which has the coherence of schist, the adherence of the particles of contrary elements. The wild within holds itself together by force of mind. Destruction is his pose, without composure. In Tennyson there is the role of the poet, in Auden the role of the poem: two forms of heroism. In Tennyson, there is the maker of things beyond the reach of their tension, under another music, which belongs to the words. In Auden there is the expressiveness *of* the tension, in rough music that compacts as you hear it over, within its form of words. In Tennyson the poems at best unite with, lead to, or are graced by *their* images. In Auden the images habitually participate in, are functional parts, of the action of the poems, and are themselves the grace. Of both we might say, There is the beauty in his daily life, that makes mine ugly. In Auden it is the rugged mass that just escapes the habit of form. In Tennyson, the habit of verse keeps warm the inner form. Tennyson perpetuates clichés, or what must become cliché, by the very nature of the process by which he leaves things out. Auden constantly re-expands cliché by what he puts in. Tennyson tells anecdotes of myth, Auden sees anecdote become myth. Tennyson must find room in this turmoil for his culture, he must find convenient form. Auden must present or express or enact the internecine warfare of behavior (the turmoil) out of which culture might be *made*. Tennyson lived in an age of balance with new weights to be distributed. Auden inaugurates the second phase of the age of the techniques of trouble, the age of anxiety, as one of his books reminds us, taken not as melancholy but as ferocity or gall—something more forcible than mere "spleen."

It is along the lines of these comparisons that Tennyson and Auden acquired their characteristic moods. The mood of a poem is as much a part of its thought as its conventions or its predilections or its ideas. The mood is the mixture of the elements of the experience and the approach, the perception and the sensibility. Mood is the mystique of poetic thought: the medium of participation. Tennyson ached for finish, which made his mood. If Ezra Pound roughened the expressive surface of a mind already, and badly, made up, Auden roughened the mind itself, raw for adventure; and that is *his* mood. But all three submit, accept, assent to the force of words and all take advantage of and succumb to the prosody of their language.

Partly for the sheer pleasure of the contrast let us think together of Lord Byron and William Carlos Williams. Neither of these two men ever reached mastery of the medium of verse, towards which their attitudes were vulgar. There was the vulgarity of aristocratic carelessness and there was the vulgarity of the baby-doctor in a run-down North Jersey urban-rural community. In each the felicities are of raw perception (or unappeased sophistication). In Byron a raw (jocular) formality; in Williams a raw (gusty) magic. In neither case was there any intervention (or assistance) by unity of apperception. Byron saw no need, Williams was, and is, against it. Each had plenty of the violence of talent (the aura of genius): quite enough to require the control of style; but neither saw the requirement as worth taking up. Therefore their "thought" runs towards what with a view to poetry we call prose. In Byron, the ideas are other peoples', the attitude a pose, but the rhymes are superbly his. He rhymes his attitudes and his "thoughts." In Williams, nothing is his except the magic of his direct perception. We could not come much nearer bottom, except in the absence of talent.

That is to say that both poets depend on the rhetorical forces in language at a low state of cultivation and under a minimum state of control. Byron had a sterile state of control over a very ordinary state of emotion. Williams had a vigorous and unusual state of emotion with control vested in the fallacy of expressive form. Byron has the sneer of position, Williams the cry of sincerity. Byron is the snobbism of conventionality, Williams its primitivism. But each has his powers to an unusual degree of competence, and each in his own way to an unusual degree of freshness, to an unusual kind of immediate persuasiveness, with, in addition for Williams, the occasional *pang.*

Byron is a kind of sensorium of attitude, Williams a kind of omnibus of sensation. Remember, though, as Eliot said of D. H. Lawrence, both were careful about what interested them: Byron the rhymes, Williams the sensation. Both were prolix as only the little gift can be; neither ever found a subject to command his own powers of attention; both were spontaneous, though each from opposite ends of the rhetorical spectrum— Byron ultra-violet, Williams infra-red. These were their interests, and these the ways they worked. One wishes that both had taken deeper forms.

In the poetry of Eros—the force from below, the impulse that satisfies itself only in the instance—we see emphatic cases of the experience of thought where, if you like, the experience comes very near becoming thought—as near as symbolic action can come. This is one of the great examples of tautology: where things become their own meaning: which is the condition of poetry—however great or narrow the selection of experience may be. It is how many-modedness becomes one, how we reduce the many to the one—sometimes to one Sphinx, sometimes to one Grand Inquisitor. We think of Eros, and we think of John Donne and of García Lorca as specific examples of this kind of thought in poetry.

We say of Donne that he thinks with his feelings and then go on to say that he feels his thought. The famous figure of the compasses we take as the feeling of thought. Yet we should remember that Donne needed his "platonic" thought and his scholasticism to make a structure for his feelings, but he could

53

not trust his thought unless he could feel it. His true thought lay in the area where the jointure was made. He could not trust either his senses alone or his figures alone.

When we come to Lorca something has happened to the western mind. It has come to insist on the authority—in words, in thought—of the senses, and particularly the authority of sexual sensuality. Poetry became sensual in this fashion with the French symbolists, but hardly reached its present level till after the First World War. It was only that in this respect words had come to resemble the mediums of the other arts. Sensual experience became in poetry what it had often been in painting, sculpture, music, one of the great substances of thought; and Lorca is an example. Where the older eroticism mainly merely pointed, Lorca must present, as in these lines: "Her thighs escaped me like startled fishes, half filled with fire, half filled with frost." The feelings *are* thought, in a new way: they affect directly some of the other types of thought as another kind of the same thing. The revolution here is merely letting something in at an operative level which had previously been there at a kind of *known remove* from the words.

To think of Rilke let us also think of Robert Herrick and Emily Dickinson.[1] All three are nuptial poets. Herrick marries the created world, Dickinson marries herself, Rilke creates within himself something to marry which will—which does—marry and thereby rival the real world. In Herrick the direct experience was always for the sake of something else to be found in the plenitude of God's creation of nature. Thus it is that this clergyman played at wearing great costumes in which we must acknowledge the union of God and Nature. His order is the world's order of his time, his poetry what he did with it.

In Dickinson, one spends all one's life finding a role apart from life, in which one creates one's own role in despite of the world. Born in unity, one cuts oneself off, and cuts one's losses in the role of one's own immortality. What was sensuality in Herrick becomes in her the blow of deprived sensation on the

[1] This and the next paragraph have appeared in a slightly different version in the course of my review of Johnson's edition of Emily Dickinson.

quick. The direct experience was for her always for something else which would replace the habit and the destructive gusto of experience itself. This is the best that could be done with the puerile marriage of the self with the self: a sensorium for the most part without the senses, it is sometimes the vision of sense itself. In Rilke, one spends all one's life in a constant succession (almost simultaneous in experience) of withdrawal and return; withdrawal from the actual world and return to the same world, with no loss of response to it, but with something added through the figures which inhabit his poems. I think of the Angel who makes his peremptory apparitions in so many of the poems with the frightfulness of the absolute, which if one is to survive into death, must be accepted. Put the other way round, Rilke transformed, not himself, but his life into an approach to death. His books built his own death all the way from a noise in the valley to the crashing permanence of the world. This he had to do because life—God's creation alone—had lost its plenitude, its habit of continuing creation. It is the chain of being that is our own, the plenitude is for us to *find*. This is the pull in Rilke that makes him a great poet and draws us after. His order is his own: what he has done with the world in adoring it; and we use it, in those moments where we resemble him and where he creates our thoughts, as *our* own.

Yeats and together with him Coleridge (who will help us draw the picture in one more comparison) is of the same great school as Rilke, but with differences which are enlightening. Yeats is nearer the ordinary world than either. In Coleridge the dream is numinous and its cultivation is meant to discover that reality. In Yeats there is another reality made up out of the chosen rituals of soldiers, hunters, poets, wicked ladies and wenches (as earlier there had been the "false" Ireland and the "false" Joachim of Flora) and also made up out of the *poète maudit,* and the dandy. In 1900, says Yeats, we stopped drinking absinthe with our coffee. Compared to Coleridge, there is nothing numinous in Yeats, there are rather fetishes, obsessions, infatuations such as engage us all most days and hours.

The matters of curiosity in *The Ancient Mariner* and *Xanadu* are mere masking fancies, here secondary creations, which fall off to reveal the reality of what is sometimes called the sacramental vision of life, and the whole is indeed a means of discovering what that reality is. In Yeats we create reality in terms of our fancies. This is what is meant by the celebrated phrase, "In dreams begin responsibilities"; and it is best commented in the late cry, "What shall I do for pretty girls now my old bawd is dead?"; or again, in "I was blessèd, and could bless."

One concludes that the power in Yeats depends very little on the machinery of his Vision (we keep it only for purposes of scaffolding, for hints on how to ad lib, and how to run the frame of the dramatization of an idea) and does depend very much on the fancies of flesh and piety on which he seized. Yeats was an erotic poet with regard to his objects, not a sacramental poet. Homer is my example, he says, and his unchristened heart; but he also needed shenanigans. Thus he had the image of a beautiful woman predominant, and the image of Dante's face, with the hollows of our own soul sunk in it, as our christendom and politics and religion; and had also the phases of the moon and the great year and *anima mundi* and larky séances; thus he had fairies; and thus he had Swift and Goldsmith, Berkeley and Burke. Yet his vision is what he saw, the actual world to which he added, but which he did not wish to rival.

One concludes that the power in Coleridge's poetry depends very little on the sensations of the actual world and very greatly, in the end exclusively, on the substance of vision—which was not his own, but with which he united through a communication of spirit. He saw what his vision compelled him to. His fascinating personal life has almost nothing to do with the power of his poetry—which may be why he wrote so little where Yeats wrote so much of worth—or only so far as he found himself revealed in his vision. There is nothing erotic in his poetry; his work is *agapé*, without either *eros* or *philia*. So in the end, we see in Yeats, character moving in the flesh, emotion trespassing on and conquering spirit, and intuition seizing hold on the whole life, including the nameless life within us; and in Coleridge we see what moves character from within, including the nameless power.

I know no sharper contrast than this to bring us to direct contemplation of the sensuality of the irregular metaphysics of the poetry of our time, or what was once our time. We have had too many comparisons and perhaps most of them were of qualities of poets which ought not to be compared. Let me hope only that there was some creative virtue (which I would prefer to the critical in any case) in the analogies the comparisons may have suggested. To close let us drop comparisons and quote three examples of what I mean by sensual metaphysics, one from Eliot and two from Yeats.

From part V of *The Waste Land,* I take these lines:

> A woman drew her long black hair out tight
> And fiddled whisper music on those strings
> And bats with baby faces in the violet light
> Whistled, and beat their wings
> And crawled head downward down a blackened wall
> And upside down in air were towers
> Tolling reminiscent bells, that kept the hours
> And voices singing out of empty cisterns and exhausted wells

The exegetes tell us, and it is true, that we are in the Chapel Perilous and the Perilous Cemetery is no doubt near at hand, and it may be as one of the exegetes says that we hear something like the voice of John the Baptist in the last line. But for myself, I muse and merge and ache and find myself feeling with the very senses of my thought greetings and cries from all the senses there are.

Here is the sonnet called "Leda and the Swan":

> A sudden blow: the great wings beating still
> Above the staggering girl, her thighs caressed
> By the dark webs, her nape caught in his bill,
> He holds her helpless breast upon his breast.
>
> How can those terrified vague fingers push
> The feathered glory from her loosening thighs?
> And how can body, laid in that white rush,
> But feel the strange heart beating where it lies?
>
> . . .

> A shudder in the loins engenders there
> The broken wall, the burning roof and tower
> And Agamemnon dead.
> Being so caught up,
> So mastered by the brute blood of the air,
> Did she put on his knowledge with his power
> Before the indifferent beak could let her drop?

No doubt we have here the annunciation of Greek civilization and the turning of the Great Year, but it was not this that disturbed the churchmen of Dublin when the poem first appeared; the metaphysics was deeper than that of any existing church. It was the staggering, vague blow of the knowledge and power of the central, spreading, sexual quick: the loosening of thought into life and into itself, with a gained life.

Here, to end, is a small poem of Yeats called "A Deep-Sworn Vow":

> Others because you did not keep
> That deep-sworn vow have been friends of mine;
> Yet always when I look death in the face,
> When I clamber to the heights of sleep,
> Or when I grow excited with wine,
> Suddenly I meet your face.

Here the senses have given a new order to thought of all time and all eternity. It is not from wine to sleep to death, as thought without the senses might say; it is from death to sleep to wine, which the senses create the thought to say. In these poems we have what Milton wanted poetry to be: the simple, the sensuous, the passionate. We have made the potential, within its own limits so endless, real; it is the thought which was *first* in the senses.

4

Contemplation

AT THIS POINT I should like to carp at myself a little. What we have been talking about as the literature of the twenties, with its grasp of the irrational, its techniques of trouble, and its irregular metaphysics—with its fear of syntax, its resort to arbitrary orders, and its infinite sensuality—may very well turn out to have been an aberration, a mere intermittence in the great heart of literature. The true current of literature may have flowed purer through other names which we have hardly mentioned. Robert Frost rather than Eliot, Robinson rather than Yeats, De La Mare rather than Rilke might be the objects of poetic study. The line of Galsworthy and Maugham, of Jules Romain's *Men of Good Will* rather than Proust's *Remembrance of Things Past*, of E. M. Forster's *Passage to India* rather than Joyce's *Ulysses*, perhaps Heinrich Mann rather than his brother Thomas may turn out to have carried the true Cross. I would not wish to presume on the judgment of another generation, but I would insist that if E. M. Forster comes to top Joyce in aesthetic estimation, it will be because another aspect of imagination than that with which I am familiar has taken over. I know some names will go up and others go down, but not that far; and as for myself, I expect the unity of literature will include them all, for unity in literature is what we feel together—as any bookshelf will show us, whether it be the books of one man or of fifty. I speak here by my bias in the presence of other biases which have shaped mine, or repelled me, or to which I have been indifferent; and I hope that they too will unite into one historical bias at an appropriate time.

At the moment I should not care to define my bias, and rest on Aristotle's ground that any occasion requires only its optimum degree of definition, usually rather less than other people think; but I will make a suggestion or so. When Eliot published *The Sacred Wood* he prefixed to the first essay—"The Perfect Critic"—this sentence written by Rémy de Gourmont: *Eriger en lois ses impressions personnelles, c'est le grand effort d'un homme s'il est sincère.* I do not recollect having seen this epigraph commented in relation to Eliot's criticism, and I rather expect that most comment might refer to its irony. Yet the sentence was placed there before the age of irony and paradox had begun, and now that the age of irony has passed I must insist that I do not see any irony there at all; I see rather a relation between ambition and honesty when confronted with the critical task. But I would put against it a sentence drawn from Erich Heller's admirable book, *The Hazard of Modern Poetry:* "That which is systematic in a system is merely the trivial aspect of true order." And from that I would turn back to another passage in the same book which illustrates the particular effort I have been up to in these papers. "Poetry," says Heller, "heightens and cultivates the creative element that is in experience itself. For experience is not in the impressions we receive; it is in *making* sense. And poetry is the foremost sense-maker of experience. It renders *actual* ever new sectors of the apparently inexhaustible field of *potential* experience. This is why the poet is . . . an easier prey to doubt and despair than people content to live with the sense made by others." We deal with *potential* experience in poetry, or as Ortega y Gasset says of the novel, we deal with potential psychologies; observations which have critical implications to which we shall return. Here I want only the sentiment, the possibility.

The structure of *Ulysses* seems more fully identical with its words every time it is read and at the same time (by means both of words and structure) far more fully expressive. It will bear even the falsifications of structure we put upon it and our mounting ignorance of what the words mean cognitively. In fact it is through these that the expression is made. This then is not pure expressionism, or incomplete or impure expressionism; it is a rational and traditional art. To exaggerate only a little by way of repetition, *Ulysses* is the most structured book in English since at least Milton and it does as much to maintain and develop the full language as anybody since Shakespeare. These may not be desirable features in a masterpiece when the audience cannot *apprehend* the structures, or some of them, and cannot *recognize* the words, or many of them, and when the audience is unwilling or unable to perform the enormous labor to do either—unless it be done as a parlor-game with all the counters provided and labeled. Joyce knew this very well; he expected people to work, and was arrogant in requiring maximum work—as much as he had done himself; but he had a means of commanding attention which carries the reader well on his way to the work.

The means is triple. His basic patterns are universal and are known without their names. His chief characters are interesting and alive and parallel and completing to each other. And he had a story that is gradually told in immense bursts of vivid detail good whether or not there was a story at all; the detail makes the sense of the story. What unified these means is his always availing power to raise the language to the condition of glory or beauty. Beauty is the condition of things when in apprehension they are reduced to one; so Pythagoras says. I

61

should rather than "reduced" say, "carried away or along": given the *élan* of one, but an *élan* which sweeps in more than one direction, though one cannot say how many directions. Stephen Dedalus and Leopold Bloom are swept together, are merged or confused, and are then swept past each other, forever, in their directions, like winds at different levels in the sky, or waters of different temperatures in flooding tides. Molly Bloom's direction is different from either of theirs, but somehow both theirs rest upon hers. Each partakes of the other. Again it is something like this in the movement of tidal currents with respect to the major tidal flow.

It is our business as readers to bring as much of the structure into performance as the story will bear and at the same time to illuminate the structure with the story. It is unlikely that we shall end with a uniform action; but it will only be because we have the sense of such a uniform action that we shall be able to proceed at all. We must have a sense that what happens in Telemachus, Nestor, and Proteus and what happens in Calypso and the Lotus Eaters (these are the first three sections on Stephen and the first two on Bloom), will have, when read, a created mutually illuminating correspondence. There are weights which answer each other. The balance tilts, teeters, veers, slides, trembles and recovers; then begins all over again. It is a balancing of weights which are alive, like bodies hefted, and shift the sense and the sentiment within themselves. They correspond, at a series of given instants, and as a function of being in motion. Correspondence is the flash of vision or the pulse of feeling; never permanent, and, once had, never quite lost. There is the mockery of the Mass in the very first two pages of the book, and there is Bloom's wrongly articulated grasp of the mystery of the Mass in the Lotus Eaters. Stephen is fascinated by heresies because he knows them; Bloom has heretical notions (as all experience has) almost without knowing it—though he wishes he knew more about it. So Stephen dreams of a creative sea, Bloom of an erotic bath. Again how deep is and is *not* the correspondence between Bloom watching the cat's eyes in the dark (dark eyeslits narrowing with greed

62

till her eyes are green stones), and Stephen's darkness shining in brightness which brightness could not comprehend. Again, Stephen devours himself with *amor matris* and Bloom rescues himself with *amor patris*. Still again, Stephen combines in one image the poet Swift and Saint Joachim of Flora; Bloom combines the idea of metempsychosis and his lost son. Can you balance these without running one into the other?

Stephen opens on all that goes by *tradition* of mind and flesh. Bloom opens on all that comes by the *qualm* of emotion and flesh. Joyce, being both, opens on all that is maintained by form and symbol. Stephen does Hamlet by algebra, Bloom wonders whether Hamlet was a woman. Each is full of the language of Hamlet: Stephen wincing, Bloom unaware of it: a part of hope and a part of speech: each with a frustrate obligation. Stephen, so to speak, knows that he has a prophetic soul —which will abort or obliterate his prophecy; his friends will walk on the track of his ashplant by night. Bloom is unaware that he is an enacted prophecy. Neither has remembered the key home when setting out on the long day. Both remember, and exchange, the ashplant and the potato, which are their symbols. Stephen calls his the augur's rod, Bloom does not know his potato is the moly Hermes gave Odysseus to protect him from Circe. Pride is consciousness, humility beyond it. Yet I think Bloom is a deeper mimesis of Hamlet than Stephen, for Bloom's form of the role existed before Hamlet did. Bloom represents, is the very taste of, the orthodoxy that we plumb; Stephen is the rising fall of that orthodoxy the mind erects. Stephen Dedalus marks what is martyrized and fashioned new in words; Leopold Bloom what grows and what things grow into. I suspect that Stephen got to be a good poet after Bloom caught hold of his ashplant and made it bud like Aaron's rod. But if that is the case, it must also be true—a true potential of psychology—that Stephen got the benefit—safety of conscience, certainty of identity—that went with the possession of the potato. Bloom had these all along, without knowing it.

Joyce has somewhere the remark that great art is concerned with the Constant and the Grave; and of these qualities Stephen and Bloom are constant analogies. Bloom adverts constantly and gravely to Molly and Rudy, his lost son. Stephen adverts constantly and gravely to his mother's death and the missing role of the father. It is the rhythms, in their constancy and their gravity, that prove the identity. This is the substance upon which the structure is reared, and which warrants its many-mindedness. I mean of course those occasions when more than words are given to their thoughts, more than gesture to their actions; so that words and images seem themselves to be moving actions. With Bloom it is more in images; with Stephen it is nearer to words; but it is the music of action moves us. All this is clear tone.

But Joyce also knows that the constant and the grave may be ambiguous and minatory, and it is for this reason that he introduces the apparition of the Man in the Brown Macintosh: he who is the incubus of death, the visitor by night, the other fellow, round the corner, up the stairs, on the slates, he whom you will momently become; the stranger that is indeed yourself, engulfing yourself. He is no doubt related to the vampire mouth in the poem Stephen wrote on the beach. For each the figure comes in day-sleep, the creative aspect of thought. Stephen asks, Why did I write it? Bloom wonders where he came from. The vampire mouth is a poem made; the man in the brown macintosh is an image thrown up out of the *nous poetikos* (the talent things have to assume meaning).

The man in the brown macintosh turns up first at the funeral, where he has the number thirteen at the grave, and his name is put down as present. He is seen eating dry bread and passing unscathed across the path of the viceroy's cavalcade. Bloom wonders who he was. He loves a lady that is dead. He is called the Walking Macintosh of lonely canyon, and we are told that we will see him today at runefall. He is the Nameless One on a jury. He springs through a trap door and identifies Bloom as himself, and a little later Bloom is seen wearing the brown macintosh. He is Mac Somebody, Unmack, I have it. He is What do you call him, Strangeface, Fellow that's like, Saw him before, Chap with. He is said to have been at the funeral by name. Lastly, for these citations are in their order of appearance, Bloom apprehends him not comprehending, but comprehends where Moses was when the candle went out.

Are not these two, the vampire mouth and the man in the brown macintosh, precisely our closest familiars, always there or at hand, not constant and not grave but rousing in each of us the yearning for the constant and the qualm of the grave?

But let us see the constant and the grave where they make action in the very music of the psyche. To introduce that action, I have a sentence from a letter of Kafka cited by Heller in his *The Disinherited Mind:* "No people sing with such pure voices as those who live in deepest hell; what we take for the song of angels is their song." Here are two forms of the action, both in the second chapter of the book, called Nestor, rather like Polonius and no more easily to be distrusted, in the guise of Mr. Deasy the headmaster. Stephen Telemachus is collecting his pay, resigning his job, and preparing to do Mr. Deasy a favor. Mr. Deasy is of good sense and of dangerous platitudes, of another persuasion, requiring a scapegoat, with conventional prejudices and good will and public spirit: he keeps the world going: he is the brightness which cannot comprehend the darkness that shines. He is one of the conditions of life that must be accepted. In his office he has a tray of Stuart coins, apostles preaching to the gentiles, world without end; he has also a stone mortar full of shells, especially a scallop or pilgrim's shell, and a savings box for small coins. He has much to say to Stephen. He speaks of Iago's "Put money in thy purse," and says that it was England's creed: I paid my way. I owe nothing. He says that the Jewish merchants were the death of England; they sinned against the light and are wanderers of the earth till this day. He speaks of the hoof and mouth disease and of backstairs intrigues, and of the women who brought sin and downfall to the world of man. To him Stephen answers aloud. I fear these big words which make us so unhappy. . . . Who has not sinned against the light? . . . A merchant is one who buys cheap and sells dear, Jew or gentile, is he not? . . .

History is a nightmare from which I am trying to awake.
. . . God is a shout in the street. And to himself Stephen says
that he can break the bond of bargain and money; that it is
the Harlot's cry from street to street, not the Jews, that destroyed England. And as for the Jews, *he* sees images of gold-
skinned men on the Paris Bourse, with their unoffending gestures. He asks himself: What if that nightmare gave you a back
kick? And when he has agreed to get a letter put in the paper
about the hoof and mouth disease, he says that Mulligan will
call him a new name, the bullock-befriending bard. These are
Stephen's correspondences. Against them Mr. Deasy is money
and sunlight and humor. "I have always struggled for the
right," he says seriously, and at the end of the chapter runs
after Stephen with his story as to why the Irish never persecuted the Jews: because they never let them in. "On his wise
shoulders through the checkerwork of leaves the sun flung
spangles, dancing coins."

Here is the other form of the action of the psyche. When
school broke up one boy, Cyril Sargent, stayed behind in Stephen's class with a copybook, the word "Sums" written on the
head line, and it is sums he has been copying at Mr. Deasy's
orders.

"Can you do them yourself?" Stephen asked.
"No, sir."

Ugly and futile: lean neck and tangled hair and a stain of ink, a
snail's bed. Yet someone had loved him, borne him in her arms and
in her heart. But for her the race would have trampled him under
foot, a squashed boneless snail. She had loved his weak watery blood
drained from her own. Was that then real? The only true thing in
life? His mother's prostrate body the fiery Columbanus in holy zeal
bestrode. She was no more; the trembling skeleton of a twig burnt in
the fire, an odour of rosewood and wetted ashes. She had saved him
from being trampled under foot and had gone, scarcely having been.
A poor soul gone to heaven: and on a heath beneath winking stars a
fox, red reek of rapine in his fur, with merciless bright eyes scraped
in the earth, listened, scraped up the earth, listened, scraped and
scraped.

Notice how the rhythm of the sentence containing Columbanus rises off the page; rhythm is the music of the soul's action. Stephen watches the boy.

In long shady strokes Sargent copied the data. Waiting always for a word of help his hand moved faithfully the unsteady symbols, a faint hue of shame flickering behind his dull skin. *Amor matris:* the subjective and objective genitive. With her weak blood and wheysour milk she had fed him and hid from sight of others his swaddling bands.

Like him was I, these sloping shoulders, this gracelessness. My childhood bends beside me. Too far for me to lay a hand there once or lightly. Mine is far and his secret as our eyes. Secrets, silent, stony, sit in the dark palaces of both our hearts: secrets weary of their tyranny: tyrants willing to be dethroned.

This is Stephen at his most tender, he transcends his intransigence, and comes on the conditions of life—which is where Bloom is all the time. If we put the two together, side by side in their fertile and permanent analogy, we have an example of the great potential psychology of which Joyce was the master craftsman. We have also one more place for the application of the words we quoted for epigraph two weeks ago. "Every life is many days, day after day. We walk through ourselves, meeting robbers, ghosts, giants, old men, young men, wives, widows, brothers in love. But always meeting ourselves." We have, I think, an irregular metaphysics of heart and head in sensual action.

Here we should come to an end, and if we pretend that we have done so we can regard all that follows as a kind of appendix. Our bourgeois humanism requires of us some account of what sort of criticism it was that surrounded its creations. What we value in the bulk of it, and in the bulk sifted out and generalized, has very much the same sources as the literature itself. Our critics became for the most part hardly at all men of letters; they became researchers, psychologists, psychiatrists, amateur mythologists, students of words in themselves, and above all technical masters of the difficulties in reading. That is, the critics used the new knowledges to apply to literature as if it were some kind of autonomous and amorphous aspect of the new mass society; but of course they did not do so purely, any more than the literature did, and there was not much more criticastry than there was poetastry. There was a renewed attention to the details of prosody and a vast new attention to the novel as a well-made object with almost mechanical rules. And side by side, and gradually, there was a renewal of a kind of neo-medieval interpretation almost fourfold in its scope. If there was no syntax in this modern literature, there was at least to be an allegorical form; and perhaps allegory goes with analogy and correspondences and symbolism generally, rather better than the logic and the syntax which the middle ages also depended on as aspects of form. One risks it that in an expressionistic art and in any sympathetic criticism of it there will be a dread of any external control over the order of the elements in which the expression emerges, and at the same time a rush towards all sorts of internal, but equally arbitrary, controls. The arbitrary external controls, such as those of syntax, are likely to predict a good deal of the meaning of the work, where the arbitrary internal controls, such as allegory in its modern anthropological guises, seem to liberate meaning on its own. In this area the critics, having easily the more mechanical techniques which were for all they knew everywhere relevant, got far ahead of the artists. The early exegetes of *Finnegans Wake,* which was then called *Work in Progress,* went far beyond anything that Joyce actually did, and touched very little of the flesh of his work. Similarly, those who have been overconcerned with the Rose Garden in Eliot seem never to have come across the thorns.

In another aspect, particularly with regard to the poetry, there is a remarkable and reassuring resemblance between the criticism in English between 1922 and 1940 and the criticism of the Elizabethan age. Elizabethan criticism is an example of the contest between medieval rhetoric, logic and grammar, and the techniques which went with what we call the Renaissance and the revival of learning. The literature and the theory tried to operate on both models simultaneously. Thus there was a complex struggle between the native independence and inner necessity of practice on the one hand, and the two kinds of authority on the other hand. There is a nice subject for speculation here, whether the very complex terms of the struggle, and the permanent inability of the English to reach any single conclusion, may not be responsible for the depth-structure of English literature in its great writers and the relatively shallow quality of its secondary great writers. Perhaps it is an idle speculation; but still, it is situations like this struggle which create deep contentions in the spirit and consequent many-moded expression. There is *more* to answer for, not *less*. I am suggesting of course that the confusion of the struggle of independence and necessity against the two kinds of authority, themselves deeply opposed, helped Shakespeare express his riches. Shakespearean tragedy and seventeenth-century pastoral as major modes in English get their forms, styles, words—it seems to me —precisely out of this confusion and this struggle. Put another way, where Dante made a generalization which released poetic power from the bonds of a learned tongue and the worse bonds of oratory, the English extended the struggle and got swept along by the momentum which underlay it. So it seems to me to be with Eliot and Yeats and Joyce.

To remind you of the details of the comparison, let me run over some of the topics that inhabited the manifestos and little magazines of our period. There was the argument for the sequence of the musical phrase as against the patter of the metronome. There was, and still is among those who bother with such things, an attempt to "restore" the sense of "quantity" in English verse. There was an Italianate idea of balance; and there were such things as neo-Websterian blank verse, the reassertion of the secret tongue, and the intense declaration of the absolute power of the word as a thing having life of its own and apart from its meaning. There was, and is, the leaning towards structure by the logic of conceit, along with structure-texture of ambiguity, structure by irony and paradox, and even the quarrel over rhyme and free verse. All these have

69

their close counterparts in the Elizabethan age. It was all a struggle, couched in rhetoric as newly understood, for a decent condition of language governed by a decent prosody, and the struggle is not over.

The moral struggle, too, has its parallels in the same period. Some of the humanists of the Renaissance took a very high tone indeed towards the arts, and were only the predecessors of the puritans. So it was with the neo-humanists in our period, and it is worth taking a look at their rejection and denigration of modern literature if only because of the offchance that they may be followed by a neo-puritanism appropriate to the new sociological conception of the virtues and vices; for if so, we must be sure to have a Milton in the midst, and a Milton warmed by the remnants of the bourgeois tradition.

Our bourgeois neo-humanists were neither so bourgeois nor so humanistic as they thought when they came to tackle literature; for they by and large only succeeded in misusing it. It is silly to quarrel with misuses of the arts beyond the point where the misuse is established. Our particular misuse was primarily American at its center, though it had many sympathizers in England and France. In the early twenties and thirties the neo-humanist movement set itself the task of making literature conform to a particular moral and philosophical view in which alone human health could be found. It was a movement of dissident professors (the new conservatives of their time) in this country. It was representative in an extreme way of the natural prejudice the moral and intellectual half of us has: either to find our own morals and ideas in literature or to condemn it when they are not there. It is a sign of the vitality of literature, and of our own minds, and of the whole enterprise of which both are part, that this prejudice should exist and should want to take action: and there is nothing to diminish this vitality in the reflection that in history what we call living literature has never met the requirements of this prejudice. It was usually some older literature, rather remote, that filled the bill. For the American neo-humanists, it was Greek tragedy—not particular tragedies by particular poets, just the lump sum of Greek tragedy—that seemed pretty nearly right in the general ideas by which it interpreted human nature. It is precisely in the light of this last phrase that this type of mind insists on criticizing literature: the general ideas by which it interprets human nature. So far, so good. If there is a misuse of literature, it is universal. But it is wrong and does a vast amount of harm to literature, to insist on finding a particular set of ideas there, and it is even worse to reprehend literature or to accuse it of having no ideas at all or only bad ones, if literature has *done something* to those ideas; if it has, for example, brought the ideas back into the realm of experience and criticized them in an imaginative way. This is the sort of thing the neo-humanists did; and the amount of literature they were able to condemn is astounding. They could never understand that the idea of murder or adultery was one thing, the experience of it another, and that a story about either was something very different: a kind of criticism, a psychological projection, of the relation between the idea and the experience. The neo-humanist wanted the police to step in where the story-teller could not properly step at all. The neo-humanist condemned what he could not correct.

This was an expected reaction of moral natures to romanticism, realism, art-for-art's-sake, and all the chain leading to our own expressionism which flourished in an age without adequate thought-police, and it ought to strike you as something similar to all the activities of the neo-classicists and the puritans. They are the same type under a different cultural situation; and the sameness lies in the habitual exercise of personal authority, where the habit creates the delusion that personal authority is absolute authority—and where the penalty is the fear of any other authority whatever. The neo-classicists and the neo-humanists were alike driven to tyranny and suffered from the tyrant's characteristic privation—the lack of direct knowledge of the actual state of affairs, whether in life or in letters.

But let us pursue the comparison in more nearly literary terms. The difference between the neo-humanists and the humanists is like that between the neo-classicists and the classicists. The neo's show a lack of sensibility where the original types worked under a rush of sensibility, the pressure of experience that needed to be formed and expressed. To make up for the lack of sensibility there is a general air of witch-hunting and exorcism; a violence of language on essentially formalistic matters; and a violence of idea employed to put down or minimize the violence that exists. Thus Irving Babbitt could pursue Rousseau as the father of all modern evil, political, social, and artistic, all his life long, and never realize that he was slaying a dead horse. Thus Paul Elmer More could exclude *Antony and Cleopatra* from the canon of Shakespeare because of the lust and adultery in that play. Thus each of them could borrow phrases from the other such as "an explosion in a cesspool," for Dos Passos' *Manhattan Transfer;* or, for general abuse: "he thinks he is emancipated where he is only unbuttoned." Or again, one humanist could get rid of Shakespeare as high art on the ground that there was no transcendence or unity in him—to which Eliot's answer was that a good mirror is worth any amount of transcendence.

In ideal these men were against the absolute. In ideal they saw the hope for grace, clear conscience, individual riches, balanced diversity of needs and satisfactions. In practice they carried a whip; for nothing in literature since Rousseau approximated the ideal unless it might be that half-hero Arnold. These men could handle nothing but the *ideas* of their own time; and an idea without its medium in life, without the shapeliness it gets in action or experience is hard to see as hero, desperately easy to see as villain.

We may think that they did not see what literature *is,* through lack of sensibility. Why did they ask of literature what it has never done? I think it is partly because they looked at the mass of contemporary literature, much of it still *our* contemporary literature, and the *mass* of literature in a given time always gives much less of what literature can do than its masters, when they have been seen, will turn out to have done. This is why the *New York Times Book Review* runs leaders on the current novel, from time to time—on the average twice a year. The writer will complain that the run of our novelists do not represent us, and will list a good number, I remember once as many as thirty. When did thirty novelists represent a time; or five; or one? When did Shakespeare or Dante or Virgil represent their times in this sense? Yet it is a real question because it points to a real need in a part of all our minds, and a dominant part in those minds which seem to canalize their emotions according to an intellectual drive.

The neo-humanists, and the leader writers for the *New York Times,* perhaps ask of literature critically what it has never done, out of a deep instinctive wish that literature would give us heroic models. It was because Plato saw that this was unlikely that he excluded the poets from the *Republic.* The affair points itself when we remember that Paul Elmer More dismissed Joyce's *Ulysses* as moral and artistic chaos. Yet it was Joyce's lifelong labor to create conscience, to create, after the fashion of literature, the kind of hero More wanted. More did not understand the fashion of literature, and I do not think very much the fashion of heroes either, in or out of literature. Prudent men and practical moralists seldom do; they want their heroes to purge them without themselves having anything to lose.

This literature will not do. The cost of a hero in literature as in life is practically everything; and commonly literature has provided us with heroes whom it would be fatal to any society to take as general models. Literature and life give us heroes whom we desperately need so that we may see what we are not and cannot be in height and depth; and even in literature we can afford them only exceptionally. It is a lucky economy of the genius that creates heroes that it is so scarce. So in religion: we could not afford very many saints; and since the Reformation the Roman Church has looked long and suspiciously into the credentials of candidates. It was Eliot who remarked that as morals are only a *primary* consideration for saints, so they are only a *secondary* consideration for artists. And in politics or history we cannot afford so many great men

73

as we have; we are always half-mired in the blood shed which they caused by being bad great men (Napoleon; who had all the greatness possible without virtue) or in the worse blood-shed caused by our inability to keep equal to their greatness. England was lucky to have only one Cromwell, ourselves to have only one Lincoln, India only one Gandhi. All were magnanimous men: "By the bowels of Christ I beseech ye, Gentlemen, consider lest ye be mistaken"; "With malice toward none; with charity for all"; and Gandhi's spinning wheel and passive resistance. It would have paid the humanists to have looked less into Arnold and more into Arnold's contemporary, Lord Acton; Acton was a better humanist than any of them, and made a lifelong study of great men in concert and conflict with great ideas. No;—by and large we can afford the gesture of greatness better in literature and the other arts than we can in life. Half at least of our soul insists on creating images of the greatness that destroys us, so near it is to our hearts' desire. We would create experience no matter how fatal it might be for us to live what we have created, but if we could not create such images we would not live at all.

But I should not have spent so much time on the neo-humanists, as such, if we bourgeois humanists did not understand them so well, and if they did not represent perfectly, or as perfectly as any criticism can, what society thinks of its arts and what it is likely to do with its artists, whenever it takes them with mistaken seriousness in the merely intellectual sense. We do not live *in* the intellect, but *with* the intellect—and this is what our arts and letters do most severely show us. Mere intellect is the mere manners of the mind, and the man who makes himself all intellect or all opinion, is all manners and no man. The intellect should hospitably make room for what it might overlook. Hospitality is imaginative, plastic, responsive, and to practice it enriches one's manners and gives them being. Here again we may make a repetition of the remark in Mann's *Magic Mountain,* that vast account of what happens to bourgeois humanism when it turns to art. When the two young heroes of sensibility have gotten to know Settembrini, the professed humanist, quite well, and just after they have heard him discourse, Hans remarks to Joachim of him: "Just as always, first an anecdote, then an abstraction; that's his humanism." Anecdote and an abstraction, abstraction *and* anecdote. Otherwise, as Hans sees in his dreams, the humanist is only an organ-grinder, with a monkey, not a man, at the end of his string.

Questions of this sort do not arise when we look at the professional or trade criticism of the twenties which stemmed partly, as in Eliot or Wilson or Trilling or Leavis, from the old traditions of the man of letters, and partly from the special needs of the new literature to make itself available to any appreciable audience outside the general company of actual and disappointed writers. It seems that the man of letters is at present disappearing, though he is much wanted, and there is nothing that has turned up to replace him. Instead we have the rising tide of the professional, the expert, the man with the technical knowledge who is expected to save us from the need of any knowledge of our own, except as we are ourselves experts, and who makes us largely the children of other peoples' research. In the very heart of our period, A. N. Whitehead took a more optimistic view than I can in speaking of our professionalized society in general. "Professionals are not new to the world. But in the past professionals have formed unprogressive castes. The point is that professionalism has now been mated with progress. The world is now faced with a self-evolving system, which it cannot stop. . . . The problem is not how to produce great men, but how to produce great societies. The great man will put up the men for the occasions." This is from *Science and the Modern World*. A little earlier in the same chapter, he declares that "the habit of art is the habit of enjoying vivid values,"—a statement to which I would adhere. But I do not think this is precisely a description of how the most of the professional criticism of our time has worked, or wanted to work, or been permitted to work either by the audience or the art. The techniques which have become natural to us tend towards the discovery of difficulties and their exegesis or explication for its own sake and largely because it would be done. Reading these critics it would seem that all our old unconscious skills of apprehension and gradual intimacy had disappeared or become useless under the far more incomplete skills of conscious analysis. One of the conspicuous losses, which points to others in other fields of society, has been the increasing inability to appreciate the older poetry except when it masquerades as new poetry.

Let I. A. Richards, whom I admire greatly—a warm and passionate man and a lover of poetry—let Richards stand for the rest, if only for the reason that he led a great many other critics and even invented some who might not otherwise have appeared, such as William Empson. Three little passages from *Science and Poetry* (1926) may serve as texts for departure. "The necessity for independence [from beliefs] is increasing. This is not to say that traditional poetry, into which beliefs readily enter, is becoming obsolete; it is merely becoming more and more difficult to approach without confusion; it demands a greater imaginative effort, a greater purity in the reader." That is one; here is another: "A poet today, whose integrity is equal to that of the greater poets of the past, is inevitably plagued by the problem of thought and feeling as poets have never been plagued before." Here is a third. Poetry, he says, is the science of our knowledge of our experience. Poetry is "a means of ordering, controlling, and consolidating the whole experience." Thus the command of words is the command of life; or at any rate the command of all that kind of life of which the experience is its own justification.

This is quite an extraordinary claim. Richards, loving poetry, made it in this way because he was a direct product of a scientific education at Cambridge: he was full of biology, anthropology, and psychology: those great *underminers* of belief, those great *analyzers* of experience. Right or wrong, these notions with their developments, are a preparatory school for the greater part, quantitatively, of what literary criticism must consist in a society like our own, and I think this is so even when we discount by half every major statement of difficulty he has made. No schooling is ever adequate to the purposes of that schooling, and the schooling afforded by Richards in his *Practical Criticism* (1929) is no exception; but that book is still a useful guide to normal failures to master what have become the difficulties of reading poetry which was to give us command of life.

Practical Criticism was the result of sending thirteen poems, without date or authorship attached, to a number of cultivated readers, and the results were stupefying. The protocols turned in showed gross failures to understand, to appreciate, or to judge the poems at anywhere near the level they required or deserved. Yet these poems had been submitted to far more than the average scrutiny poetry gets from its regular readers: which was perhaps the trouble. The scrutiny was necessary, but it got in the way. —I think it fair to add that Richards has since made other experiments which show that the cultivated experience of poetry is no worse than that of other uses of language central to our tradition.

What is more striking about all this is, as I said above, that it represents a decay in unconscious skills confronted by an inadequacy in conscious skills of reading. The forms which excess consciousness takes are—at least when analyzed—unsatisfactory for the purposes of consciousness. Our culture has always been carried in words, and especially for purposes of action; here was the use of words breaking down.

Yet clearly—from the examples in literature we have touched on in these papers, and also in our daily lives, the breakdown is only superficial and it took place when confronted with an extraordinary burst of imaginative talent, in expression if not always in communication; and I think that as we are readers—as we are critics—we had better work from that example primarily, no matter what other techniques and metaphysics we call in to grasp our unreason. In this we are saying that criticism resembles art; and how it does so seems so important that I wish it could be said clearly, self-evidently, and irrefutably. But only revelation can do all that. I think it has something to do with radical imperfection. I risk it that in

77

literary criticism you get the radical imperfection of the intellect striking on the radical imperfection of the imagination. Just as the imagination is never able to get all of itself into the arbitrary forms of art and has to depend on aids from the intellect, from conventions, and from the general assumptions of the time, so the intellect dealing with the imagination is itself imperfect and has to depend on conventions of its own, some of them imaginative, some quite formalistic. Each of these modes of the mind avows imperfection by making assertions about its intentions which it neither expresses nor communicates except by convention. It is of the first importance that we use pretty much the same conventions; it is of only secondary importance that we agree closely as to what the conventions mean, *e.g.:* in arts, the tragic fault: in criticism, verisimilitude. If we use whatever it is that is meant by these conventions, it does not matter too much if we define them differently: indeed we should use definition in the end in order to surround the indefinable. If you "define" the novel or the sonnet you will not be able to read the next one that alters the limits.

These remarks are in no way meant to be a confession of impotence on the part of the mind, but rather an assertion of its strength; and so far as literary criticism is concerned it is meant only as a precaution against substituting intellectual formulae for experience; or put the other way round, it is meant as an insistence that intellectual formulation is the great convenience for ordering the experience of the mind and, because of the imperfection of the mind, an even greater convenience for stepping in, in the guise of generalization or hypothesis, when there is not enough experience to go round. —Again: If either art or criticism—if either imagination or intellect—were relatively perfect, we should have no trouble and no problem, and the staring inadequacies of either with respect to the other would long since have disappeared. The contrary is so much the case that in practice we tend to get in literature immature intellect tampering with imagination, and in criticism immature imagination tampering with intellect.

78

Hence the "claims" made for poetry, and hence the authoritarian aspect of much criticism. When you get maturity of imagination and of intellect (I do not say perfection, only maturity: balance without loss of passion or vitality), you get great literature and great criticism—or, let us say, criticism that has become a part of literature or literature that has become a part of criticism. That you get considerably more great literature than great criticism may very well be due to the fact that the imaginative mode of the mind requires so much of its skill to be developed to the point of second nature, whereas the intellectual mode of the mind rather likes to be self-conscious in its work as well as its role. But it is more likely that the paucity of great criticism may be explained by saying that by and large only second-order minds took it up, or the second-order parts of first-order minds. Of course, I should *like* to say that it was not till pretty nearly our own time—about the time you reach Coleridge or even Arnold—that we had any need of great criticism. Perhaps this is meant in praise of past times. Perhaps it is meant as reference to the enormously increased number of persons who either try to write literature or try to tamper with literature. I do not know. But it may possibly be that those of us are right who believe that both the nature of literature and the nature of the audience have changed from previous times. The literature has become more inaccessible and the audience more illiterate; I mean, of course, that Shakespeare has become more inaccessible than previously to the audience presumed to want to use him. I mean also that Shakespeare is now open to uses to which he would not previously have been put. Shakespeare has changed: anyway our consciousness of him has changed, it matters nothing which way this is put. We now look to Shakespeare to see what has happened to us; and that is naturally a hard job to find out. The change is only superficial; it is only that we are able to take less for granted than our ancestors were; it is only that we do not have nearly so adequate a set of conventions as they. We have invented so many ways of formularizing consciously what we know that it sometimes seems we know, by nature, nothing at all. We are as bad off as Socrates complaining about the specialization of knowledge at Athens in his time; by which I do not mean to be frivolous but only to suggest that the availability of our knowledge depends deeply on the attitude we take towards it.

Part Two

PATHOLOGIES OF
CULTURE

5

The Logos in the Catacomb: The Role of the Intellectual

ONE OF THE resources of the American intellectual abroad is to meditate on the uses of the American intellectual at home, with the result that he questions a little whether he has any uses at all and tends to wish he could remain abroad where, in most countries, he would at least be accepted as a member of the intellectual proletariat without ceasing to be an intellectual. What becomes clear is, that if the American intellectual at home is in general ill repute it is possibly because his society has not for a long time assigned him any roles to play as such or given him any place to sit in, neither an ivory cellar nor an ivory attic nor any flights of stairs between. None of the politics of his society has any use for him and none of them will publicly put up with his support. He has only the chance of being a pure intellectual, and at his own expense, which is the

83

last expense he can afford. He is expected always to be somebody else. He can be a writer, an artist, a professor, a scientist
and gain modest prestige from society and considerable pa-
tronage from the foundations; but to do this he must as a rule
forego any of the dubious, uncommitted roles of the mind in
action.

Should he take up the role of intellectual appropriate, but
not necessary, to his art or his profession he becomes not an
object of need but a target of suspicion if anyone observes him
in the role, and it will be his own kind which makes the first
and cruelest observations. The intellectual comes way down in
the pecking order, since unpecked he might come first. What
happened to Robert Oppenheimer should be a leading case.
Mr. Oppenheimer, I take it, got into trouble because in his
nature, which was thereby with us a rare nature, he had to
play not only the role of physicist and patriot but also the role
of intellectual; so that he must bring to bear every relevant
force of mind. John Von Neumann, who went to Washington
as a member of the Atomic Energy Commission a little after
the climax of Mr. Oppenheimer's trouble, offered to set up a
private number pool as to how long he would last. His own
guess was not over two years, and it seems likely that had he
not died he might have won. To this extent intellectuals near
the government must talk like politicians; and that is right, or
ought to be right, but it is within the domain without suffrage
and where the rewards are often punishments—it is in the domain of the politics of culture that he talks. By putting his
thought into it, the intellectual makes talk a kind of action: as near as possible the direct action of his force of mind
upon the shape and polity of society. What are called the security restrictions upon our scientists are meant precisely to
prevent the application of force of mind, good or bad, and
again one remembers John Webster's words: that *securitie* is
in the suburbs of hell, only a dead wall between. The risk is
great in all established securities. If you are neither a scientist
nor running for office few are likely to notice if you develop
force of mind, and if you are noticed you may be lucky enough

84

to be thought a crank or a fool—as Tolstoi was—rather than an intellectual. In the mass of those in our country who call themselves intellectuals the washy weakness of pique and cant —together with their flagrant disrelatedness—obscures the genuine force, the force as near as possible without pique and cant, the force of mind itself that emerges in action whenever the intellectual can find a role to play related to his society. The sweet thing to remember is that the intellectual does not need many people to notice him for him to get his work done; the hard thing to remember is the number of lions he has to get out of the path before he can get anybody to notice him at all. The intent here is to recognize, and perhaps to budge, a few of the commoner lions.

In June, 1956, there were two lions roaring in those Italian papers which could be had in Palermo. The Khrushchev speech repudiating Stalin was at its height of réclame, and the story was spreading that our Ambassador to Rome, Mrs. Luce, had got arsenic poisoning from the ceiling and walls of her suite in what had once been a royal palace. Both affairs were outrages upon sensibility made by modern international techniques in publicity and propaganda. Neither, by any report, was entirely credible, and neither seemed entirely to correspond to intelligent motive. Yet each left its watermark upon the paper we use to record our thoughts. One was an invention of Moscow, the other an invention of the Madison Avenue version of the Time-Life building. An invention is not necessarily a lie, but it is a sound rule of thumb in propaganda that no country tends to believe any lies other than its own; a rule everywhere ignored.

The Moscow invention was designed, and did so whether it was a lie or not, to reflect a shift in mode or phase in the Russian polity and so to affect the structure of international politics, and everybody was asking the familiar question why the Russians told that lie rather than another. To what truth did the lie point? No such question could be asked of the Madison Avenue invention. To the Italian mind it seemed adventitious and meretricious in some offensive Luce-like way. No Italian believed it, and furthermore few Italians seemed to think that intelligent Americans believed it either—certainly not the American intellectuals. The small peak of Italian reaction was reached when a Communist member of the Chamber of Deputies read in the Chamber a fine doggerel polemic on the matter. But the Italians were wrong about the state of American belief. Some months later two young men from the C.I.A. journeyed all over Italy to find out why no Italians believed the story—which after all had been prepared by the best publicity people in America. The young men questioned both Americans and Italians, but their training was such that they could not accept the answers they mainly got: that the story simply wasn't true, and that it was too much like something in *Time* magazine. The young men should have been sent in the role of field sociologists, not intelligence officers; whatever else the story was, it represented an aberration in behavior dressed out by unquiet, if not ugly, Americans—and this, in effect, was what Italian intellectuals were saying.

But the point where both the American and Italian mistakes met can be illustrated by a leading article on the Khrushchev letter in the *Corriere della Sera,* the great independent conservative paper of Milan. It was important to find out at once, said the leader, what response to Khrushchev was being made by the American intellectuals because in America, as everywhere else, this was the most important response. Americans were taken like another sort of Italians, and it is perhaps worth quoting the general statement. "Il rapporto Kruscev ha scosso il mondo communista, da un capo all' altro del globo terrestre. Gli strati intellettuali, che sono sempre i più sensibili in ogni società, danno segni di un generale fermento, di una diffusa irrequietudine." The mistakes met in the empty place where the American intellectual ought to be, in the American press. Not even Mr. Lippmann is precisely there, and wherever he is it is a very lonely place. For the rest, the writer in the *Corriere* would have to wait for the first pages of *The Nation, The New Republic, The New Leader,* and *The Reporter*—though the editorial policies of at least two of these journals are hardly favorable to what the *Corriere* meant by the responsiveness of the intellectual. The role is open, but does not invite, for the American, and is not much enacted.

Americans believe in education but they distrust the intellect. This lion will perhaps always be in the American path looking about to see whom he may devour. But there is another lion perhaps more temporary and only at present more dangerous. This lion lives in some of the dens of the United States Information Agency—though by no means in all of them. If he is budgeable we must budge him out. At least we must recognize him even when he is a very pleasant animal indeed and says he knows Androcles. There was, it seems to me, a whole pride of lions of this order in and about the American Foreign Service Settlement in Tokyo. (Most actual foreign service officers are specifically exempted from any leonine reek: an exemption remembered with great pleasure and obligation.) I had accepted an invitation from the State Department to lecture for three weeks on American subjects at Nagano, Japan. It was understood that there would not be very many lectures—once it was put as five or six; and it was on this basis that I had prepared myself and my baggage for the six previous weeks in Italy, France, and England—with the precaution, however, that I took several extra notebooks in case anything turned up not mentioned in correspondence.

It was further understood, though dimly by me, from a conversation in Washington, that I had also a secondary (or perhaps it was an over-all) function to help combat neutralism in Japan. (The man who told me this also told me to take my own coffee and towels with me to that country.) It is good to have some things only dimly in mind, and the idea of combating neutralism would increasingly seem to be one of them, since when practiced clearly by Americans it has compelled the Scandinavian countries, and also Canada, to ask their foreign service people in the neutralist-minded countries to explain away what sounded like hysteria when Americans went about combating their frame of interest. I myself was, as I say, dim about the combative arts in this area, and had besides always thought, which may be thinking more dimly still, that it was a better enterprise for American foreign policy to build on the vast potential *strength* of neutralism than to combat its weakness. For me, in short, American relations to foreign neutralism seemed to belong to the politics of culture rather than to the politics of power. There was a great adventure in these relations so seen, and it was an adventure that an intellectual might legitimately take up, or even seek out. Flying through a green and orange sunrise over the China Sea I felt that my role as lecturer, though not of course that of the lectures themselves, might be regarded as a bit-role in that adventure. It was only in such a way that I might combine my assigned functions.

My plane was nearly an hour late from London when I reached Tokyo. Actually, I was myself behind by an American generation, but having crossed half the earth, I felt tremendously ahead of myself in thought and only tardy beyond redemption in the clock-movements of my body. The psyche in me labored valiantly in the vertigo between, so I had practically nothing in me capable of shaking the hands of the two young American chaps who were there to meet me and take me to my hotel. I suggested a drink, that great abettor and delayer of judgment. They were very pleasant and confident young men until they left just before two in the morning. Then one of them handed me a large envelope with nervous hand and voice saying that here were my appointments for the next day and hoping, with no confidence at all, that I would not find it too much for me, especially the broadcast. All the confidence that goes with anger came up in me full flood so soon as I had got half through the day's list, precisely the fourth item.

At ten there was the Ambassador (whom I should wish to praise if I had another context) for a protocol call, at eleven the financial office, at noon lunch with the Japan-America Society, with perhaps a few words to speak—so far, so good. Then, at two o'clock, I was to make a half hour broadcast, or a tape for future broadcasting, on the New Criticism—a subject upon which I have tried explicitly never to concern myself, and which could not inadvertently be found in my pocket. It seemed to me that some empire I had not known of must be falling, where the emergencies or the salvage were thought to include the New Criticism. Perhaps it was the American Empire, for which I was working, up to a new form of evangelism. There was no time to meditate the trap. I scrabbled notes, showered, was annoyed that the Hotel Imperial's air-conditioning had the same effect of deep and irreparable sloth as that of the BOAC's plane in fifty-six hours of lapsed time from London to Tokyo, and finished a practicable preparation by half-past nine in the morning, my angry confidence quite quite gone.

But there had been two interruptions, aside from those of napping and coffee. Both were by telephone. The first was at five minutes past eight, with a beautifully modulated voice of Japanese apology that I should have had put upon me the burden of a broadcast without warning; and so on and so on; which did not mollify me much, though I made a break in the flow by assuring the voice that it was no trouble at all, and so on and so on. After the break, my interlocutor turned to a different charge which involved an imploring request: that I must by no means let the Japanese Broadcasting Company or the Japanese people down. On the contrary, would I speak my own thoughts as I thought them? If there were any difficulty, there would be a Japanese professor, wholly conversant with my work, to preface, interpret, and explain. In closing, he earnestly repeated his request that I let nobody down.

The second phone call was not like unto the first, except that it had to do with letting somebody down. This call had an American voice and came a little after nine from the USIA office in the Embassy buildings. After a little introduction the voice came to its burden: Say, take it easy on that broadcast. It doesn't matter much what you put into it. There'll be a lot of people listening, so take it easy. And so on and so on. My American friend had asked me to let down everybody concerned, including his government and mine. As I had already decided to combat the forces of neutralism in my own way, there was nothing to answer except to assure him that all was going well. But I could not help reflecting on this my first morning in Tokyo, that while I understood perfectly the Japanese voice at eight I could not at nine understand the American voice at all. And later, when I heard of it, I understood deeply why William Faulkner (who had done my job at Nagano in the previous year) answered the Japanese reporters on leaving their country, Yes, he would like to return to Japan, but only as a free man.

It seems useful at this point to quote a passage from an English review of an American compilation of extracts from great philosophers running to a thousand pages and called *Man in Contemporary Society.*

The question is commonly raised why the popular Press, in spite of its gigantic circulation, has a negligible political influence. The answer is surely that the great questions of policy are of their nature complicated, and if issues are oversimplified so as to make them palatable for mass-circulation, they are necessarily presented in a way that makes their presentation valueless to those who have the responsibilities of decision. It is very much the same with philosophy by extract.

This quotation is meant to suggest that the American Information Agent abroad has companions among the professors at home. Neither acts with the intelligence to secure his own ends or those of the institutions which he serves, for neither trusts the capacity of its audience.

Of course, the point may have been that my American friend didn't trust me—as an author, an intellectual, a professor, or as a pest sent overseas by the State Department to bother the Information service—which is supposed, against all common sense, to be an independent agency, as the bourbon and water crowd might be thought independent of the martini set. Like them it never is. Whomever the agent distrusted he might well have been wrong for excellent reasons, and it may not always have damaged his work too much that he was the wrong man in his job. Many American authors, professors, intellectuals, add shame without apparently knowing it to their reputations among foreigners by speaking under the American aegis in as

much contempt as ignorance of their audience, as much indifference to their own abilities as insolence to others. To hear
a great man garble himself is a hard thing, to hear second-rate
men garble and repudiate every assumed responsibility is
shameful. I have heard Americans let down their audiences in
a dozen countries, and I have heard, not always but often,
their American sponsors express themselves as either content or
ignorant that the speakers had done so. I suspect that soon our
foreign audiences will regard this misbehavior as a normal
American corruption, a mere jobbery of intellect; and they
will be right.

Too many Americans believe—and hold the belief precious
—the sort of language that *American Heritage* (circulation
about three hundred thousand) puts out in search of subscrip-
tions: "Dear Reader: Your history is visible in your mirror.
And you don't have to be handsome or pretty to be grateful for
what you see: one of the best-educated, best-informed, best-fed,
best-groomed, least afraid—*and* proudly free—faces ever mirrored on earth." It is understandable then that there was nothing surprising in the eight-in-the-morning Japanese plea that
an American might not let them down. It was a plea on the offchance.

It was a plea from an institution accustomed to the recognition and regular use of intellectuals as such. Most countries
but our own have such institutions—even the English whom
we regard as so much like ourselves; and it is a charming and
hopeful fact that all these countries persist in believing that we
resemble them in some accidentally hidden way that only
needs to be disclosed. This is of course what I believe myself.
None of us could survive a single dark month did we stop
whistling in that dark; and it is very comforting to have other
people do some of our whistling for us.

One of the best whistlers in American ears is the British
Broadcasting Corporation's Third Program—though its time
on the air was cut savagely a year or so ago; and it is a great
pleasure for an American to write and give a script for it in the
freedom of artistic and intellectual discipline and without

exact limitation as to time in either direction. One runs over or under, by a considerable margin as the time of the script demands; and one runs above or below or to one side the norm of "desirable" opinion and vocabulary or level of interest precisely to the extent that the intellect demands. One is not expected to say of Dostoevsky, as I was once expected to say of him in a New York broadcast, that he was one of the fathers of democracy whom later Russians have betrayed. One is expected to have a marginal mind for the play and interest of it, for where but on the margin of things does the mind most characteristically operate? It is with animus I speak here, since in America I was once condemned to very low estate because my mind was marginal. Of course if I were British I should now proceed to damn the Third Program up and down and perhaps turn for succor to the *Radio Diffusion Française* which can do such things as broadcast [in interviews] the autobiography of Paul Claudel in thirty-eight sessions. I know how such things can go: in the course of attacking his own parliament in the '70's, Walter Bagehot once praised the integrity of the American Congress under President Grant. But I am an American regarding the Third Program with two or three things in mind.

BBC is an institution independent of the state within which and upon the taxing power of which it exists: the kind of institution upon which both the intellectual health of the state and individual intellectual liberties must depend when the form of the state is democratic. In our country it is either upon the Supreme Court, an integral part of the state, or upon such groups as the Civil Liberties Union, which is no part of the state at all, that these matters depend, to their detriment in increased precariousness. One observes, and the more so as one is grateful to them, that both the Court and the Union are variously subject to hysterical attacks, as indeed are our universities. The point is, that although BBC is pressed upon by Parliament and Foreign Office, nobody in England expects the BBC to give in or to reform its programs. That is one thing.

Another thing is the beautiful absence of the distrust of the audience displayed by the Third Program. There is no requirement of mass-appeal and no policy which aims to create it. Where the other two programs are believed to have an audience of some forty-five million, the Third Program is thought to have a top audience of a hundred thousand which shifts among members of a maximum audience of one and a half millions. The average audience for the Third Program is estimated at no more than forty-five thousand. It is the high value (and the high cost of it) set upon a small, self-created and constantly shifting national audience which I wish to emphasize: an audience having nothing in common but its intellectual and imaginative interests, an audience from which there can be nothing in return except response to force of mind.

My third point about the Third Program also makes a point about American character. After a long conversation with its director on many matters within the realm of the politics of culture—the partial realm of their practical adjudication—I was told I had been the first American professor who had not argued that the program ought to go in heavily for adult education. Once again it seemed to me that the American conception of education inherently involves the deprivation of intellectual force. In America one has constantly to go about defending the right to contemporary existence of those modes of the mind whose dead forms we study; we have to defend a contemporary Montaigne: as if there could be a culture without its living and contentious polity, or as if there could be a culture that depended only on method and training. This is a Byzantine part of our mind which Britain and most of Europe have not yet reached, and from which we ought if we can to draw back. We cannot feed wholly on the dead, though we would have gone under many times in our history, if we had not fed mainly on them. The Third Program does not want to be educational at all except by the example of entertainment, and in adult education the Program under its present direction takes no stock. Here it runs contrary to the general British drift, which is much like our own—towards distrust of the audience and towards distrust of entertainment not vulgarized in one direction or another. It seems that intellect and imagination must sometimes play the role of that Public Enemy who exists in us all, and who comes before, as he survives, every mere expression of Law, Right Conduct, and a Virtuous Life.

But intellect and imagination may also play the role of Public Friend—*Amicus curiae*—the Friend of the Court—though when he comes forward that way he is seldom liked and is often suspected of ulterior and destructive motives—like the Department of Justice when it played the role of intellectual in the proceedings at Little Rock in 1957. One might, for example, attempt to reform the editorial policy of the *New York Times Book Review*. This delightful enterprise was put forward to me during and after an excellent lunch in that monument to the histrionic imagination, the Garrick Club, but even with such momentum about my ears and such grime of the human mind at play in every corner and window pane, I could not gather up the force for an affirmative response. So I ate and listened and let my mind ad lib in the hope that force might yet gather. My hosts were the editor of the London *Times Literary Supplement* and his predecessor. It was the elder man who did most of the talking, and he said nothing in which I did not believe and nothing upon which there seemed to be any way of taking immediate action. Now you have become an empire, he said—or have taken over world-leadership —you must not repeat our mistakes. You are obligated to have the *New York Times* review from an American point of view what is possible of the books and thought of the world before they have been published in, or otherwise reached, America. It was not, he said, till his own day as editor that the *Times Literary Supplement* reviewed foreign books as such, and he gathered that even now there is still some complaint from the money-office. And so on and so on. The last thing, he said, was to have the employees of Mr. Dulles review the books, for that seemed to him no more than to me a valuable point of view. When I asked where the subsidy was to come from, he replied that *all* printing was subsidized; intellectual printing needed no more than its natural or normal or whatever share. What

94

was wanted in the United States was not an extra subsidy but strong and independent editors. He urged me when I got home to take this matter up with the owners of the *New York Times.*

My friend had made the Italian mistake all over again. He misconstrued the position of the intellectual in America, thinking that there were public places where he would be welcome to play his role. Yet he was right, halfway. It was not money that was needed by the managing editor of the *New York Sunday Times;* it was such a change of psychology as would permit him to appoint a strong and independent editor of the *Book Review* and then to abide by that editor's decisions. The *Book Review* has already a captive possible audience never less, and often more, than the general Sunday circulation, many times the possible circulation of any other existing literary review in the United States. Certainly very few publishers would withdraw their advertising from a journal which had raised its standards and increased its scope without loss of circulation. All that is needed is intelligent recognition of the vital purpose involved in such an enterprise. My best enquiries have brought me no assurance that this recognition exists in the neighborhood of Times Square.

And why, on what is taken to be the American archetype of things, should it? Here is another paragraph taken from the *American Heritage* brochure quoted above.

You're lucky. Most of us Americans are. In due humility, we usually credit our "luck" to our truly miraculous heritage—to a short, violent period of history, to a soaring idea, and to a lot of ordinary people who somehow rose to greatness when their call came. What people? See your mirror, with its shadows of your predecessors.

I doubt if Lincoln looked that way in that mirror, and there seems to be evidence that if he used any mirror at all it was the *Speculum Mentis,* the mirror of the mind at work, not the mind comatose, of his own times.

It may be that the race of editors is running out in America on account of the new and abortive functions that have been put upon it. An editor was once supposed to persuade authors to their best and most appropriate work which should influence the existing and growing literate audience. Now the editor of a book-publishing house, and indeed of such journals as *Time* and the *Saturday Evening Post,* is meant to replace the author as far as possible and to create an illiterate and uninformed mass audience. I exaggerate very little and only to rouse response. A few years ago the *Saturday Evening Post* distributed among the professors, and I assume elsewhere, quite a large bundle of documents in facsimile which together made a full account—conferences, notes, scripts, revisions, and so on—of the stages whereby an article on the city of St. Louis got prepared for the press. Notice I do not say written; and this is deliberate, because the published article differed widely from what the author—presumably the only true authority concerned—had himself written. Again, I know a man for many years a foreign correspondent for *Time* who always carried with him copies of his stories both as filed and as printed; this because he had to defend himself against charges of ignorance and incompetence and lack of authority. It is by such instances that we learn what editorship is.

But we had better, in the search for charity, look to see what sort of training young men and women who become editors might get from their textbooks. It is not charity the search comes on in the example I think of. Some two years ago a leading textbook publisher received an invited manuscript of a textbook in one of the social sciences designed for advanced students and written by three professors in good standing in this science. The book was contracted for publication if certain revisions were made, and an editor was assigned to make suggestions and to see the book through the press. As there was a good deal of the bad writing to which social scientists are prone, the editor did a certain amount of rewriting and discovered quantities of plagiarism, which also had to be rewritten so that it would no longer be plagiarism within the law. Then it came to light that many of the illustrations were also stolen, and the "authors" refused successive requests for photo credits. After many months' work, the "editor" turned the script in to the boss, with an adverse report. The boss, nothing fazed, got in an outside or free-lance editor who for five hundred dollars was to make a publishable script. I saw many parts of the script with the multiple penciled revisions of the first editor. The original, except for quotations, was illiterate under any definition, and it was quite impossible to make out either the contours or the substance (I will not say the thought) of what the authors presumed to say. The editor had evidently guessed, and when guessing failed substituted the nearest noncommittal cliché—that is, substituted another form of illiteracy for that of the authors. Thus the outside editor had two forms of illiteracy to go on in making a competent upper-class textbook. It should be reported that the authors joyously accepted the earlier revisions. Whether or not the book ever was or ever would be of any authority whatever, even as a concealed plagiarism, was apparently at no time a matter of consideration. The needs of students and professors alike were ignored. I would suppose that the needs of the authors in their careers and the financial interests of the publisher combined to make this scandal plausible to those concerned. The publisher made an advance on royalties, spent a good part of a year's wages for one editor, and then got lost between total loss and grander perfidy. This is the treason of those who do not care. It is also one example of how the new illiteracy degrades our intellectual life and adulterates our knowledge. Further, it represents one of the principal causes for the high costs of publishing—costs which in part must be borne by the literate authors whose books are relatively cheap to produce.

I regret to say that not only commercial houses are thus corrupt. One of our older university presses recently had an editor rewrite a book to free it of the plagiarisms made by its learned author. This book, by its subject-matter, should not have been theirs in the first place. Further, it ought to have been returned to the author as a violation of that part of his contract which dealt with plagiarism. Lastly, in my opinion, the press and its editor deliberately compounded the felony of plagiarism. The intellectuals seem to find one of their chief roles now-adays by assisting in, and insisting on, their own betrayal through their disloyalty to every interest that gives them ex-cuse for being. They are the lions in their own path. But of course I should not say this if I did not know that it need not be so, if only we refuse to accept it as some simple corruption like the sale of office.

These considerations perhaps add up to the suggestion that in our mass society it is for the intellectual all lions and no role, but this is an unprofitable exaggeration, and we had bet-ter assure ourselves of the greater likelihood that most roles for-merly open to the intellectual are still open to wit and energy and force of mind and above all to play of spirit—are still open, perhaps with different risks and under different, but no harsher, conditions, as much as ever they were. This openness is a condition of the lively mind at least as much as the tempta-tion to the moral suicide of stoicism or surrender, which is also a permanent condition. The writer should be the intellectual most aware of this openness. The writer's role is to play what-ever role he can put himself into from emperor to clown, from saint to hunchback, without prejudice of anything but the pos-sibility of the glory and the ignominy that may appear, a last-ing image, in the playing. For this playing, too, is the play of the force of mind. To enter a role is to make a fiction—either for a better understanding of the truth as it is, or has been, or to make a new truth nearer our sense of our own need, to cele-brate either memory or aspiration, our spontaneity or our chance. So we make the judgment of Paris or practice Hamlet's soliloquies; so we approximate the images of our possible selves in our own fictions.

If it were only for himself it would not matter in what lan-guage a writer made his fiction, which is to say it would not matter if a writer had but a single self. The truth is, a writer requires an audience, perhaps that only of his other or his next selves. Most often he wants at least the image of the great audi-ence of all who can read his language, and he must therefore enter into the role of that language, which is his only in so far

as it is also that of others. He must, like Dante, set his fictions
to music, and must, like Mallarmé, purify the language of the
tribe. He must play Ariel putting to the music of language
the grave errands of Prospero. This is the primary role of the
writer, which in the past could often be taken for granted, but
which tends to be obliterated today when so many millions of
words are printed in which no music can be heard and no er-
rand can be discerned. Hence the writer today who is also an
intellectual had better write, as Eliot says, as if the whole history of his words were present in each use of them. He must by
Plato's noble lie believe the fiction, hear its music, think as the
Indians thought that the reality in words is both superior and
anterior to any use to which you can put them. There would
be no literature else.

Nor would there be any scope for the other great historic
role for the writer, which is the role of prophet, of seer, of
leader—lately that strange hero the artist as outsider, the
young man angry or the still younger man beat, but angry and
beat with ebullience. Indeed there seems little scope for this
role in any present circumstance. The trouble with literary
leadership is that it always gets out of literature and yet uses
the prestige of literature in its new and alien territories. Bar-
ring the master, it does so ignorantly, adventitiously, arbitrar-
ily, as we see differently in Colin Wilson and Jack Kerouac. It
becomes a partisan rather than a statesman, and never heeds
the cost. At worst, it makes a methodology that obviates experience while pretending to equal it; at best it creates a method
that passes for experience. It is hard to maintain an audience
so large at a level of standards where discrimination is still
possible, or indeed anything but contagion. I speak here of our
own day, and of the great risk that the contagion of the state's
example may become a methodology for us all, as with the
Byzantines of the fifth century or the Holy Roman Empire of
the fourteenth. If there is anything that will insist it rests com-
fortably on ignorance it is omnicompetence: a frame of general
mind such that he who is made a leader takes on himself the
undoubting face of omnicompetence along with the pretense

of omniscience and the illusion of omnipotence. It is then that all greatness is lost and magnanimity seems a shabby fraud. The fly of private intellect struggles in the marmalade of rhetoric and sees our leaders as necessary scapegoats. A scapegoat is not a panacea. These remarks are meant to apply both to literary and all other kinds of leadership. My politics counts the cost.

I say this here because literature and the arts alone are enabled—and can by their inheritance afford—to escape the frustrating predicament of rhetoric and omnicompetence. We tend to forget how many times the overwhelming force of mind has concentrated in single men or small groups of men and has compelled at least the convulsion of response in us all. Even the fact that mind is a force is forgotten, and it is argued, rather, that the literary man is necessarily political or social or religious or philosophical in the same way as his society is. So indeed he may be, but not *as* he is a literary man, but only as he is a man in general, a statistic and not a force. To the literary man as such, politics, society, religion and philosophy may, or may not, be part of his experience—it is amazing in how little of our general experience an individual can share; and he had better not pretend in his work to experience he does not have.

If he does so pretend, he will obscure his special role as intellectual. It is not at all a detached, or Olympian, or Ivory Tower role, though in order to irritate action he will often pretend so. He lives between the Gates of Horn, but in a critical and playful dream, like Homer and Virgil. Here we touch on the proper leadership of the literary man: of the intellectual, which is the large class to which he belongs; he is *critical* and *playful*. He seeks truth and he plays with it. He dramatizes and plays one of its fragmentary roles. And this is the first of the two pleas—which I think intimately related—for leadership in literature that I would myself make.

The intellectual is committed to society and participates in the commitment according to his talent, but not for immediate action; he does not wish to struggle in the marmalade. He is

committed for the purposes of reaching understanding of the
grounds of action and of finding a frame for decision, or alternative decisions. It is his obligation to see what is likely to
happen and to be prepared to deal with—to respond to—what
does actually happen. He will therefore keep himself a little
outside the avowed interests of the society—or the institution
—which he serves. His true allegiance will be to the contentious, speculative, imaginative nature of the mind itself and to
the dark, problematical, reversible nature of the experience
with which the mind deals. That is to say, his allegiance is to
the whole enterprise of the mind, and far from being remote
from it, it will move him from both without and within. That
is why he will be skeptical of any particular commitment and
will be rebellious to any attempt to make conformity a simple
or narrow thing. Like Dante, he will be rebellious to merely
social or political authority. Like John of Salisbury, he will
know that rebellion to tyranny is obedience to God. Like the
young Jefferson, he will say that if he has to go to heaven in a
party he would rather not go at all.

This is no doubt an impossible ideal but it is the ideal or
desired form of something actual, flexible, provisional, and re-
newable. It would seem the frame of how we have best got
along. With it in mind, we can always take up again, always go
on, and understand why it is worth doing. It is nothing against
the ideal that Dante was the chief imagination of Christendom; that John of Salisbury was Bishop of Chartres and president of a very good college; that Jefferson became President of
the United States and head and heart of a great party. The
honest thing that rebelled remained in them, and is our best
inheritance from them so far as we are intellectuals.

Now the writer as a man of letters—as critic—as public figure—as an image of prestige—belongs among the intellectuals.
His best leadership will be in exemplifying that role so far as
the life of his times does not damage him and drive him from
it. He may do something else very valuable; he may seek and
gain power, and he may use literature in doing so, but he will
to that extent have ceased being a man of letters. I do not say

that this is fatal—only that it is different; as in France every statesman sees himself as a novelist, and every novelist sees himself as statesman—when neither should be premier.

Here is my second plea about leadership, and it is related to the first. If the writer as man of letters belongs among the intellectuals, the writer as artist belongs even further outside all official aspects of society and yet is ineradicably blood-kin to the intellectual just the same. He is even more critical, even more playful, and with real things too: he deals with the great enterprise of society as a poetic experience. He exhibits, expresses, dramatizes it as it actually is experienced with all the shortcomings and turbulences of consciousness and conscience. He shows, let us say, both what has happened to the institution of marriage, or the Church, or whatever it is, and also what the persistent experience is with which practical society has to cope through its institutions and its rituals. It is by these means that morals get into art; it is also, and much more important, by these means that art gets into morals and is thrifty there. Art refreshes our sense, art reminds us of "the Medusa face of life" —or again it protects us from that face by playing with it; lastly it criticizes what we do with life in order to carry it on—which I suppose must be what Arnold meant by asking art to be a criticism of life. It is life not at the remove of manipulation which many people confuse with the real thing, but life at the dangerous remove to the quick of poetic experience.

As the writer as man of letters is the intellectual skeptic coming to decision and understanding, so the writer as artist shows the basis—whether in aspiration or in experience—of the intellectual's rebellion against the mere present form of society and all its institutions. The artist shows that society like the arts has to be remade every generation or so, and what the stresses are. It is by showing this—it is by the critical play of the poetic imagination—that art constitutes in its practice what small share of leadership it may properly have. So believing I cannot help thinking that the critic who forwards this view in his actual critical practice—whether on literature or on public affairs—will be himself practicing his most appropriate kind of leadership. He will be showing the nature and will be justifying the fact of the total irresponsibility of the art to any particular set, or phase, or trend of society. Otherwise, like Plato, he will be suspicious of admitting the arts to the Republic; and that, the record seems to show, is a position at least as untenable as my own, which I take to be a development of Aristotle. Plato, I take it, would lead us out of the wilderness. Aristotle would make us at home there.

There is then lastly the role of the writer in relation to the wilderness of behavior—to human relations—the very quick and the very quicksands of experience. Life, as Shakespeare was constantly observing, is an imperfect play. Consider Eleonora Duse. She had such a demon in her that she spent her life transforming bad plays into masterpieces of acting. She assumed the role to which the original playwrights were inadequate. Is it not possible that the writer must do something like Duse? He plays the role of behavior as it actually is. He takes— it is Henry James' phrase—from the enormous lap of the actual. He formalizes behavior to celebrate it or to make it tolerable or meaningful, and this is his supreme role as intellectual. He may turn behavior into pure play, either to escape from it or for opportunity to develop it, or both. If he does not do this (and perhaps obscurely if he does) he will discover with the pang of actuality that he has joined the role and the temptation of the intellectual and will find, as Rebecca West has said, that "those who are the children of light are irresistibly drawn to assume a task which changes them into the companions of darkness." But the Logos will always emerge from the catacomb.

(*1959*)

6

Ara Coeli and Campidoglio

Iт мах ве that Rome is no longer a capital city, but for an American abroad looking to see where he started from and also where he is, there is no city where the pang of things past seems so strongly the prong of things to come, where indeed it is possible to feel the American conscience taking new and premonitory shape. Looking homewards, here, one is taken aback, is adrift on the momentum of old forces, and gathers sudden way in the sea of old enterprise and new being. Rome, as Edwin Muir says, is the city of resurrection and of incarnation; in which the shapeliness and the possibility of our world of cities make the embrace of shadows which may yet become real. Capital city or not, Rome is the city of all our survival in the midst of all our abandonment. There is in the Museum of the Capitol a stoic mosaic which is a comfortless reminder of all this:

more or less of a negative X ray (black with the bones in white) of a figure more or less reclining over (but not on) flames and spikes. Only his left elbow is at rest. His right hand points with a very extended forefinger into another territory. No doubt he had been there once, but he will never go there again. He has ceased being an explorer, but he knows the role and the cry of exploration. He cannot accommodate what he learned there, but he wants you too to grasp the feel of disaccommodation. The territory is represented only by the imperative motto, in Greek: Know thyself! This is not Socrates up to his tricks; this is as far from Socrates as the psyche can go, and there is no sort of trick about it. This is what Shakespeare saw in *Lear:* the poor bare spirit of unaccommodated man; and it is the constant nightmare of possessive and imaginative natures. This spirit is the creature told that he has become, or always was, responsible for his dreams. Looking at this image in memory, I hear also the sound of the bronze doors of Purgatory—*alto* and *basso*—in the Baptistry of John Lateran, and do not know whether I am shut in or shut out, or if I wish either. In Rome there are incarnations and resurrections over both shoulders. From Rome everything may be explored, and especially the Cities of Man's Making. Rome is the vantage of conscience.

So Rome seemed in 1952 and 1953 and again more deeply in 1956 and 1957, a retort, and exploration, and a vantage of conscience; and it began to seem to me I had a permanent reservation in the Piazza Ara Coeli, or at least a bench there (and in old pictures there are several benches, though only my spirit could find one available now) where I might look at the two flights of steps, one leading steeply up to the Church of Santa Maria of Ara Coeli, the other flowing widely down from the old Capitol. Cities of man climbing and flowing. Roman education is visual and massive, sharpened or distorted by historical focus and the history of private hopes construed somehow everywhere as the public monster lurking and shining within or beyond monument after monument, but always climbing or flowing, whether at Ara Coeli, the Pantheon (where sound itself is a kind of vision, echoing), at Tivoli (where all the waters in Italy flow to climb), at St. Peter's or along the Via Veneto. Rome is no longer either a capital or a capitol but is full of the great forms. St. Peter's is the Grand Hotel on the beach of Christianity, the Via Veneto of the Cross: style à la mode, the moving animal, the spectacle without final order which keeps one in immediate order—as in the great tide of people flowing towards the altar on St. Peter's day at the time of vesper mass, with Peter himself, not at all a rock, but all robed half benign and half uniform. And against this the flow of women on the Via Veneto at much the same hour, but every fair day; and altogether the thing here and the grace possible, resurrection and incarnation, with sinkholes, and gaps, and missing steps in flow or climb.

Rome was an image of the polity of power and culture. The Paris I saw, with Rome fresh on my mind, is not a capital city in any old Roman sense, but is a capital city of a lower-middle-class country with aggregates not consummations of power, with people visibly not equal either to the beauty of their city or to their human possibilities. I saw hardly a well-dressed woman or a decently dressed man except those whose occupations or role it was to be so. Sloppiness and dirty feet never make enough style to control, only enough to smirch, the human violence of talent. This is why everything costs so much more than is given in Paris. I speak only of visual impressions, and I do not forget the powerful visages of old women and the haggard visages of old men, remnants of the Third Republic. But even the visual could not be understood in Paris till escape is made into the green Connecticut and quiet of the Île-de-France, not forty miles away. There the green quiet of the country was almost opulent with the style farmers make ever and ever for succeeding selves out of the violence of the land. There I saw clearly, again, how Paris more than London is victim to the Revolt of the Masses. The wooded reaches alone were enough to show it; my friends' little duck pond alongside their swimming pool and the sheep-fold beyond that, gave another emphasis; my country hotel with Margaux 1925 another.

The piety of the rural is all the greater and the very riches and heart of the true city when seen against the impiety of the mass city: against the swarming impiety of all human movement which is merely administered.

It is not the center, it is the city that cannot hold. It is the concept of the Great City or of the True City that does not hold. Even the tower may no longer be as visible as it was to Dante the Pilgrim in his dream of polity. The great city— Paris, London, New York—is where we are most vulnerable; the great city is a spreading world as well as a spreading stain, as the waste tissues around them proclaim. What does one not think? Here in this village—Rochefort-en-Yvelines—is the tattered bill for a circus now gone: *plus vivant que le théâtre, plus réel que la cinéma;* this tells both lies at once. Again, the very same vegetables are sucked from this rich farm area through Paris, and back to the same place in contaminated form to be eaten. So it was in Cairo, but a little worse, for in Egypt none of the farmers ever ate, except by theft, an orange or a strawberry or a fresh vegetable; they ate dried beans, dried lupins, and if they could afford it hashish once a week; Cairo was a city of other peoples' hopes, with a future imperatively futureless except by hysterias. Tokyo, with a vaster swarm than anywhere in the world, was bursting rather than shrinking on its impulse, showed the very maw of the future. Tokyo says at once why Japan is precarious, as New York says of America (I see with affection why Washington, that city not a city but only the administrative chimera of one, is of possible good for America), and London says of England. Our modern cities draw on their land as near as possible without return, where cities should draw on only what is genuinely exchangeable, on the usufruct not the substance. In America we have turned everything into something purportedly exchangeable, so that if money is the instrument of our freedom it is also the image of our freedom; and so with England. Confronted so, it becomes a vital instinct to lie about our incomes on our tax returns. We know deeply that in the next genuine depression our tax systems will crumple the country as well as the city.

Twenty years ago there were vast so-called marginal areas in America which were actually so prosperous at bottom that they paid and levied hardly more than courtesy taxes; but now the margins have been be-tided. According to rumor and the financial police, the rich in Italy and France do not pay taxes; it occurs to me that the poor can afford to pay taxes only when the rich are let off. But with us and the English we go right on abolishing the poor no matter what the cost. No wonder the universal American and English wish is to create security. The curse is, we must do it on a money basis and on a money necessarily as unstable as the snowball it resembles. There being no way to reverse the process, the need of intelligence seems very great to imagine a viable society in our insecure cities. If these fragments of thought have any force it is because they come from the green fields of the Île-de-France: the human fertility that must not be injured.

There are associated fragments as well. Eugène, the gardener at my friends' place, one afternoon tried chatting with me through my non-French, and among other things gave imitations of the cries of birds and animals. When he came to the crowing of the cock he *said* (did not render) *co-co-ricó;* and for a second I thought he was quoting the *Waste Land.* I thought of the "flash of lightning. Then a damp gust/Bringing rain." But there was only the warm gardener with his dented scythe, and the image of the Chapel Perilous fell away. I thought of the cows in the outskirts of Palermo just after dawn delivering their milk at different houses a few squirts at a time; I thought, too, of a Roman friend quoting I think Silone that in Italy the intellectuals come in small groups, no group too large for a single *terrazzo;* and again I heard the cock on the rooftree: Co-co-ricó! I looked round me, hearing cock-crow as word: above me and visible is a romanesque church from the eleventh century with a modern clock in the tower, just out of sight the old chateau in ruins, and beyond that its enormous replacement of the nineteenth century—the only new grand building in town. My friends' place, "La Tourelle," dates only to the intimate bloodshed of Joan of Arc's time. The birds are brighter than air outside.

That night, to find me a different fragment, to find fragments shoring together, I read the whole of Montaigne, II, 12, the Apology for Raimond Sebond: that chapter which is the great livest image of Pyrrhonism, or the technique of fragmentation as the form for survival in treacherous times. If Montaigne is a city of the mind, it is in that essay a city where every highway is suddenly a purlieu and every alley or private path is broader than the highway. There was no Ara Coeli here. But in this city of Montaigne I found once again the word I had lost since 1934: Epecho: I will not budge, I will suspend judgment. Montaigne says this word was a motto for the Pyrrhonists, and he himself put it on his ceiling. It is this motto which is the beacon and horn and bell in the great fog of his doubt—with which I feel my clothes permanently damp and clinging; and this word is what Pascal *should* have said to himself, even if my memory that he did not ever say it is wrong on the fact. All minds should contain several vocabularies. Reading the Apology for Raimond Sebond in this French and largely sixteenth-century village made me think of the late Plantagenets and early Tudors and of the account of the Sicilian campaigns in the Seventh Book of Thucydides. I had thought of these before at Palermo where I read the Italian accounts of the Khrushchev report on Stalin and its consequences elsewhere. The religious wars in France were of the same pattern, and I like to think that it was the impulse of St. Bartholomew's Day that gave strength and Pyrrhonism to Montaigne's essays. He had both Henrys as friends in power; there are times when one doubts not to find the truth but in order to dissipate it till it appears in new form. Trust and confidence are not parts of our dependable expectations, but we cannot move at all without them, even at their most undependable. One learns to be elastic even to the thinning point—to the Zero at the Bone.

Possibly that is the spring of behavior and response in the Curé of this village. One night the Curé was guest at La Tourelle by invitation together with the plumber by inadvertence of occupation. The plumber runs like a Japanese or German actor to open doors, and gets frantically in the way. When the john got stuck he worked alone in it for an hour, then emerged upon the company with his bare arm raised. "I've had it in woman-shit to the arm-pit," he cried; "that's good luck to us all!" With the Curé he makes a pair. The Curé likes to drink and has a motorcycle. On this night, between one drink and another he rode helter-skelter back to town to turn on the illuminations for the old church (now a state monument) just for his host's pleasure, and his own. At midnight, he rode away again and turned them off. They are not fancy lights, but they made the Church look triple its size, so that it might dominate even electricity in this town where eight out of ten of the people are *non-croyant*. What an elite the Church has come to be! Is this, too, a product of the new illiteracy? Soon only poets and Americans will be believers—and the twenty out of a hundred whose muscles flow that way.

In the yard of my hotel in this village I sat to work in company of a peacock who screamed and danced, a poodle bitch who dropped stones on my feet, a puppy who worried my ankles with baby teeth, and two guinea-hens who snapped up my cigarette ashes almost before they fell. Meditating after a lunch of nearly four hours—melon with a pool of port-wine, blood-sausage, lamb chop, fruit, cheese, with wines and cognac to make the proprium—it seemed to me that the luxury here is in grand indifference to anything the city can do; in the absence of hot water an ignorance; in the cry and dance of the peacock both a transgression and a surmounting. Too many hopes are impious, too many despairs a mere chattering of teeth and decorum; the only shame the shame of not taking up the possibility.

With this for a most private fragment, it lay upon me to go to Chartres on a bright crisp day only less blue than a Roman day: Ara Coeli and the Queen of Heaven: what a salad of inspirations for historians! It is true, as Eliot says, that the words do not matter, that the poetry does not matter, but it is true

only when you already know what the words called for and out
of what the poetry was made. This is the proprium of what
does not matter: intimacy, the sense of which is the only
primer of ignorance except the peacock's cry.

The day was stronger than the place and on the whole I
prefer Ara Coeli to Our Lady of Chartres. It is the sculpture
and the glass, not the church as architecture, that seemed
strong and beautiful to me. As architecture York is stronger,
Placidia's tomb at Ravenna is more beautiful, and a four-
teenth-century mosque of which I forget the name at Cairo is
fuller of the fear and love of God. But nothing was more all
there than the French countryside on this heavenly day. I was
not only a generation or so later, but a whole incarnation back
of Henry Adams. I felt I must try for Adams once more (for
this was my third try): to see if I too could feel the cult as well
as the beauty and relish and fecundity of glass and color and
figure, or if I could not do that, I must at least bring my own
disturbance to clearer words. I know more than my present
words can see, I think I know that the feeling I got was
not particularly Christian; but perhaps the Christian is never
really strong except when drawing on powers other than and
radically alien to itself: when it deals with the non-Christian
world in which all Christians must live as they are Christians.
The Cross is never more than a partial piety. Ara Coeli and the
Campidoglio taken together surmount the Christian without
ever having touched it. Chartres was soaked in the Christian,
but in its independence it is something else as well.

In the necessary recess between the morning and the afternoon visits, I saw how the town too was beautiful, and ignored
the cathedral. I remember I had a Montrachet for lunch, a dry
Pouilly-Fuissé for supper: supreme products of French natural
piety in the observation of which even strangers may join even
as in the sunlight and the wind. These sentiments were an
emollient for my fractions in looking at the church, where I at
once saw a great many little boys chipping with the most noise
they could raise the wax off the candles in the Lady Chapel
where it had fallen on the spikes as on thorns, and seeing, was

distracted. There was lateral space everywhere except in the church proper. But in the church the vertical or lifting space was enormous—and led nowhere; there was no Virgin looking down and I do not think most of us can look up much farther than the glass. In Ara Coeli the steps lead every possible where, solving nothing but leading. I suspect that Chartres has for too many people solved too much, and to others has presented solutions they cannot accept. I do not like art which solves technical problems for anything but itself. I do not like Sancta Sophia, where all the beauty is gone and only the secondary or technical beauty remains: a skeletal beauty, like the present general Turkish effect. I adore Ravenna.

Cradle-Catholics are like Ravenna; they solve no technical problems, but are the effect of a balance of many beautifully solved. Cradle-Catholics should be able to take Chartres as a lift in their stride: as a cult they did not know they practiced and of which they do not need, therefore, to understand the convulsive or aspiring movements. The rest of us can perhaps understand nothing—and need not—unless we have created it within us. Chartres tells me how far away I am from such a creation; precisely because I am in no way indifferent to what I feel there as its various darknesses bloom in light and color; what pushes at me and commands my attention is not Christian, and I have too little in me of the donkey sniffing at the straw of the manger that Henry Adams saw himself to be.

Yet, between the cathedral and the town, Chartres did give me a lift, or a vertiginous drop, or a simple convulsion of spirit that I cannot forget and upon which these present writings depend. I was thinking at lunch of a possible analogy between Chartres and, say, democracy and its evangelical imperialism (its unacknowledged cult), when the waiter brought me a copy of the *Figaro*. It was June 1956, and there was Eisenhower re-announcing that he would run for President: reaffirming, that is, his own cult. My apprehension of his cult is as alien to me as the Christian cult of Chartres. The cult itself is alien, and the act evil; and the substitution of self for intelligence equally a surrender in both. It is, we see in Mr. Eisenhower, the power we do not cultivate that takes over. For centuries people have yapped to speak for the Virgin. Mr. Eisenhower yaps to speak for a self that has been created by others, and has only a little of the old self he had built till the Days of Columbia to prompt him. Inshallah!

Thinking of Mr. Eisenhower as a diet of words, I reminded myself that we survive ourselves in alien forms, and that no one would murder us sooner than our own children or those who have stopped loving us because of a change in the focus of instincts; and this seemed a great warning that I may find myself expecting society to continue to be dear to me, and I perhaps dear to it, merely because I have an interest in its future —in the changing shape of its immortality. But I did and do have the interest, and I do not much trust any particular apparent shift of instincts. The vision of Mr. Eisenhower at Chartres made me go one better: to write a polemic against the monster polemic which is destroying the city.

Such a polemic impulse naturally required a little vision of formality, so on the day after resolving upon it I took with glee a visit to the gardens of Rambouillet with my friends and their three little girls. Glee was both rejoiced and eroded into earth, with the twittering and rubbing of all the formal bedded gardens and alleys and vistas: over water, woods, paths: over all: running always eventually beyond formality to the saving form of forest and field. The odor of cat-piss in box hedges remains with me: as if the box were getting back at the formality with which it had been trimmed; also the three little girls dribbling their ice-cream cones on the borders; and the tendency of public gardens to look like classic pattern indices at an elementary level, and the tendency to cerise in color—to which so many flowers want to return. But also I remember the very lovely lawns, lovelier than Henry James at twilight, and the creation of nature against nature within nature. The walks were swept and everything except my soul was garnished. Suddenly I knew what was missing and needed for soul's safety—the voice of Mozart. Only Mozart knew what to say to make these monsters lyric. The French could never have a Mozart; for he was at the forward edge of form, they at its cracking. Nevertheless, in these gardens, the daughters of Minos and Pasiphaë sang within me. All about the forests were beautiful; Ariadne's hair was tangled all over my face. I resolved to make no very black sails and to make no more perjury than I must to keep alive. I was the forest not the château.

Versailles was needed to project the form. If the colors of the formal beds at Rambouillet were like anatomical plates, those at Versailles were like small crushed animals on the highways in the Carolinas. Versailles goes in for dwarf topiaries and vast gravel expanses and flower beds that look better at a distance. There is a little intimacy at Rambouillet: one might meet a woman there; at Versailles one could meet only an intrigue. At the Villa d'Este, I suddenly remembered, anything might happen. Thinking of Versailles: Only the Sun King could have done it: only that aggrandizement of power and that gluttonous distrust of merits. Nowadays one aggrandizes only one's hopes of sensuality; in the ceilings I kept seeing mistresses with pink nipples and inquiring fingers. But there is neither power nor sensuality there today, only their empty apartments, only the waste grandiosity and puerile splendor of a deserted World's Fair. This was why the peace of 1918 was a waste splendor: even the hall of mirrors could not magnify it to the dimensions of reality. On this day there were American Girl Scouts and their grey mistresses going bored among the gilt and the marbles: all pimples and dead blood: wan pilgrims. Kafka could have invented Versailles.

But it was history, not Kafka. That evening there was a visitor for dinner, one of those men who make history possible and even desirable. A teacher of English in the Lycée (and in two or three other places as well); was in the Resistance and in Spanish jails; is healthy, in his forties; married to a little money and has three children in the Sixteenth Arrondissement; a good citizen with a fine air which said he could not be frustrated. He believed that America had solved the economic problem for herself and for those countries which can imitate her. After a few more troubles, he believed, America will make the solution permanent. One heard a Greek admirer of Rome speak. He also believed that Morocco cannot govern or defend herself under modern conditions, but that Tunisia could. Of Algeria he said nothing. The two sets of beliefs seemed equally deeply lodged. In French education, he said, there is no taint of Deweyism or any other progressivism. What France wanted, he said, was thoroughgoing technical education.

I began to think of the American solution: how we have abolished poverty by fiat and largely in practice, but are required to support the farmer by subsidy along with our housing. Our necessities have become luxuries in themselves and furthermore require the worse luxury of administration. Again, I thought how precarious we have made our shifting stable states by expressing them almost wholly in services and dollars, almost not at all in stable goods. The convertible value of food and housing runs out like clay banks in a flood the moment the luxury of perpetual administration costs too much or presses too hard for other reasons. Our energies and our techniques are ahead of our skills and our intelligence; are ahead of our hands. The furniture and the mirrors at Versailles made that plain for France in another century—as plain as the piles of wheat in Manitoba: two poles of energy that no longer attract but repel each other. Possibly the Sun King himself planted the seeds. At any rate I could not join my new friend's praise for the American solution. We will survive, but it will take a doing in the hands we hardly itch for now. The great threatening evil in our energies and our techniques—in our cities—is that we do not, and cannot, release them in an order consonant with our policy: or in relation to any other policy. Henry Adams seems often to have thought we had better trust in our inertia than in the intelligence we cannot muster. But *Epecho,* as Montaigne said, I will hold back. I think of Ara Coeli again and how Adams said that the steep steps pointed to a discontinuous process and not at all to the substantial anarchy of administrative order. The steps led to the temple, the church, the plague, the unfinished thing, the saltatory pressure of images, to flames jumping. I thought it would be better that the French citizen should think, not of America but of La Sainte-Chapelle where Man says truthfully to the Lord, Look what beautiful things I can make! What a mirror in another phase! But I did not tell him so and he went off in the dark towards Spain.

I myself the next day went off to London and thence to Tokyo and the provincial city of Nagano where there was another temple with very different steps to climb than any seen in the cities of Italy or France but leading nevertheless to much the same place: to where no man can stay no matter how hard he dreamed he could, since the dreams are dreamed always through the ivory gates—or at any rate have been ever since Penelope suggested as much to Odysseus when he came home. Zenkoji Temple, like Chartres, is a point of pilgrimage, both in general and in especial for those who may feel themselves nearing death. Thus on my first visit within its clear absolute magnitude and its risingness and endless space, there was a great trough full of ancient women prostrate and little girls knitting. More very old women were coming in constantly, some of them cripples. There were very few men visible except priests and monks. But there were three enormous drums and one smaller one and several gongs; and the noise of these made the whole temple alive with space moving into the sanctuary. The power flowing from people to temple and temple to people was clearly alien to me (the only foreigner) but seemed in no way inimical. With regard to it I did not exist; regarding it I felt the risk of extinction within it: death was indeed very near upon me as well as within me, within me as well as within the gongs and the drums, their strike and their beat. Since I knew nothing of the decorum, I felt the blow. It did not restore me that I was photographed by an eminent Japanese poet as I stood against the wooden figure of a healing Buddha in a red jacket before leaving. It seemed to me as I went out, and I cannot explain the sharpness of the seeming, that the Japanese would never build great cities in the western sense. Their cities would be vast agglomerates, in *any present* world, sprawling, as indeed Tokyo does sprawl, between the world of the ancestors and the world of eternity. This troubled me and I went back many times on my own to see if I could understand at the temple gates the vital habit and pattern of eastern cities; surely it could be only ourselves in another phase (as La Sainte-Chapelle, Placidia's tomb at Ravenna, and Monreale at Palermo are); but what was the phase? What was the fourth phase to add to water, ice, and vapor? Surely it could not be a more refined phase; it was no false dream like those of Porphyry's Cave, nor was it a coarsening of spirit into extinction such as we like to think the Russians show. These people were alive in absolute spate in this world, not another, and the beauty of their children was like that of ripest plums. And where, geographically, did the phase end running west? It did not go so far as Cairo, Beirut, Damascus, or Istanbul; but, whatever it was, it was present in Calcutta, Delhi, Hong Kong, though in a far less attractive form than in Tokyo and Nagano. A great fear ran through me, thinking of Rome, Paris, London, and New York, and their future, that these eastern cities were cities still, and that their difference from ours lay in the infinitely longer eastern experience of mass populations—in a more profound and feudal arrangement of the Revolt of the Masses. I had the living fear that the east might fertilize the west; and there was no help from the healing Buddha, worn though he was with salutation.

My final visit to Zenkoji Temple was even more formal than the first, but the formality was shattered in literal dark, in a kind of Luna Park crypt at the end of a descending maze: where at the bottom of the darkness there was both the key to paradise and what felt like a girl's body. I turned the key thrice, as instructed, and the girl's body evaded me as if I had tried to embrace the ultimate shadow of flesh—which, as the eyes of Dante's Beatrice in Paradise were still eyes, in its evasion was still flesh, and I was puerile terror.

This took place during an inspection of the temple made under the guidance of the priest Junsho Hayashi (he was also a member of the Provincial Assembly of Nagano), a man of perhaps sixty, wearing a lovely violet net surplice over his

117

white cassock. Hayashi lent me some both of his humor and his dignity as we proceeded from the outer gates through the precincts into the temple and inside the sanctuary—and indeed everywhere except through the remaining six of the seven veils in which the sacred statue of the Buddha is hidden. Hayashi was able to keep balanced belief and unbelief on a fulcrum of laughter, but with an extra reserve of belief should he need it: superstition and belief were two phases of the same behavior. Monks might equally well smoke on the floor in a side chapel or chant and strike gongs; one might as well bring sickness as be healed; look for the key of heaven or a lover's body in the crypt—unless, he said, you had gotten too old. The meaning of the gong, he said, was obscure, but it was thought its striking was the command to abstain from evil. In that case, he added, he hoped there were two secret gongs in the world—one in Washington, the other in Moscow. . . . For my pleasure and instruction he had performed a service of the raising of the curtain with chants and gongs and the beating of soprano wood for a family of four who desired to "see" their ancestors behind the curtain. The family knelt, parents and two children; the priests did their work; we sat in differing comforts on the floor. The curtains did not stay up long and I do not know what the family saw. Hayashi looked abstracted and alert; I, attentive and empty, felt my ancestors behind my shoulders.

Hayashi came out of abstraction to ask me which I thought came first, the curtain of the theatre or the curtain of the temple. Does God show or reveal himself? There were lights, incense, mats, gilt, a marching forest of symbols all about. He said we should go down into the crypt and see: down darkness in steps through stocking feet turning always to the right, one's right hand on centuries of polished wood, left hand in front to ward and find. It was long in the dark, breath sharpened in the nervous domain. Just as I touched female flesh (the young were down there within their own eternity), Hayashi took my right hand: Here is the key! I turned it, and was not old enough to die—and was *pursued* by the blackness as I got out into the faintest shadow, the haunted edge of light.

Zenkoji Temple has been burned ten times since its found-
ing and the present building is of the sixteenth century and
was finished in five years. Being of wood there are very few very
old temples in Japan and none which took centuries to build.
Thus their style seems not to be composed enough, but are all
of a breath. I think of Monreale, Chartres, Modena, York; and
I feel a little sad that the temple in Nagano could not partly
have been of stone and free of fire. The center of an aspiration
is in its transformations; and the style which is of a thing made
outside the mind should have as many breakthroughs as possible. Here is too much of the style of a thing which is preserved, or asserted. There is no melding. The best patina is the
green mold on the sweeping undercurve of the pagodalike
mansards. Here my prejudice for the cumulus asserts itself, for
it is Clio who smiles best within me. Not that Buddhism is not
a cumulus and a hospital: the curio shops with their objects
and figures from eight and ten centuries and countries tell me
that at once: each arrests time and space another way, and
one's own mind can make of them an order and a shifting
composition.

—Suddenly I see the legs of three men running—in black
bloomers and black stockings under the billowing gathered
bottom of the curtain in the Kabuki theatre—faster and faster
—the very fastest that they can go. So between every act, too,
drums, gongs, and wood are struck. This is what Hayashi the
priest had wanted as a boy; now there is the raising of the
curtain in the temple. Thus he is willing to have the Buddha
unsealed for scholars of the dark.

After the temple I went to the mausoleum with its little
quarter-pound packets of the ashes of a million dead, a temple
enclosing file cases. Then the university, which did not fail to
look both grimy and flimsy except for the beds of flowers, all of
which, as in France, I knew: otherwise the endless empty bar-
racks which I also knew. Then the Prefectural Library with a
great reading room full of black heads in the hot August: full
full full. And the forested mountains all about, fuller of their
own life, and ours, than temple or mausoleum or library. This

is a provincial city and the relation shows more sharply than in Tokyo or in Paris: as clear as it showed a century ago to Henry Adams in the relation between Boston and Quincy: mountains temple library in sweet triangulation. Ara Coeli and the Campidoglio were the more visible for being here.

Japan is sweet as experience ripens into memory, the sweetness of energy, resilience, transforming power, and intelligence. Except for the greater pressure of population, she makes a country much like our own. I knew this by the sweetness—after Hong Kong, Delhi, Karachi—the amazing sweetness of London. London smelled sweet: a sweet almost too fine to breathe into nostrils that had for some time hardly been able to breathe at all in territory that seemed hardly to have anything but the stain of the city spreading onto greater and greater areas of land, and spreading in the medium of poverty. At twenty, in 1858, Henry Adams learned a permanent lesson in the railway sight of the Black Country in England; at fifty-two, I learned another lesson (which I had thought learned in Cairo four years earlier) in the hideous brown stench of one hundred and twenty-three miles of rural poverty between Delhi and Agra, between an emulsified humanity at Delhi and an emptied humanity—empty of all but vain pride—in the monument of the Taj Mahal. The lesson was, and is, its own meaning, and will remain so no matter what I may be able to say about it. The meaning is like the cows wandering in traffic; like the water buffaloes with only their noses showing in the water holes; but it is still the meaning of poverty. Suddenly I understand the sanctity, and the hollowness of St. Francis of Assisi; and I see, and smell, how it is that all the world-denying religions sprang from this part of the east. We westerners have our poverty within us, where we abase us. In the east poverty is the only condition of life which is not false; poverty is not even a curse, but wealth is. When we plead for poverty—for the poor in spirit—we emaciate ourselves in the illusion that we emaciate the curse within us. We divest ourselves of the love of created things because there are indeed no created spirits in such poverty, only the uncreated—and the *other* people: the governors, the rich, the money-lenders, those who are happy or harsh in love: those fictions without which we could not exist at all. Thus I *see* how it is that in the *Cantico del Sole* St. Francis told the greatest of all human lies; the others are for God to tell. No doubt this is what St. Augustine meant saying we have lost nothing when we have lost everything since we still have God. Augustine was indeed writing poetics, not theology. In other words I see how it is that the great spreading religions find the world intolerable, and how it is also that each has aggrandized riches and power and how it is that each has over the shoulder an image of theocracy. Poverty is the condition for these manipulations, as near absolute poverty as you can come: nothing less will do. This perhaps is the terrible lesson of Render unto Cæsar, the more terribly so, if taken with the Sermon on the Mount echoing in the other ear. When the western world began to reduce poverty with one theocracy (for it failed of Hildebrand's Christian Republic) it got the Renaissance, followed by the theocracies of the Reformation and Counter Reformation. But it is better to look at this poverty of India another way: the way in which it sheds light on the problem of government in our American empire. The last natural talent to develop is government, and perhaps the most fantastic practical assumption is that a people can develop that talent. In America the governing class is too much like the people as a whole and has only the bureaucracy between. In India the governing class is being abolished, expropriated, impoverished, and is becoming only a bureaucracy. Mr. Nehru's government, the immediate heir to the British, increasingly uses police powers to best the bureaus. When Nehru is gone at worst the succession is gone; at best there will be increasingly explosive fragmentation.

But what I meant to note more firmly is, in the analogy of India and America, the illiterate poverty our politicians use to avoid the labor of governing in all those affairs outside their home interest. At home corruption and interest and intelligence make sufficient incentive to do a tolerable job: even enough is the wish to stay in power. But when the affairs are external there is no incentive proper to get the work done, so there is all the more incentive to mere adventure or mere evangelism or the mere intermittent flutterings of good will. These do not make proper imperium. Hence our impatience, our hysteria, our distrust of others, and our imputation of bad motives: these with our tendency to make rigid the untenable positions in which we find ourselves, and our tendency to believe our own weaker lies—especially the ones that insist that laws and methods will solve all problems. India, if you like, is ahead of us in this respect: she is the great advance warning that we must reverse our roles.

What a difference to remember the tea-ceremony performed so devoutly for me in Nagano: harmony, respect for others, tranquility, manners, and the sense of beauty over all. I see the girl making tea in her meditation, my host a little elevated beside me, myself turning my cup six times in unknown admiration. There were John Von Neumann's five terms, not for physics, not even for poetics, but for the sweets of human behavior: rigor, simplicity, fruitfulness, opportunity, and the sense of the aesthetic whole. Between the two, clock-time disappeared as much as in any intimacy. Also: I was being tested without a grade.

If India seems too far away for American attention and the two Delhis too much in abstraction, let us look at the two Berlins. In that city I stayed in the Hotel Am Zoo, and I have never been nearer and more in a zoo in life—a zoo of animals, of ruins, of captive hopes, of energies undirected and worse energies (not only in East Berlin) misdirected, not one of which was not emphasized by my bedtime reading while there: *Old Mortality* and *Heart of Midlothian* by Sir Walter, and Graham Greene's *Quiet American*. The border warfares and the frantic ideologies of the Scottish seventeenth century and those of our own time, each with their sanctified cruelties, are too much alike. Passing into East Berlin through the Brandenburg Gate into the snapping silence is a reminder of which the explosive force is only held down. The ruins and the rubble—the effort to *abolish* history—are to the East Germans, or to their masters, not worth tidying up in terms of their present earnings in their labors to testify to a new history. Only the memorial graveyard to the Russian dead has space that ends anywhere: green green green and to a cenotaph. Thus the streets are deserted on a Sunday afternoon—when the bus stopped for minor adjustment there were more rats than people visible; and the great graveyard was full of wanderers from the west, exercising their distaste with the available monuments after the miles of unavailing ruins. The master race has above all the talent for submitting to the taxes of an alien master. East Berlin is a poem that gives one more example of what surrenders of the human spirit are made under the force of insight which finds living itself intolerable now, and sees in the future an inhuman heaven. Santayana would mention the barbarism of the dark north (but his reference was an ideal of the Mediterranean, so that his scope of vision was parochial in its classicism). I would rather call it, for poetic purposes, a barbarism that insisted on the efficacy of its own insight; and it is lucky for the world that the present American insights are a great deal more emollient than those of the Russians in their present form. We are both races of fanatical evangelists, each depending on our technical classes to enforce our revelations.

Thinking of that medium of conflict: in East Germany the technologist can earn, by secret bargain, luxurious life, up to $15,000 a year and more. But what is a technologist or technical intellectual? He is not a technocrat, though he may live in a technocracy; and he is neither oligarch nor aristocrat; and he is by no means the manager. It seems unlikely that he can seize his own power for himself, and he is likely to be separated even from the forms of power, at least in Russia and Europe. In the Middle East he feels communism as a warm invitation to power, but not here, and not yet in America.

Another way to put it lies in this plain mystery: that Russia cannot administer East Berlin successfully, even in her own interests, from any western human point of view. Therefore the pretense that the rubble and the rationing and the poverty don't matter; and the other pretense that there is something false about the comfort and order of West Berlin; and the third pretense of the future—and this last might come true if they let the momentum of things alone for a bit—that suddenly everyone will be fed and housed and clothed and have other people's money to spend. *Suddenly:* for this is to live in the constructive hope of a miracle, when the Second Coming will be, not judgment, but earthly paradise. Meanwhile they have technology in puritan form. New England had a similar experience; the first millionaires were produced by local treason in the War of 1812—and very nearly wrecked every dollar in the country in the making, including their own. But here we are not on the level of millions, but on the low level of food and tidiness. West Berlin has the flowers and lawns and the suburban middle-class prosperity without a trace of architecture in the good sense (and less in the bad sense than the stinking concrete of Frankfort and Munich—or Milan, for that matter). This is why Berliners agree that the bombed Memorial Church of Wilhelm I was beautiful when the whole church was undistinguished if not ugly, and I am sorry to have watched them pulling it down with great skill.

The mystery of the two Berlins has yet another form, and it needs meditation, and even to be brought to the Ara Coeli and the Campidoglio. The Germans, east and west, have vast force from indestructible energy; they are mass in motion; but they have not broken through into the style which is power—which is, as Toynbee might say here, the power and the glory. Force can be dangerous, even to those who express it in mere action; but force cannot do its holder human good until it has taken the form—the identity—of power: which is style. As I saw in Egypt six years ago, talent is violence (or force) in the soul and only style can control it. We might say of Germany between the two wars that her style—her power—collapsed into force. Memory was abolished, and so the ground of reason. Germany here reminds America of a common risk. Either country or both might lose all but technical memory; lose it, I mean, at the level of decision. It might—and does—happen all the time to individuals. I mean the style which is the man, not the style which is the rote of composite production. This is what my Swiss friends in Zurich may have meant by saying there was plenty in the heads of the Germans, but they, the Germans, did not know what it was. We must distinguish the composite and what is composed, and if so in Germany, the more so in ourselves. Always we must attend the force of things that they become force of mind.

Once at a Sunday breakfast in a Yorkshire village the small son of my host broke into a quiet moment with the question to me: Please, sir, what are the Holy Cities in America? As I could not answer Salt Lake City, I could not answer at all. The boy meant something on the lines of York and Canterbury. Whatever they may have been in the past, I find it hard to think of them as Holy Cities today in the sense that Rome remains one with its evidently infinite capacity for resurrection and incarnation, or even in the sense that Florence remains one. For Florence is a holy city, especially if seen from Rome, and more so than when one is there. If Rome is five times as large, Florence is five times as holy. Perhaps I mean that five times the holiness has run out, pretty much all that was in the people, along with the vices of holiness, which are crime and pride, the virtues, which are art and thought, went too. The city draws life from its remaining holiness, and not only the city but a good part of the countryside about. The Uffizi, the Pitti, the Medici Chapel, are alone almost enough to feed, clothe, and house a third of a million people. The leather goods and lace are nothing but cheap barter. The foreign colonies are the same barter. The river Arno seems a good symbol for what has "actually" happened to the superficial city: it is a river with a past which occasionally flares into the present. It may even be enough of a river in spate to cast one's murders into for hiding, but that would be ostentatious display. But there is another and numinous vitality which affects all those who can feel it and perhaps many others indirectly who do not feel it at all. Florence is the holy city of the numen which is no longer cultivated; the numen cultivates, at a remove, those who inhabit it. If you like, the numen cultivates the monsters within the city who have otherwise taken over. The monsters think it the business or the pleasure of tourism, but the monsters are as usual mistaken in their premises. The blessed blue sky is the grace of holiness which cares nothing for faith or indifference in those on whom it falls, since these, receiving it, feeding on it, maintain the source.

There is the vocabulary of Florence, which we use when we are the creatures of history; but there is also the vocabulary of Rome which we must learn to use when we are the bearers or creatures of history; and in Rome there is especially the vocabulary of the Ara Coeli and the Campidoglio. I do not know that they are inexhaustible, but their voices have been pleading for a long human time. If I feel any gratitude to Mr. Dulles at all it is that by canceling American passports for the Middle East during the Suez crisis in the fall of 1956 he kept me within earshot of those voices for a good four months. Though I cannot always hear the voices, I have seen the two buildings side by side, with their contrasting flights of steps, so clearly and with so much feeling of possible piety, that their image is part of my daily eyesight. The Church of Santa Maria Ara Coeli was built in the fourteenth century, though never finished, on top of the ruins of a temple to Juno (though there is some disagreement about that) and the steps leading up to it are steep and without question to a height. The Campidoglio —the Roman Capitol—was built in its own times, and is the monument of a perfect ruin. The steps which lead down from it were designed by Michelangelo, and were meant, not as steps, but as a waterfall forever flowing; hence their width and ease, but they are harder in their aspiration, to my mind, than those to the church. One leads to an unfinished Christian church, the other to an unfinished pagan state. Gibbon sat on one flight of steps meditating his history, Henry Adams sat on the other flight (or so I like to think) meditating on Gibbon. There was confusion in both their minds, but it was the confusion which is almost like a liberation since it comes as the beat of history; so we may sit there, too, or across the piazza, and summon our own confusions.

—When I tried all over Rome, and elsewhere, to obtain a good copy, or any copy, of either the first or second edition of Piranesi's print of these two flights of stairs, I had endless bad luck. The reason, I was told, was that for a long time young girls had got married in Ara Coeli, and the prints had been used up as mementoes of the place of marriage. Adams, if not Gibbon, would have liked that. I may add that when I got to Boston I found and bought the very day it had been released for sale an excellent example of the second edition which had spent some seventy years in the house of a maiden lady across the street from where I grew up.

(1958)

7

The Swan in Zurich

Standing alone in the bar of Covent Garden at the second interval (my companion was elsewhere for the moment) I found myself filling with the warmth made by the Sadler's Wells Ballet: warmth and sweetness and ease, nowhere embittered by any redundant sauce of expertness and nowhere laid waste by efficiency, and altogether I felt very free. Freedom is what one feels in intimacy when there is no need to worry about any of the labors of translation we call understanding; and here I had been made intimate with a style—in this case a style of theatrical dancing—so that it became a part of my own meaning. I had known the skills of this dancing all my life, and from the belated presence of past lives as well. My mind ran to Tokyo and the great Kabuki theatre where just a month before I had seen a day of plays with the sense of intimacy and little chance for the labor of understanding but had been pressed by color and movement, especially in the dance scenes (as in the whole fourth act of a play called, for short, "Onna Seigen"). In the Kabuki theatre there was clearly style; the style assaulted and intruded on me, with knives that left no wounds; the style was its own meaning, but like everything which, being unfamiliar, seems stylized, was no part of *my* own meaning. I knew only what I missed, just as one may be aware only of what has been forgotten. It was a world of brilliant impersonations where since I did not know the persons I could enjoy chiefly the alien brilliance. Here in Covent Garden I was at home—rather an older one than Hawthorne thought of— but there were other and more expert Americans than I here, who were at home only in the sense of being abroad together. Two of them stood behind me, pressing their opinions into the form of reactions: ". . . and the ensemble has no technique— or what there is, is sloppy. Fonteyn is all right, but for the rest—these people should see the City Center a few times." His friend answered in mollifying confirmation.

Hearing this—something to the effect, "Yes; it is true they have no style"—I wondered what they would think of the Russian ballet with its ragged and athletic exuberance, and indeed I wondered how I felt about it myself—aside from the great noise of it with which London burred and bristled. Would I say of the Russians, Yes; it is true they are a fortress state and they have no style?—But the second bell had sounded, just as my companion returned with her English warmth—which no doubt in expert American opinion might also have been called sloppy—and with its aid I was able to recover in good part the warmth and sweetness of the Sadler's Wells Ballet—but only in good part, for there was a triangular piece of my mind which retained the prompting of opinion and fussed with what style was and particularly what American style was. It fussed and bored so brownly, and kept on so, that at dinner afterward —as I remember, it was a Greek dinner with egg-lemon soup, vine leaves, and resinous wine at the Akropolis restaurant, surely all appropriate to the subject—I got myself sworn at least to surround, if I could not define, American style, and I supposed, so swearing, that I might be surrounding my own otherwise indefinable self. At any rate, for six months afterwards, and with the pressure of the three previous months, I set against everything American I could remember and see and be, whatever luck and travel threw in my way which might surround—which might illuminate—the limits and scope of American style. I was an American self-conscious because of the rest of the world, a thought which seemed a little too characteristic until I remembered that Hazlitt had defined the Englishman best in his "Notes of a Journey through France and Italy." When we are abroad we bring with us the conspicuous part of what we left behind, and can sometimes learn to see it, as in Cairo when I found that the Cairenes had no difficulty in singling me from the British by my American walk, I got a sight of my own legs going ahead of me never since lost. One's gait, when not an oppression, is a part of one's perfectible role. In harness racing there is a difference in gait between the 2:12 and the 2:15 horses which is radical but not unequal. In ballet, then (and if so, of course in other things as well), might there not be a radical difference in gait between the City Center and the Sadler's Wells company which would be one indication of the difference between the American and the British national styles?

In London, with only memories of New York, Boston, and Bar Harbor to prompt me, I knew only there was a difference in speed: the Americans were much faster than the British ever wanted to be. The Americans kept their eyes on the ball, and were stripped for nothing but action. The British were rather absent-minded because they had so much else than the ball to attend to, and gave no effect at all—not even the slenderest ballerina—of being stripped. In them, stripping would have depleted the quality of their action. In the Americans, only the stripping made action possible. In Zurich—where I went to lecture the following week—these sentiments were fortified and developed, for it happened I got there on the afternoon of the last night of a series of performances of the City Center

Ballet, and of course (at a price which annoyed and in pretense outraged him) the concierge procured me a seat on the aisle in the seventh row. It seemed to me, but not from the almost entirely Swiss audience, that I was about to confront a company of very old friends, of whom I might therefore find a sudden distrust—a distrust which might sharpen my eyes through the double blur of London and Zurich.

Going into the Stadttheater I had room to think how for twenty years I had regarded what is now the City Center Ballet as the joint enterprise of Lincoln Kirstein and George Balanchine. The boys and girls were Kirstein's chicks but to a school of indefinable ardors and intensely precise drills where the chief professor was Balanchine. Parentage was as important as the teaching in this school. The ardors, one thought, might be American, the drills European—or from Moscow by way of Paris. Certainly nobody could be more "American" than Kirstein; his many and long exposures to "Europe" and to South America had only weathered him down to a native rock to which they had then administered a durable and variable polish. His glitter reflected many lights but his glow was his own —as much as his figure with its delicate balance a little off plumb and his walk that came straight from "Alice in Wonderland" were both his own. Balanchine could be nothing but European in the buoyancy and revolving balance of his figure and in the contained energy of his character and his momentum; all his *élan* was European, yet he had made himself magnificently at home in New York and had indeed been a force for transforming hybrids into natives there. What then would Zurich show that Kirstein and Balanchine had made out of chicks and pupils? What was Madison Avenue on the Zurichsee?

The audience was on the formal side, much more so than at Covent Garden, and had nothing at all of that air of affectionate disorder, of interlacing and growing commitment to the performance, which is so becoming in a London audience. The Swiss, as audience, are chunky in contour and bourgeois in frontage, and do not unite well; though looking about me I saw many pretty girls of salad age, a number of striking women near menopause, and a scattering of men with saturnine or sandy faces—all incurious. Of European theatre audiences there is none so incurious as the Swiss; which is perhaps an effect of their keeping history so in its place (say with Zwingli and Calvin) as almost to do without it. Even the Swiss houses do not give you curious regard; they seem to have no history in conduct of their own; and if you find the Swiss watching you in public it is not from curiosity or practical interest but out of that decorum which requires an exercise of the eyes. If Balanchine should look through the peephole in the curtain, though he might be pleased with the solid occupancy, he must surely shudder—it was so far from a warm house.

The question of warmth disappeared with the Bach-Balanchine "Concerto Barocco" into the terrifying vision of proficiency beyond conceivable impulse, and exactly equal to the reason which propelled it. One felt like tap dancing in a smaller and smaller space until one's self disappeared, and one understood at last what Kirstein and Balanchine must have been up to, sometime around 1935, when they had Paul Draper at work tapping to Bach. It is not necessary to think of the Dehumanization of Art but it is advisable to take a sidelong look at that thought; the dehumanization was an international game, but America in New York had her own development of that game. It was a magnificent technique for expunging the psyche—who is slow, and stubborn, and always purposeful with however much uncertainty—from the body which danced. I saw at once (or in the intermission after I had seen what this company could do with Britten-Rollins' "Fanfare") that here was high art (which may as well ignore as affirm the psyche) made out of American habits and predispositions into an almost totally characteristic, and indeed almost "closed" performance. We Americans have the technique to bring something to performance so well that the subject is left out. There is nothing we throw away so quickly as our *données;* for we would make always an independent and evangelical, rather than a contingent, creation. This is why other people in the

132

world in part take us up and in part repudiate us; and it is why they find us both abstract and hysterical: we throw away so much and make so much of the meager remainder. We make a great beauty, which is devastated of everything but form and gait.

In all this I was caught up, a fly in invisible eddies, and whirled in the moral vortex of art, fascinated with what I abhorred, seeking what I must shun: my own abstraction modulating my own hysteria. Abstraction comes on form in the guise of principles, and hysteria creates everything but the substance of disease or well-being—as in hysterical secondary syphilis the power of abstraction is great enough to produce lesions perfect except for the spirochetae. Being so caught up, I understood both what my American friends in London missed in Sadler's Wells and what I missed, in my incompetent distrust, in City Center here at Zurich. The Americans did not like the softness of the Sadler's Wells girls. They missed the hardness of the American girls, hardness of flesh, of face, and the scrupulousness of motion so hard it inched on the brittle—as if every gesture were secretly fractured, but finely joined. There was also the hardness of pace or gait. What is so hard as hysteric exactness, unless it be abstract exclusiveness? And what, when one has learned them, comes so to be the habit of demand? My American friends were out of their habit and thought the intimate order they saw was sloppiness where rather it might be called a different optimum of precision. In their habit they were used to American hardness and no doubt thought the London bobbies too gentle for effective police-work; they expected to be bitched instead of welcomed. This hardness of ours runs along the whole road: an external hardness which comes from wearing our cultural skeletons on the outside. The English are soft on the outside (they call it being empirical, or making arrangements) and complain of the French logic that misses so much of what is sweet and gets into an external muddle; but French logic has nothing in the capacity of missing compared to the American logic of hysteria. What the City Center lacked in its excess of virtue was what I missed in them.

133

There were all those beautiful legs and no one in the company who could walk except Diana Adams and none but her with a proper face. All the rest of the girls made up a ballet of pinheads. I do not speak of what these girls actually were off stage, which is very attractive, or what they would be like in love, but of what they really were under the transforming powers of their technique or—so far as it is the same thing—their style in the dance. In that reality they had no faces and no legs that were inhabited. Some kind of sex was missing here—the tenderness—the predatoriness—the sexuality itself. To look at their faces was to look at what under other circumstances they would be if only the technique of the psyche echoed in the technique of their bodies. The men were a little better than the girls, as if their technique required some stigma—some echo—reflected in the face. But the girls were echoless technique. This was not so in Covent Garden. Of those girls I knew many faces, and of all of them I knew what their legs did as a grand exercise of all my sentiments—the very exercise, as it is the very knowledge, which can never be made perfect by any technique of body or any technology of sensibility. Technique has ultimately to do only with performance, and to the degree that a particular stage of technique is depended on alone it will exclude, because it thinks it stands for, what ought to be performed. We Americans—and in our ballet as much as anywhere—tend to stop when we have reached "technical" perfection; that is, we decide on our perfections ahead of time. This should, I think, be called whoring before the arts with only half our natural skills and wiles. What is forgotten is that all true techniques draw on the chthonic for their substance—as the best carpenter scribes with his eye and knows his square is in its live part a magical instrument; as a gesture comes to birth beyond, and *with,* every skill of nerve and muscle—and likewise draw on the heavenly only for the last form: which is the other end of the chthonic.—But how shall the great initial beauty of the City Center be brought so far?

Only, I suppose, by meditations analogous to those which

prompted the question. My way to bed—after going backstage for a moment to admire the private beauty of the American girls: and so to reassure myself of *all* possibilities—led from the foot of the lake along the Limat Quai to the third bridge where across the river stands the Hotel zum Störchen. The night was soft September with only the inner articulate skeleton of chill. I could not see the snowy mountain which I saw every clear day from my balcony up the river and far beyond the head of the lake, but it was enough in me from this day and from others in other years so that I knew it was there, and it gave me a remote resistless strength. I could not tell what it might not do to me. I could not see. I could not tell. Below the rail along the parade I could not see nor tell but knew the quiet swift sweep of the Limat River: "wide water without sound," as Wallace Stevens says, but here also all a-flowing. By a pair of steps to a float stood a man all dark but his face, which gathered darkness to its white, his shoulders in the last stages of irresolution. At any moment he will go away, I thought, as I passed to leeward of him. The airs were soft that blew round him. A hundred yards down river they blew round me, leaving a caress of chill on cheek and shoulder. Below me was one of the swan pens, and a swan, head under wing, drifting swiftly on the current that eased through the outer half of the pen. As the body came just short of the lower barrier, the head came nearly erect from under the wing, the renerved swan gave two thrusting paddle strokes—enough to carry it almost to the upper barrier. There, already drifting, the head went under the wing again for four or five seconds of sleep. Of the hundred odd swans who live on the Limat Quai, this one alone, at least on this night, was with skill deeper than any technique rehearsing in gesture the quality of its life in the quantity of the element it lived in. In the meaning was the precision, in repetition never altogether the same, always a little loose, unique only in the instance. As hysterical, as abstract, as anything New York ever happened on, yet a progressive echo of nature and of herself in nature, this swan was in analogy a model of how the breakthrough into style might be accomplished, without loss of quantity or quality of the impact of what was meant to be controlled.

But there is no sense exaggerating the value of a swan, least of all in Zurich. In Berlin ten days later there was again the City Center Ballet and a very different foil to put against them, in the same theatre on successive days, the Ximenez-Vargas Spanish Ballet from Madrid, which I have heard spoken of as very low stuff indeed as ballet goes. The same theatre, but you would not have thought so from the feeling of the house. For the Americans the house was bland, friendlier than Zurich and more aristocratic than bourgeois, but on the whole more correct than welcoming; hospitality was a grace one had learned to practice solo, on either side of a barrier, nothing mutual. For the Spanish all was heat and rejoicing of participation and release into (not from) common action. People pounded and yelled, not for admiration of technical energy, but for the deep skills of life bursting into momentary form; and indeed the audience had to be darkened out of the house into the light rain. The contrast is worth making clear. There was no lack of admiration for the Americans and it was in no way perfunctory, but one was not related to what one admired, and very little of the self was involved in the admiration. As in the kinds of love, the Americans might express a form of eros and might even reach for agape but there was in their dancing none of the warm vibrancy of philia, of which the Spanish had so much, and without which eros is hysterical and agape abstract and hence persuade something less than the full self. Thus seen in the Spanish contrast, the sense of American hardness was reinforced with the sense of American abstractness: as if Lincoln Kirstein's boys and girls danced in organized abstraction fits. Again, only Diana Adams kept enough warmth in her while dancing to supply her face with life. If there was unity in their dancing it was the American unity which is achieved by cutting away; unity by privation or deprivation; unity by technique—by action precipitated in the kaleidoscope and learned in the muscles which could operate without the pressure of the person. Where other faces than Adams' were visible it was by intrusion—as the boys looked like college boys with crew cuts and the girls showed as puny in the face. Yet the legs were very beautiful in abstraction, quite beyond participation, with movements that could be repeated endlessly the same.

In the Spanish dancing you feel, what is not true, that the next time a given passage would *necessarily* be done differently —like the Zurich swan in the pen—and that the necessity of change was in the particular motion. This is like Santayana's doctrine of essences: the eternality is in the instance. But it is the fullness of deep skill I want to emphasize. The Spanish used face and voice and body (and the guitar was all three). The "aesthetic distance" was there all right, but something in you crossed the distance, into the living unity that flowed in face and voice and body: as one crosses, and is crossed into by, the warmth of a stranger's body, sometimes, never calculably, in a bus or walking side by side—or as in the beginnings of love. Only, in the Spanish dancing, the crossing is precalculated. The beauty of face and voice and body was the same beauty: the building, rather than the reduction, of all these things into one. There was nothing abstract except what ought to be, the pattern of the movement, and nothing hysterical unless it was the sense of greater force than what the dancers used: as if they caught both the violence of the soul and of the stream of time into their spatial movements. Their technique was only what they needed. Was not all this an image of force finding style? Was it not, too, force passing through without losing the sexual phase? Face and voice were of the body: body was *of* face and voice. If I was withdrawn, I was withdrawn into them and their clamor: into intimacy which was also access of knowledge.—No doubt one would tire of all this, or would no longer see it, if too often repeated; but on this occasion I was left tired ahead of time with the City Center girls and boys, and thought again in the light Berlin rain outside the Titania-Palast Theater of the Zurich swan. Might there not be a whole brood of ugly ducklings in New York, but guaranteed at birth to be swans, if the Spanish and American ballets were bred together? They would make something warmer than Sadler's Wells and would have gained a violence of talent worth controlling. Then at last mere technique could be forgotten.

Mere technique is what anyone with intelligence and docility can learn and it represents what can be repeated from one work to another without regard to substance or gift, and it has to do with style only when we use that word to represent the habit of using a particular set of technical devices in a period or body of work. Surely no country in the world has less reason to overestimate the value of mere technique than America. We have Hollywood with its incomparable technical resources and its preponderance of bad pictures which not even the personal techniques of its best actors and actresses can save even by Hollywood's own standards. I say Hollywood; I might as well have said the name of almost any one of our cultural or intellectual enterprises, though without the same air of inexpensive contempt we use for Hollywood. Hollywood technique when good —when possessed by the Muses—is very good indeed and transcends its self-imposed limitations. I do not refer to the vices but to the characterizing habits of American culture, as they make themselves plain against the habits of other cultures, and one of these is the excessive commitment to mere technique which carries with it not so much a failure of value as the exclusion of some values and a blindness to purpose. I could have talked of our symphony orchestras which make Italian, French, and even German and English orchestras seem as sloppy as my American friends thought Sadler's Wells, but which as the cost of their proficiency transform the music, to say the least of it, somewhat unexpectedly. It loses reference, which is another way of saying purpose or rational urgency or individuality; and if you think I exaggerate you may substitute your own terms or ask the ghost of Toscanini. My own substitution would be to say a good word for the virtuoso; which I say in warm feeling for having heard Rubinstein once again, after thirty years, in Rome, and because—now I exaggerate again— his mere technique had no values comparable to the overriding force of his body's purpose and play. Virtuosity, when worth itself, plays something expressive on purpose, and I am glad I grew up in the end of the last great age of virtuosos. I would add that every cultivated man must be something of a virtuoso in several fields, but as addition that would be too much; and yet—what else and what better could general education encourage in a young man?

If three ballet companies seen in contrast can come up with the idea (only superficially paradoxical, and mainly a truism) of technique as opposed to virtuosity, we had better go to another country and find examples. The Folies-Bergères might do, but the Folies, like so much else in France, affect more the social and sociological style of Americans and especially the style of the cultural roughneck, than the high art style that here concerns us, and had therefore better be treated elsewhere; and besides in the Folies there is not much dancing, a matter we are not done with. Rome will do better and gives us this time the contrast of another American company with the Italian company which two or three times a season intersperses the Rome Opera, and of them both there is much already said that needs only the briefest repetition. The Americans were the ANTA-American Ballet Theatre and came to Rome on emergency engagement to replace the Russians who were no longer welcome after the Hungarian troubles began. Ballet Theatre, at least on tour, was a company with no style of its own, and in effect with no *corps de ballet* really a body. Not that these are required, but it is worth commenting that when Sadler's Wells and City Center unite the racial diversities in their companies into single styles almost as firm as the Spanish, Ballet Theatre in action calls attention to the individuals and their origins. After the performance, such was its effect in the full-bodiedness of Italy, that when I stood outside to watch the girls come out I saw them in caricature: as young and promising pinheads and bird-women for the side show in the country fair: as if they had been specialized by long training to do without heads and without complete figures. This was my reaction becoming opinion, a response rather like that of my

139

American friends in London but moving in the opposite direction; and I suppose it arose and hardened in the process of watching them dance the utterly or at any rate deliberately "American" "Rodeo" of Aaron Copland and Agnes De Mille. As a musical comedy number it would have been better, for something would have preceded and followed it; as ballet it was dull and pretentious in the direction of folklore of the kind which is the vitiation of history and culture. If the dancers had been chorus boys and girls they would have saved me (and the Italians, who were bored both in the audience and the next day's press); but neither they nor Aaron Copland knew how to bring that about. For the rest, the cowboys and cowgirls of this rodeo were strictly Brooklyn allegory, abstractions that veiled nothing; and it seemed to me that the choreography had been supervised by a folk-culture vulture. What was good in the program was the work of individuals, particularly Lupe Serrano and John Kriza (Latin-American and Slavic) dancing "Il Combattimento" by DeBanfield and Dollar. Here I could have wished for the music of Monteverdi and for a little more of the substance of Tasso; we should have been nearer Tancredi and Clorinda, and Serrano and Kriza would have had a chance, not to display but to enforce their virtuosity in a true *combattimento*—in the "clashed edges of two words that kill." As it was, their superb virtuosity could only be displayed, as in vaudeville, in a struggle that did not greatly matter.

The kind of virtuosity that does enforce itself in struggles that do matter showed in three of the four numbers on the program of the Miloss-Argento Ballet of the Rome Opera, "Pétrouchka," "Bolero," and "Estro Arguto" (Miloss-Prokofiev) with Attila Radice dancing in all three. (The fourth number, "Bacco e Arianna," seemed more efflorescent than properly flowering, more verbose than of the word, and belonged to that part of Italy which is best not thought about away from Rome or Venice.) Signora Radice has been dancing a long time out of the evidently permanent youth of her energy not of her physical years, and in this she is like Margot

Fonteyn, and is in the line (though not the stature) of Pavlova or (in the theatre) Nazimova. Here she undertook a masterpiece ("Pétrouchka"), what craved to be a masterpiece ("Bolero"), and a *jeu-d'esprit* of the body ("Estro Arguto")—a ballet, as the program says, without story, "without scenes or special costumes"—"a choreographic concerto inspired by the music." Each was unruly, technically, and had edges that, however clear, trespassed upon each other, unruly because of the rules that *had* to be broken, because what they generalized was insufficient to the intent; and each was unruly, too, like a torch struck and showering in the wind, unruly by the far rule of the northern lights that makes them seem a flamboyant ambience. This is the classical spirit of virtuosity maintaining its constant surprises of the possible not thought of but found. I thought of the swan in Zurich and I thought also of a passage in Valéry's dialogue "Eupalinos" between Socrates and Phaedrus, which seems to me to take care of what virtuosity is up to. It is Socrates who speaks. "But the Fates have decreed that among the things indispensable to the race of men, there must figure some insensate desires. There would be no men without love. Nor would science exist without absurd ambitions. And whence, think you, have we drawn the primal idea and the energy for those immense efforts which have raised so many illustrious cities and useless monuments which reason admires, though she would have been incapable of conceiving them?"

That primal idea and that energy are virtuosity. "Pétrouchka" and "Bolero" could not come to full performance (and every performance is different) without it, and "Estro Arguto" requires it in each performance in order to exist at all—for it is hardly even notation without what every dancer in the company does with his or her virtuosity. Of the first two it needs be said here that, by virtue of the performance, the first has something to do with the turmoil before the First World War and the second has something to do with what was left after the betrayal after the end of that war. Each assaults us savagely and each haunts us humanly; each gives us the phrases, and beyond the phrases, the composition of our inner actions of what we once were and what we can never become. The frenzy in each is solid creation, the extremes of the waking and the sleeping swan in its pen, and with the current under it, the head under the wing. Of the third ballet— the "Estro Arguto"—it can be said with more justice than usual that here Attila Radice was indeed first among equals and more equal than the others, for this ballet gives to the body itself full virtuosity in commitment to its own action. The bodies of these dancers are haunted by nothing and we are haunted only by the bodies and by our own sexuality— without regard to any of its gods—as we find it glowing in them: the light and warmth our own flesh would make in unimpeded action. It is possible that all the livest young girls in all the dancing schools in Italy had been brought into this company that that virtuosity might show itself forth. Even so, it would have been nothing without the ripeness some call maturity in the prima ballerina.

Abstraction, hysteria, hardness, formalism in every kind—all were as absent as may be; the concretion of the psyche in gesture, the purpose that comes from choice, the softness that gives response, the form that keeps these together in the loose federation of interest we call composition—all these were present and made warmth in the Italian ballet. I do not know whether it is in the present nature of American ballet to forget its extraordinary proficiency for the sake of undertaking such perilous adventures. I think not, for it would require a nearer approach to actual behavior and a closer addiction to the Muses than seems to fit any American predilection of this long moment in creeping imperialism which so preoccupies us. We are like a complex of new physical and spiritual forces let loose with our laboratory managers always a little behind in the understanding of the forces, in either their likely behavior or their possible aspirations. That we run to abstraction and hysteria is almost appropriate in the present phase of our natures. The ballet is only one extreme. Abstraction is where we ignore behavior and hysteria is where we replace it; both are modes appropriate for daily creation but there is more than the usual

uncertainty about them that their creations, however beautifully articulated and however technically—even technologi-
cally—exact, will conform to anything like enough of the native impulses which taken in balance—in experience together
—lead to purpose or choice or the delineation of these. There
is no conformity which is exclusive, no order which is complete, and there is no conforming order worth mustering which
does not invite, for its life, the constant and random supply of
fresh disorder. Chaos is not what we must exclude; it is what
we do not know, or ignore, of the behavior which, in all the
versions of space and time we can manage, forms our lives, and
order is how we arrange them with the behavior of lives past or
to come. This is why society is immortal and immoral, and in
the stature of our genius we give forms to how it is that this is
so to the individual mortal and moral man. This is the role of
man as virtuoso as it is the role of nature as herself, for she is
nothing but the play of that role just as we are much less than
ourselves if we do not play it.

It is in this high language that I would have us look at the
ballet and its styles in the present western world, and it is similarly that I would have us look at our other arts and faculties.
If we cannot or will not from some superior compulsion correct
ourselves to common experience we can at least understand
ourselves in terms of the behavior we believe not to be ours;
and if we cannot be intimate with ourselves (short of some
new dispensation on intimacy) we can look at the swan in
Zurich.

Here we might proceed to look at the theatre and test our
delineations of American style in that art which is committed
(more than the dance is in gesture) to the concrete and sticky
looseness of the spoken word and the even stickier business of
what we call the communication of thought. The Comédie
Française, Théâtre de Poche, and Théâtre en Ronde in Paris,
with Molière, Yeats, and Pirandello respectively, all point
gravely and with opening hands hospitably seduce Broadway
in the direction of looseness and softness. So does the Schiller
Theater in Berlin, with "Don Carlos" and "Measure for Meas-

ure." And so, nearer home, does London with its young plays like Osborne's "Look Back in Anger," but most of all with London versions of plays already seen in New York, such as "The Chalk Garden" or "The Young and the Beautiful." There are the same (with appropriate differences) contrasts in pace and gait and hardness and warmth, and the same inexpugnable realization of the abstraction and hysteria in the American examples. Perhaps the sharpest example would be to compare Williams' "Streetcar Named Desire" or "Orpheus Descending" with (in the Berliner Ensemble production) Brecht's "Mother Courage and her Children" or "The Chalk Circle"; in Williams the hysteria makes the action, in Brecht it heightens what was otherwise made, etc.

To explore the theatre is always a long and thereby a delightful task; one would rejoice in describing the acting of Miss Lehman as an invalid harridan, or Osborne's handling of tirade nearly soliloquy; but there will be here a more economical presentation—to be taken as representing the risks the Americans have perhaps not calculated—of two images, one predominantly of hysteria, the other a superlative abstraction, both from Rome.

One image is from the Flea Market where every fair Sunday morning the Neapolitans in many dubious and unseemly and some merely commercial varieties invade and struggle to corrupt Rome. There is no reason why everything for sale there—and almost everything is for sale—should not be either stolen or fraudulent or worthless; it is the market of bargains in every sense of that word and every bargain has dubious issue. One Neapolitan in evening clothes and a dirty shirt under a top hat seemed the complete corruption of animal man (man, not the tiger, can be less than himself, as Ortega says), and declared unexpected possibilities, with which, once seen, I knew I had long been familiar. The eyes were all black and glowed with blackness, and indeed there was a vitality of black abandon which wired his whole body. I was unwilling to keep looking at him for fear I should be invited to some action which I should never afterwards be able to reject. Also, I could not stop looking *again* at him, lest he should take some advantage of me. All this he saw—rakish and raffish—and saw it, not with the skill of consciousness but with a skill of being. Had I struck him with a long lash—the only possible weapon—I am not sure there would have been any wince except of pleasurable pain in his response. A little down the alley was another Neapolitan in evening clothes and top hat in bright noon; he made the hat stay on with a wad of paper and so turned clown; and in him was no harm—for he had only the adventurous corruption of a child, and looking at him I was blessedly aware of the stainless sky and the warmth of the sun. But of the first man I got the dread of all behavior which is predatory, sexual, and without compassion.

So much for the incentives to hysteria. My other image is of abstraction and consists in the memory of taking a little girl to see "Die Fledermaus" performed by the Salzburg Marionettes. They—both marionettes and the girl—left me deeply unbalanced, as if my weight like theirs was all upwardly administered, and all the movements of my feet on the ground were idle gestures, jokes in the earth: like the terrific sliding split one of the dancers did. We agree at once on a theoretic form for feelings which mocks us by exaggerations and reductions (abstract deformations) of the motions we know so well. To the little girl there was no deformation. Most of the motions the marionettes made are part of our manners: courtship, parade, cancan; but each has a new balance, a new axis, a new vertex or vortex. Some are new creations, new abandons, such as the quivering of a single buttock, or the leap upwards to a seat: as if one had new degrees of fever. I do not inquire why children extend themselves in marionettes: I expect they find other people's lives very abstract and think the abstractions true to life. All of us glory in abstractions that need no wisdom of head, heart, or body.—The real secret, though, is that marionettes are run from above, and it is nice to have one's center of gravity in elbow or neck.

Otherwise there is the swan in Zurich.

(1958)

8

Reflections of Toynbee

TOYNBEE'S TEN VOLUMES do not seem at this moment of thought to have made a masterpiece; neither do they make, as one reviewer said, an obsession to be examined and allowed for, to be troubled by and dismissed. They make rather a possibility of a coming masterpiece in each reader's mind. They make possible a major action of mind. I suppose this is why so many reviewers and critics (for the two are not the same) have asked of Toynbee that he now write a book. I would suggest the possibility that Toynbee, like Plato, thinks of an intimacy, of a fire of contact, other than those that take place between books and readers, books and books, or even readers and readers, as the intimacy out of which alone can be bred a masterpiece. In quoting Plato's letter to that tyrant of society and of the psyche who wished him to "write" his philosophy, Toynbee rejects Plato's argument (or rather his indignation) as a matter of practical urgency, but accepts it in every rhythm and cadence of his comment, as a possibility of superior spiritual urgency. I suspect that Toynbee like Plato could have written all his life in the multifoliate form of the Phaedrus, and I believe that in fact, in his own way, his own vocabulary, and out of his own time, he has so written. He would study and report and lay out the history and conditions of his story, but would not himself stop to write it all down. He would rather give himself in prospect than give himself away, but in the meantime he will both insist on the practical urgencies and envision the spiritual urgencies. The true voice is in his throat where the two urgencies collide and concert but do not come forth. Let them who have ears listen and speak in their own throats.

A Study of History. No title could be more apt to these ten volumes. Here is Toynbee studying, gathering leaves—those fallen and those about to fall—against a winter work yet to come that will never come since, for all the halcyon summer in the heart, it is already that winter now. In this respect the Study is like History herself; the meaning is not yet—like that of the Christianity which some think transformed history into the dominant form of human imagination, a kind of theology of human behavior, a prophecy of conduct, and a form (the limiting identity) of human action. Let us say, History is (what Toynbee says) our effort to ask how this came out of that, and make what answers we can. But let us not consider our answers revelation until we find out (in the flow of history, in the coincidence of understanding and fate) that they are— or were, if only we had seen it in the closure of time. Our most of arrogance must be to look for that conflagration of thought and emphatic fact which we call miracle, when in some answers revelation might cry out: when we see some new tragedy of man in perspective, whether backwards or forwards. It is, as the poetry of history discloses, in these conflagrations that the psyche, like the Phoenix, seems in the moment of holocaust to preside upon her own fate. It is the Phoenix and the historian who together most know that the whole job is always to do over again, and that it is dangerous to know too well how to do it. This is how Jesus, and all saviors, all scapegoats, are the advance historians of our souls. To follow the moment of illumination, without having seen it, 'tis to follow the Wisp of the Will and come to sudden grief and hear the scream of the aunt upstairs. This is perhaps what Plato meant in indignation, Toynbee in regret. For the most part, unsafe and discontent, we must say merely that history is the lies we tell until the meaning of our roles becomes plain; and we must proceed, as a physicist has lately said with quiet fire in my ear, with rigor, simplicity, fruitfulness, opportunism, and a sense of the aesthetic whole. We must understand why it is that we, as well as our enemies, tell one lie rather than another, and hence never characterize our lies as epiphanies and yet hope that we tell our lies nobly, rather than ignobly, because of our radical imperfection. We bear the truth in our psyches, and the weight of the burden disguises us: we bear up with the best lies we can tell: those that reflect, in their dark glass, the reasons of the heart. This is to say that the student of history, like the student of poetry, recognizes the voices of rival creation in the acts and thoughts of men. Only by rivaling creation can we tolerate it. (What else could Eliot have meant, in terms of *behavior*—not incentive, not ideal—when he said that we live in an incredible public world and an intolerable private one?) The sense of our roles compels us to adapt the tone of everything we do to them, and when we cannot—when the heart or the head refuses out of reason—we add partial creations of our own which sometimes affect the original ones by becoming part of them for all aftertime. Our lies have a creative relation to the truth: they make another approximation to that same truth we were not previously able to tell, and are indeed a partial incarnation of it: truth taking the urgent form of action: precisely as near the truth as our improvident psyche can come. This is the reading of the ten volumes of Toynbee's *Study*.

This, that is, is the quality, but not necessarily the order, of the reflections of Toynbee that rise in mind thinking of the whole ten volumes carried from room to room in two hands looking for what place to put them. All the culture of present and past news rises and inhabits me: all in which I live and move and have my being. I am a green study.

But I think of something else. I think of the Yalta agreements: the communiqués of some ten years ago, just now, at the moment of writing, given in fresh and irrelevant activation to the public press, the voice of a psyche, never a phoenix, and by nature dead, and I think of the ghastly chimeras which we so often misconstrue as representing our roles: of our horrible human habit of refusing to bury our dead and our insistence on telling lies which no longer reflect the truth and are neither noble nor ignoble but hysterias clutched at like straws. It is in these hysterias that we drown, and only straws save us. Suddenly, thinking again of Toynbee, I see how this comes about. Hardly a year after Yalta, Toynbee came to Princeton to help the Bicentennial Celebration of 1946-47 of that University. I was at that time chore-boy to discussions and drinks and had therefore to read in advance the prepared scripts of the various speakers, lest there should be a falling off in discussion or a failure in human relation among the speakers. The more we believe in our own rituals the more we prepare for their success in a particular action. The script dealt with the possible, even the probable, destruction of the entire human race except for an island or two of Central African Pygmies and Arctic Eskimos. It was written under the lacerated banners of the prophets and roared with their minatory gloom. Habbakuk was alive again, and it seemed right that he should be, for there was another Testament come to a close, and one I knew almost as well as Toynbee. Nothing could be more in order than a service of Commination, for those capable of hearing and suffering the *wrath* of such a service. The western world which had flowered till 1914 had only recently endured its second death—the *Second* Adam had only recently gone down into the hardly wetted ashes of Hiroshima in a smuggery of soul and wanness of spirit as yet unequaled—in public display—among the descendants of those who had made the mind and the language of our psyche. We had not so much become aware of our unconscious as slipped into it. I was therefore prepared for a harmony of disaster and emergency, the chorus of the last gasp, and all the more so when it became evident that Toynbee would have to speak in our largest hall, for people were flowing in to hear. But it was not in this harmony that the audience received the address. Such was Toynbee's charm of person, and such the poetry of the motion of his mind, that the audience (who of course had not seen the script) laughed warmly at his warmth, so warmly that the snow fell the more warmly outside and I began to feel that all the frontiers of the human mind were eroded. At the moment I sat aghast, but I have understood how the audience was at least half right. Toynbee had so vital a sense of role and so buoyant a sense of the affair of the mind —of human action in the mind—that he radically changed the burden of his words by the action of living speech from something frightening to something warm, and carried with it the weight of the whole civilization which was about to perish. The audience understood the warmth in his words—and perhaps the story in them—but not the words themselves, and certainly not the fury that had, in reading, lifted them. I was in a brown study, a scholar looking towards the dark, and no rest for the animals on earth.

As if that were not enough to remind me of the necessity that men hear chiefly only the echoes of their own imperfectly familiar voice (and indeed it was not enough), another reminder was three times given me in the bar-cars of Continental trains with a volume of Toynbee's *Study* set before me. I found that, as echo, the voice of Toynbee was abroad in the land by reputation and publicity and éclat and by an élan that had nothing to do with any word he had ever written, but which rather had to do with the hopes and pieties that lingered from beyond some horizon that had just closed but still haunted. There was a magic that might still be at work but the spell of it was in a lost tongue. My interlocutors without exception regarded me as an initiate in an art of the mind now regrettably but irretrievably lost; but they wanted not so much initiation as representation. None of them had any axe to grind, and this—which is why I reconnoiter the event at all—is the chief difference between them and the Historians in Class whose reviews of the *Study* I have read: they too know that there is a force abroad in this *Study,* which is not theirs, but they regret its presence and wish it were lost. They all, both those in the bar and those in the academies, would do better to take rise from this latter-day version of lost art. And I think that Walter Lippmann, in his recent book, *The Public Philosophy,* would have made a less strident cry for Order had he studied his History as Art: the perpetual drama of the emergence of Creative Minorities in long but sometimes intermittent tradition; rather than as the issue of the mandate of heaven. If we look at Lippmann and Toynbee together, we see that there is too much Arnold (and perhaps too much Irving Babbitt) in Lippmann, too much of the Northern Renaissance, too little of the wildness of the Greeks and the Italians. The will of God is certainly not Jacobinical; neither is it strident and single.

I bring Lippmann in here because he is exercised by the urgency of intellectual action, which is a laudable thing, and has taken chiefly only intellectual means to determine the nature of the urgency of our societies in our times. This is perhaps natural when the heart takes to polemic and is inevitable when the maximum interested audience is sought; but it seems to me that the polemic gains vast access of being and meaning if taken in the perspective of Toynbee's *Study of History.* The *Study of History* is the study of urgencies that led to action either in tragic or anaesthetic form and to the succeeding revivals, rebirths, and formally new creation. As we look at the long series of these we begin to feel that it is the rhythm of successive and various urgencies that communicate life and shape to the desperate labors of the psyche to drive on into fresh fields while losing nothing ever gained on old pastures. The rhythm is the beat of opportunity and need, of necessity and freedom, of death and reincarnation, of behavior and fate, none of them ever complete. The *Study of History* is a Poem in Action.

Lippmann's doctrine of Civility, which I approve, gains in persuasiveness greatly if held as shifting deeply under the pressure of many-voiced rhythms; for it is that pressure that makes new action possible as a shape to our purpose or as desirable to the rhythm of our own hearts. Mere mimesis, as Toynbee uses the term, only thins the doctrine of the past and is likely to prevent rather than initiate fresh performance; we are ourselves, if we can discover it, what is live in our old action; and we cannot be what is already dead. Lippmann knows all this, though his book does not always acknowledge it, and if we think of Toynbee we feel how the poem of its weight moves in his words. But I do not want to put Toynbee vis-à-vis Lippmann to correct or to supplement him. I want the presence of *another thing alongside*—what analogy would be if it were not in words—which might persuade, not Lippmann who has no need of it, but his readers of the sense of the creative leap which goes into real action of the mind. I want the sense of the moving bodies of history—what makes the air of Monreale or Taormina—alive with all our dead—and I want the sense not of chimeras but of actors seized of their roles, with and against whom we must take action: we would see how our violence charges our tenderness, and how imperfect the love is we bear towards our own violence. I suggest that the little studies (only because they are near enough our knowledge and our urgency) of the modern experiences of Japan, China, India, our own Civil War, and, especially, of Israel, constitute a method of understanding, assessing, and predicting our own action. The method is poetic but ignores no other mode of the mind which Toynbee is able to handle; indeed, I suspect he would subscribe, with only his own reservations, to Dante's statement to Can Grande of his method in writing the *Divine Comedy* which included ten carefully distinguished terms of which I have written in an earlier issue of this Review. But we do not need Dante here, except in the background, for we have Aristotle frankly at work in Toynbee's version of his *Poetics,* of which the terms are already our own, at least at the tips of our tongues.

For Toynbee constantly sees the action in his history in the terms of Aristotelian poetics—especially in hamartia or the tragic fault by which we explain and even excuse but cannot justify human action, in anagnorisis or the blinding recognition by which we see the motives of our own actions and natures, and in peripeteia or the reversal of role where we find both our motives and our fates were far deeper in ourselves and outside ourselves than we had known; and the passage of history in each of the countries named above as seen through these terms comes alive as praxis or action. It is Toynbee's version, but we know almost instinctively how to make it our own. The *forms* of action in which history emerges are always our own. The forms are our way of seeing, our history, our theoria—which is in the end, as the Greek form of the word tells us, our means of contemplating the Oracle; and from which sometimes, if that is our bent or the consequence of our training, we are forced back into the immediate urgency of our own action. Toynbee, obsessed as he is with the notion of Withdrawal and Return, at one place suggests Plato's Myth of the Cave as a paradigm for the journey between theory and action. One learns to see again in the dark: with greater difficulty but also with more penetrating vision: that is, with vision itself, and in his citation Toynbee somehow gives the effect of the experience of that journey; and once again we feel at home in a strange place newly made.

Plato and Aristotle are the terms of our oldest creative dichotomy and our most permanent creative impasse. We do not need Plato's cave, nor Plato's sense of role, whether of the Ideas or of the mind that uses them, but it is good—it is livening—to have them present when we apply Aristotle's Poetics as a light on history. Aristotle's terms were not really commodious enough for Greek tragedy, or were so only for one tragedy, the *Oedipus Rex,* but the terms nevertheless cast light on all tragedy; they were parts of a theory which has persisted ever since it was first thought of in returning to earth. They compel the contemplation of action; of praxis; and they compel equally action to take the form of contemplation. All action is tragic because all action is taken in perspectives we think we know, or which we believe must at once reveal themselves, but which always contain moving figures that are alien and even inimical and sometimes even monstrous: and these act upon us to the detriment of our conceived vital purpose: our survival and—tragically—our prevalence. We can prevail only against the enemies of the Lord, never against our own enemies or against our deracinated selves. Our malaise comes from the imperfection with which we meet our recognition scenes or our reversals of role. Formosa and Israel seem to me monstrous examples of that imperfection. We misconstrue our encounters and the encounters we generate among others. We confuse our recognitions with reversals we will not accept; and we are unwilling to *see* in any fresh form of dark. Yet any painter—Piranesi or Rembrandt—could tell us that *chiaroscuro* is a great mode of imagination; and it makes little difference whether we see the dark streaming in the light or the light heartening the dark with silence. We have the urgency to see, as the poem sees, the current of our own action. How, if there were not *that* urgency, could a mind which has once made embassy to contemplation, which has once been haunted by the Muse—let us say here, Clio—find urgency worth taking action on at all? Only saints could.

Only saints, or perhaps lovers: those who in the details of faith find opportunity to make rigorous poems in fruitful simplicity: those who know that the imagination is never pure, but must always be topical, even autobiographical, compassionate even as it is predatory. The historian as poet knows that history is the study of urgency; and he knows equally that if he is to study history as poetry he must create a taxonomy, precisely as lovers and saints do. Surely Toynbee is one of the greatest taxonomists since Freud and Jung of major human urgencies in action, and he has made himself so for a similar reason: to enlighten the details of action. The risk in these taxonomies is that in the rhetorics of the late western Roman Empire: that in the absence of the lover or the saint the poetry will all run through the sieve and there be nothing left but rhetoric; and indeed that sometimes happens in Toynbee, in those places where taxonomy heaps into jargon and the words have stopped being words. Toynbee both protects himself against the risk and fortifies himself within by constant resort to the "archaic but familiar" language of the English Bible and the Book of Common Prayer threaded and patterned with phrases and quotations from the Greek and Latin classics: words that have a guaranteed existence so long as our particular form of post-modern western culture survives. The Bible and the classics are themselves a taxonomy of the affairs of spirit and of conduct, of inspiration and incarnation. There are pages where every word has been heard from time out of mind and where every word, thus, not only points a nexus in the story, but also establishes currents of thought not otherwise present. It is interesting that Toynbee refers to his education at Winchester and Oxford, which made this taxonomy possible, as an *Italian* classical education. This is not a gratuitous ascription—there is a part of Italy which is contemporary with any western vantage of time—and the presence of the word *Italian* here only makes emphasis on the multiple and multivocal contemporaneity which it is the purpose of Toynbee's taxonomy to secure. It is one of the ways in which the remembering psyche cuts under the overweening intellect, and if we make this way one of our ways there will be no hubris in such terms as Rout, Rally and Relapse (in religion, in the individual, in a civilization, or in any encounter of active mind); nor in Withdrawal and Return, nor Challenge and Response, nor the Reversion to Animalism, nor Truancy and Martyrdom—to repeat only a few of the classifying forms which Toynbee has invented or adapted. It is rather by the use of such forms that we can understand and tell the story of the "conflicts of incompatible visions" which make so much of the concert of history.

The reader can see a viable schema of possibilities if he will only look at the three copious, interlinked, and detailed indices which inhabit good parts of volumes three, six, and ten of the whole Study. From the index in volume ten (which covers the last four) we learn, for example, that Tamerlane (Timur

Lenk) used human skulls to build minarets, and that there was a Nemesis (a pursuing fate) upon his policy. Also we learn that the external proletariat is irradiated by civilization, and that the internal proletariat is alienated from the dominant minority and sometimes creates higher religions. Again, we learn that religion may be taken as the solution of the problem of leisure. It would be possible to write a reasoned essay out of the index alone, but Leonardo, as Toynbee quotes him, was against such efforts. "Fuggi quello studio del quale la resultante opera more insieme coll' operante d'essa." In his translation Toynbee calls "fuggi" eschew. "Eschew a line of study in which the work done dies together with the worker." It is only in book reviews such as this that we do not need to flee such temptations; and we will so proceed.

One of the most interesting words in the indices (for it has copious fertile entries in each of the three) is the word proletariat, which we have unfortunately taken in the reduced definition made for it in the usage of Karl Marx: the congeries of displaced and impoverished industrial workers in the first third of the last century. Half the remaining population of Europe after the Black Death constituted a roving proletariat; in America we long since made the Indians a proletariat. These populations were "in" but not "of" their societies. In this distinction Toynbee revives and matures the full meaning of the word. For me it has a tragic attractive force, and I feel that force all the more strongly from this fresh reading of Toynbee because I see the type of mind which Toynbee represents becoming, in all but its highest and luckiest exemplars, precisely a proletariat if we do not reform our education to run contrary to the declared purposes and clear actions of the universal state which now administers without governing our affairs. I suppose it was this state Toynbee had in mind some three years ago when he said, reportedly, on his return from America to England: No annihilation without representation; and I would suppose that it was equally well represented in the peculiar form in which the State Department chose to publish half a million words (but not all the words, at that) of the discourses at Yalta. If this thing be done in the green tree, what shall be done in the dry? It will not smell sweet, neither will it blossom in the dust. (But I should remind the reader that I am in political affiliation a species of tory-anarchist, which I suspect was the party which wrote and got ratified the Constitution of the United States.)

What I am saying is that many of Toynbee's excursuses on the proletariat seem to me to enforce the observation we all can make that as a direct result of our very nearly free college and university education there is a rapidly increasing mass of minds trained to be addicted to the fine and rational arts for whose livelihood, within the area of training, the society will not pay and has not the means to patronize either as rentiers or entertainers. The labor is desirable within the central purposes of a literate society; but it is not worthy of its hire within the articulate immediate purposes of this society. The old proletariat in the Roman Empire was counted only for its progeny. After citing the etymology of the term, Toynbee goes on (Vol. I, p. 41): "To say that 'proletarians' contribute nothing to the community but their progeny is a euphemism for saying that the community gives them no remuneration for any other contribution that they may make (whether voluntarily or under compulsion) to the common weal. In other words, a 'proletariat' is an element or group in a community which has no 'stake' in the community beyond the fact of its physical existence." But this is not all. A proletariat may be in its early stages called an intelligentsia, as in Russia a century ago, or in India under the British, and is usually thought of in inception as useful. Thinking of these, Toynbee observes (Vol. V, p. 157): "The process of manufacturing an intelligentsia is still more difficult to stop than to start; for the contempt in which the liaison class is apt to be held by those who profit by its services is more than offset by its prestige in the eyes of those who are eligible for enrollment in it; and the competition becomes so keen that the number of candidates rapidly increases out of all proportion to the number of opportunities for employing them. When this stage is reached, the original nucleus of an intelligentsia becomes swamped by the adventitious mass of an 'intellectual proletariat' which is idle and destitute as well as outcast." The tragedy of Russia and India need not be repeated in the west; but the tragic perspective is clearly there. We have already the "spiritual malaise which is the occupational disease of an intelligentsia" (VIII, 207). We have at one end the Lonely Crowd and at the other the Isolation of the Artist and the littler Little Magazines; and if we let the process alone we may find ourselves repeating Toynbee's further observations on Russia (VIII, 342):

> "odi et amo: quare id faciam, fortasse requiris.
> nescio, sed fieri sentio et excrucior.

These two lines of Latin poetry enunciated the inexhaustible theme of a nineteenth-century westernizing Russian literature whose masterpieces ran to many volumes; and this testament of a Russian intelligentsia that had been able to relieve its own malaise by the masterly exercise of a singular gift for self-expression faithfully mirrored the experience of other intelligentsias, sentenced to the same psyche's task, whose unuttered woes might have been ignored if they had not found Russian spokesmen. . . . The intensity of an alien intelligentsia's hatred of the western middle class gave the measure of that intelligentsia's foreboding of its own inability to emulate western middle-class achievements."

Since we do not have a "creative minority within a privileged minority of leisure" (IX, 604), we shall have to create as much spirit in morals as we have intellect in technology (Idem, 753) in the great class of unprivileged leisure; it is there that our consciousness and our will must labor on "the face of the waters of a subconscious psychic abyss" (Idem, 169). To return to Lippmann and his plea for a Public Philosophy, it is to this class, which exists only as a population and not as a form, that his plea is addressed; and indeed Lippmann twice in his book quotes what he calls Toynbee's "terrible" phrase about those who are "in" but not "of" the society they dominate. If the philosophy of Civility is not theirs it is not likely to be anyone's in this country, or any western country.

It is to this audience, this class, too, that Toynbee addresses himself, both those in the lecture hall and those in the bar-cars of Continental trains; he is for them an unrealized and shadowy Sacred Book, much as for Toynbee the classics and the Scriptures are moving and sacred books. Toynbee knows that there must be no Division of the Labors of the Mind but that there must be rather a doubling and a set of doublets for all the mind. He knows that history is a poem and that each of us is his own poem. He knows that the scholar is an actor, a force moving the actions of men. He knows that we are a congeries looking for action, and must needs only know our urgencies and our terms to find that action, as an amoeba takes shape and color from the forces that attract it, and also as love colors the beloved to its own warmth. He knows, too, that the secular world is the necessary condition for the operation of a living faith. This is what the poem of history tells him, in the triple order of what is personal (for this work is an intellectual autobiography), of what can be studied in our records and stories of action, and of the final compassionate disorder we call, with varying credence, the Holy Ghost. Taken as such a poem, one rejects or assents to his Study, depending on what one brings with one and on the simplicity of present understanding.

Finally, on page 127 of Volume Ten, Toynbee comments on certain passages in Job and Psalms which illustrate the divine concern for man's vanity. Man works with and against his poetry, in and out of his history. History like poetry is an irregular metaphysic of the dark and the light as they join in action.

(*1955*)

9

San Giovanni in Venere: Allen Tate
as Man of Letters

GEOFFREY SCOTT, at the end of his *Architecture of Humanism*, writes of the church of San Giovanni in Venere—a very old church indeed which still stands in the Abruzzi, deserted but a monument, "The Baptist lodged with Venus." In a footnote, Scott says that "The structure is Romanesque, the name more ancient still; but not until the Renaissance can its patrons have achieved their perfect reconciliation, which now the browsing goats do not disturb." And in his text he has this image: "Virgil attends on Dante, and St. John, in the solitude of the Adriatic shrine he shares with Venus, may ponder if ascetic energy is not best mated with classical repose. The architecture of humanism has on its side the old world and the new; it has this repose and this energy." The reader who cannot browse with the goats of Fossacesia and is not content with the photographs in the Abruzzi volume of *Attraverso L'Italia,* will perhaps browse even better on the longest slopes of his own mind. There is an image here for the human reticulation of art, life, and religion. If one meditates one sees and is sometimes able to say what literature is all about. As Scott observes, "Every art that finds a penetrating pathway to the mind, and whose foundations are profoundly set, must needs have precedent and parallel, ancestors and heirs." But my reason for setting this image of St. John in the arms of Venus and making these quotations from Scott, is that they make a good shadow and a good light in which to see the occupation of the man of letters. We see under what impulse he administers and reflects the world of letters in relation to the other human affairs of the mind, and in certain individual men of letters it seems the intermittent best animation which redeems the waste of drudgery and the worse waste of polemic which every man of letters finds fills his life. Allen Tate seems to me such a case.

If Mr. Tate does not object to such an alignment I hope he will not object, either, if I put him for the sake of my own sense of immediate history also in the company where so to speak I found him pretty continuously, and where everybody must sometimes have found him, over the past thirty years, the company of Ivor Richards and John Crowe Ransom. It is the company I have myself kept and it is a pleasure to think of still doing so. One would like to think that it is the company that makes the members human and their speech understandable of each other by the wonderful force and virtuosity of presence: it is in the *presence* of another that one follows the contours of his thought, as the Phaedrus taught us long ago. But I should begin to dine on reminiscence if I did not proceed to the less tipsy thoughts that get turned into vocabulary. All three of our men of letters were faced with what had happened in English to French symbolist poetry and to its connections with modern technical society in a world which seemed to have become less and less human. Let us remember only a little of the vocabulary of reaction—what is contained even in the titles *Practical Criticism* and *The World's Body* and *Reactionary Essays.* Our vocabularies are among our desperate inventions. Ransom invented structures and textures, architectures and qualifications, and he did so along the lines of that school of poets and readers of poetry who were raising the reputation of John Donne, but he did so with a wider and more cantankerous taste. It is interesting to see that when he tackles Shakespeare's *Sonnets* and Milton's "Lycidas," the sonnets largely disappear because he has not the means in *his* structure and texture to get at what Shakespeare's structure and texture were *of,* while on the other hand "Lycidas" comes out, after a vast amount of argument, rather well. "Lycidas," of old poems, has the characteristic vices of modern poetry, and like them may be taken as virtues. The structure and texture afford the chief access to the private world of that poem. The different temperament of Tate—more active, more engaged, more cavalier—responded by inventing tension, or in-tension—the relation of stress between the halves of irony and paradox,—the stress by which structure is united with texture. Similarly he has also opposed the committed operation of imagination to the operation of the unseated will, the action of the lyric to the asserted action of the allegory (though I doubt he would use now just this vocabulary for just this purpose, and I notice he does not reprint the essays where he made the original opposition). That is, he slew allegory of the kind he thought to be mechanical manipulation of figures, and raised pastoral (as Empson was also to do and as, in effect, Ransom had done in treating "Lycidas") and the pastoral he raised was the ambiguous allegory of the pastoral that suited his needs, as we see in his poem about Aeneas in Washington; it was the way that to him knowledge could enter poetry: the struggling morals of felt life.

Richards was dealing according to his training (as charged by his temperament, so much more hopeful, so much more immediately evangelical than either Ransom or Tate) in psychology and linguistic metaphysic with much the same problems. Out of the *Meaning of Meaning* and the International Library of Psychology, Philosophy and Scientific Method (a noble experiment which should be repeated in a new tone of rational skepticism) he invented the supreme difficulty, fascination, and necessity of reading. That is, he put himself deliberately into the destructive quarrel of the vocabularies where with the fanaticism which substitutes for vital difference people refuse all common ground because the words are different. Richards is the supreme methodologist, in the good and the bad sense, of the situation of the loss of unconscious skills in the use of words which constitutes the new illiteracy. His counsel of desperation was the Basic English which would debase us all until we could rebuild our vocabularies. But to him, always, words were real things (both primed and stuffed with unconscious skills, with the *presence* of thought) and poetry the fullest form for reality. And so on.

What have these critics in common?—an ancestry in art for art, belief in the independence, or autotelism, or the absolute sovereignty of poetry, as these may be taken to agree as well as to conflict; with a distrust of rationality as the cumulus and discrimination of skills, and a tendency to make the analyzable features of the forms and techniques of poetry both the means of access to poetry and somehow the equivalent of its content. None of them would admit this as conviction or purpose and each of them would fight it; yet this is how they write when they write well, though each with a different addition, and each with a different flare for the fling of reality and the flash of the actual to hand and eye. One thinks of Goethe in their context. "One should explore the explorable and calmly worship the Inexplorable."

But there is more to say, and two little passages from the last pages of Richards' *Science and Poetry* may serve as texts for departure. "The necessity for independence [from beliefs] is increasing. This is not to say that traditional poetry, into which beliefs readily enter, is becoming obsolete; it is merely becoming more and more difficult to approach without confusion; it demands a greater imaginative effort, a greater purity in the reader." That is one passage; here is the other. "A poet today, whose integrity is equal to that of the greater poets of the past, is inevitably plagued by the problem of thought and feeling as poets have never been plagued before." These are relatively early statements (1926), and if Richards made them now it would not be in the same form and they would take a different emphasis. They were made from the curiously neutral position that "science" was able to take in those days: a neutrality in which conviction and belief, will and choice, were thought of as getting in the way of action and enjoyment, and required, for vitality, to be transformed into some other kind of knowledge, free of beliefs and impervious to the assaults of psychology: some other kind of knowledge which, for some, poetry stood ready to supply.

Richards, in 1926, followed Arnold explicitly, both in his epigraph which quotes one of Arnold's paragraphs about poetry replacing religion, and in his own last sentences. If psychology should win, he writes, "a mental chaos such as man has never experienced may be expected. We shall then be thrown back, as Matthew Arnold foresaw, upon poetry. It is capable of saving us; it is a perfectly possible means of overcoming chaos. But whether he can loosen in time the entanglement with belief which now takes from poetry half its power and would then take all, is another question, and too large for the scope of this essay." Richards has largely occupied the rest of his life with this problem of re-orientation, of the disentanglement of belief from poetry. He has been chief public relations officer in the whole program of saving man by poetry. Poetry to him is language, the highest form of language, and language is the medium for communicating, expressing, representing knowledge. This is an old idea; it is what individuals have done with poetry when they loved it, and the worst poetry lovers have done it most, but collectively it has not been done except for entertainment or ritual or magic or hocus-pocus. Sir Winston Churchill, President Conant, and the Rockefeller Foundation for a long time stood behind Richards, and it is not immediately clear that these institutions are likely to support anything we mean by poetry, or at any rate poetry as such. I suspect that poetry was assigned a new content in this program, which is much more likely than that poetry itself should have changed as radically as the program made out. The program looked as if the mental chaos Richards was afraid of had arrived, the chaos in which salvation seems possible by a trick of learning.

There are kinder things to be said; here all that is wanted is to lodge Richards firmly in the long train of criticism that believes culture to be breaking up and that believes poetry has thereby acquired new and difficult social tasks. For Richards these new tasks had to do with knowledge in the sense that science is knowledge. Poetry is the science of those knowledges not properly in the physical and social sciences, including especially some knowledge improperly claimed by the social sciences: to wit, our knowledge of our own experience. Poetry, said Richards, is "a means of ordering, controlling, and consolidating the whole experience." Thus the *command* of words is the *command* of life; or at any rate the command of all that kind of life of which the experience is its justification.

This is quite an extraordinary claim. Richards, loving poetry, made it in this way because he was a direct product of Cambridge at the end of the First War: he was full of biology, anthropology, and psychology, those great underminers of belief, those great analyzers of experience. Richards accepted the relative destruction of belief—or did accept it; but insisted on the power of poetry to reorganize, without belief, and as self-justified, the experience belief found precious.

Tate and Ransom also made claims that poetry is knowledge, and made them partly, as Richards did, as a result of the assaults of science on belief. They lived in the same world and suffered the same monstrous growth of the possibility of consciousness without conscience. Both of them, also, came heavily under the influence of Richards' ideas and methods, which indeed had by 1925 become a part of the haze in any literary atmosphere, and both made considerable use of Richards' critical vocabulary. But they responded very differently to the complex of Richards and the times. I suppose at bottom it may be from differences of personality which are insoluble, but it is more interesting to think from that sense of controversial possibility which keeps the mind alive. Tate responded by keeping up a running battle this quarter century, until, behind and around doctrine, each so to speak capitulated to the common ground between them. It was a feather bed they had been wrestling with. Tate's battle was against the Richards ideas, against any ideas not found directly in poetry itself, and in the particular poem itself, and against any positive or organized theory of literature. In short, he made the argument that poetry should be used only as poetry—not as *pure* poetry but as the poetry of experience. What poetry did to experience was the criticism of life it afforded, for there is a *practik,* to use a word Tate later coined out of Aristotle's *praxis,* a substance of action at the heart of poetry. Ransom responded by adapting and transforming Richards' ideas and vocabularies for the examination of poetry to correspond to his own purpose of both directly examining poetry and relating that examination to a theory of poetry allied to one or another branch of systematic philosophy. Neither Tate nor Ransom has ever taken serious stock in Richards' dominant preoccupation with language— with the general problem of expression and communication in which poetry gives only the highest instances. Let us run over a few stages in these matters.

Tate very kindly stated his deliberate position in the title of one of his volumes of essays (indeed each of his titles states a position): *On the Limits of Poetry.* His essays make a series of opinions, organized (or I should rather say *composed,* for to compose an opinion is better than to organize it) as near as possible on the unconscious skills of the mind, about what happens, what actually gets into, poetry, and how it was treated after it got there. It is to these skills that Tate refers, I think, when he uses the phrase historical imagination. Otherwise he makes a series of attacks on people who handle poetry in other ways and for other purposes. Here Richards regularly turns up as the friendly enemy.

"For poetry does not explain our experience. If we begin by thinking that it ought to 'explain' the human predicament, we

shall quickly see that it does not, and we shall end up thinking
that therefore it has no meaning at all. That is what Mr. I. A.
Richards' early theory comes to at last, and it is the first assumption of criticism today. But poetry is at once more modest
and, in the great poets, more profound. It is the art of apprehending and concentrating our experience in the mysterious
limitations of form." This was in 1936, and in the next paragraph he says it again. "Poetry is one test of ideas; it is ideas
tested by experience." And here he is in 1940, when he characterizes *The Principles of Literary Criticism* in these words:
"Literature is not really nonsense, it is in a special way a kind
of science . . . a kind of applied psychology." He goes on that
"there is the significant hocus-pocus of impulses, stimuli, and
responses; there are even the elaborate charts of nerves and
nerve-systems that purport to show how the 'stimuli' of poems
elicit 'responses' in such a way as to 'organize our impulses'
towards action; there is, throughout, the pretense that the
study of poetry is at last a laboratory science. How the innocent young men—myself among them—thought, in 1924, that
laboratory jargon meant laboratory demonstration!"

All that Tate forgets here is that Richards, too, in 1924, was
an innocent young man; but what he remembers is much more
important, that these ideas of the innocent early Richards
which he attacks are the dominant ideas of a whole school of
criticism—the school which works through the techniques of
psychology on one hand and the techniques of the logical theories of signs on the other hand; and Tate himself handsomely
recognizes that it is Richards who has slain the dragon of psychology and the worse dragon of semasiology or semiotics in his
Philosophy of Rhetoric and his book on Coleridge—that is, if
they are slain. Only the mind which has been through the
temptation of the gross application of an idea where it is
meaningless can come to reject it with force and persuasion.
Tate had hardly felt the temptation, which may mark his limitation. Just the same, it is at the end of his handsome gesture
to Richards across the dinner table that he makes some of his
own finest remarks about poetry and its criticism: "If rational

inquiry is the only mode of criticism, we must yet remember that the way we employ that mode must always powerfully affect our experience of the poem. I have been concerned in this commentary with the compulsive, almost obsessed, application of an all-engrossing principle of pragmatic reduction to a formed realm of our experience, the distinction of which is its complete knowledge, the full body of the experience that it offers us. However we may see the completeness of poetry, it is a problem less to be solved than, in its full import, to be preserved." This is pretty packed. These are the limits Tate finds in poetry. They are pretty pure, pretty independent, pretty free of the entanglements of belief; and aside from that they are free of theorizing. Richards and Tate eat one bread.

For this is the singular virtue of Tate that both in his verse and his criticism his mind operates upon insight and observation as if all necessary theory had been received into his bones and blood before birth. That is why what is controversial in him is so often a matter either of temperament or temper, and there is a strength to his language superior to any ideas that may be detached from it. From this one virtue stem his two talents as a critic: one, to see through or around or beyond the methods of other critics into an image or insight (for an insight is seen like an image, that it gives light) of what those methods left out; two, when he is practicing direct criticism, his extraordinary skill, surpassed only by Eliot, at illuminating quotation, especially those made for the purpose of exemplifying what he calls the tension between the different elements in a poem. Anybody who writes poetry will understand what he is up to, even if disagreeing; anybody who does not write poetry will feel as if he did. Tate is the man who is concerned with poetry as it always was. His taste is deep; hence the love at the bottom of his contentiousness.

Ransom is a different mind. He makes no running fight on Richards but (in *The New Criticism*) makes rather a hundred-page essay, which is in itself too long, but which shows Ransom coming to terms with himself, and how he came to substitute his own texture and structure for Richards' tenor and vehicle.

Structure is how you get there and texture is what you do with it or how you stay there. The remainder of *The New Criticism* deals with Empson, Eliot as historical critic, Winters as logical critic, and ends with a plea for an ontological critic along the lines of close analysis supported by the new logic of signs as illustrated in the work of Charles Morris of Chicago. The volume represents and composes a part of Ransom's education, and we can share it (since none of us has ever found out what education is except by exposure to it in the minds of others); it exhibits continuously the processes of digestion, but nowhere, except indirectly, the processes of judgment or elucidation. Elucidation and judgment are there, but for us to put together. How this would be we can see by turning again to his essay on "Lycidas," which he calls "A Poem Nearly Anonymous." I assume this essay is familiar enough to need no quotation.

You will observe that there are no statements of importance in it as to what "Lycidas" is about; only statements about formal aspects of structure and texture and formal names—such as "wit"—for the values to be found in the texture. There is no sense at all of that side of Milton which made the poet a builder of cities and maker of men or which made a good book the precious life blood of a master spirit. Nor is there any sense of the yoking together of violently contrasting themes. There is only a mention of *The Waste Land* as a poem comparable in our time to "Lycidas." This seems to be highly characteristic of the kind of criticism Ransom stands for and of the kind of philosophy—nineteenth- and twentieth-century—which bends its attention so almost exclusively to the problem of knowledge. Epistemology and ontology are the media through which Ransom experiences the problem of the relation between thought and feeling. Here once again is the solipsist trying to find out how he knows the only thing he can trust in the world he creates—the formal aspects in which it appears; but trying also to find some formal means, through the relation of texture to structure, of discussing the actual burden of knowledge as also a set of formal relations. Ontology is being: being, one

169

supposes, is not a relation at all, nor a form; and what Ransom is really after is what inhabits form and what suffers relations.

If Tate enjoys the power of received philosophy, Ransom enjoys the fascinated power of that mind which is concerned with manufacturing the mode of a philosophy that has not been received. He creates the scaffold of system after system for Tate to see through and beyond. This is why Tate instigates insight and why Ransom instigates practice, instigations which multiply each other's value.

Richards—not personally, but as a convenience—may be called responsible for the ways in which Tate and Ransom have shown their mettle. I think he has done this largely by arguing and demonstrating the difficulties of reading poetry with the new self-consciousness and the greater difficulties of reading poetry in the absence of old skills. Together these became the enormous difficulty of reading at all and the almost certain futility of supposing that the reader ever reads what the poet wrote. This is the situation which compelled Tate to abandon a theory which prevented the purpose of the theory: to explain what went on. It is also this situation which compelled Ransom to insist on the genetic importance of logical structure in poetry with which Richards until lately has had nothing to do. If Tate and Ransom are right, where then is Richards' value? He is a preparatory school for the greater part, quantitatively, of what literary criticism must consist in a society like our own, and I think this is so even if we discount by about half every major statement of difficulty he has made. If this is so, it explains why those who make most objections to him are those who make most use of him. No schooling is ever adequate to the purposes of that schooling and each is even less adequate to the purposes of the pupil. Let us take as example of the schooling in difficulty offered by Richards his *Practical Criticism,* published about thirty years ago, and still the most useful guide to normal failures to master what have become the difficulties in reading—let alone thinking or understanding or even arguing at a serious level where action is urgent.

Practical Criticism was the result of a controlled experiment where thirteen poems were given anonymously to a number of students at Cambridge over several years. The readers were interested, and were of as high a cultural level as may be found. The commentaries ("protocols" Richards called them) they turned in showed gross failures to understand, to appreciate, or to judge: that is, they had failed to *use* the poems at anywhere near the level the poems required or deserved. Yet the scrutiny they gave the poems was far greater than the scrutiny poetry gets from its regular readers. (I think it fair to say here that other experiments of Richards show that the readers of poetry are no worse than other users of language. Nobody seems to know with what angel Jacob wrestled.) These scrutinies Richards submitted to the rigorous and varied analyses of which he is the master when it comes to any question of the movement of thought into language or the shedding of thought upon language by words. What is most striking about all this is that it represents a decay in unconscious skills confronted by an inadequacy of conscious skills in reading. (Tate gives the example of the graduate scientist who could not use his wit on Dante because he lacked grammar; the student was unaware that, as Psellus remarked in the eleventh century, Rhetoric is necessary to raise man to general thought—but let us not parade rhetoric here.) The forms which excess of consciousness takes are—at least when analyzed—unsatisfactory for the purposes of consciousness. This is what Tate rejects as the secularization of the mind. Richards has two palliatives for the situation, both secular—one the deliberate creation of a thoroughly understood or mastered basic language, what he calls basic English, with vocabularies of different sizes for different levels of mastery. The idea there is the re-duction of our divided knowledge back to a universal vocabulary. It was his work in practical criticism that led him in this direction, and the history of our time only pushed him further. Our culture has always been carried, and especially for purposes of action, through words, and here was the use of words breaking down. This palliative Tate rejected, if I may apply words written in a different context, because it led to communication without prior or following communion, and was only another example of the demon of secularization in action.

For the élite, Richards had another palliative which comes near being a placebo, and that he proposed it suggests how straitened was the desperation in which he found himself. He went east to Confucius and came back with a "technique or ritual for heightening sincerity," which for Richards means the absence of self-deception and perhaps a freedom from entanglement in beliefs; but the ritual was to be applied only *after* every analytic effort had been made. I would suppose Tate would reject this palliative as also smacking of the secular.

I myself like better the more rational eloquence to which the study of Coleridge led him (towards the end of *Coleridge on Imagination*), and I like it better because it imposes a task with its own tests and checks on the sincerity of him who practices it; but I do not mean to discount the ritual method either. And in thinking of Richards I want to keep them both in mind in order to remind us that the man who has spent his life in applying the methodologies of the new consciousness to poetry and to language has done so with such a passion for life and for poetry as can alone justify the new consciousness at all. It is a combination of the method and the passion that makes his work a good school for critics. And it is this that makes Ransom meet him in the beginning, and this that makes Tate salute him in the end.

Tate's salute is from another territory, the territory which contains in its soil and communicates to the air the expressiveness and the oppressiveness of history—of what is time out of mind in the movement of the hand or the reservation of the eye—what is present in us of the past and which, being present, we cannot ignore; but the history of the soul as well as the history of the land. Of all this Tate is exceeding aware, with a kind of Mediterranean awareness; and it is this awareness that has modified his peculiar role as man of letters. Thus we find him saying: "What modern literature has taught us is not merely that the man of letters has not participated fully in the action of society; it has taught us that nobody else has either. It is a fearful lesson." And at the other pole, where he is meditating the Angelic Imagination in Poe (the imagination with direct access to essences, and therefore divorced from perception): "Perhaps this discrepancy of belief and feeling exists in all ages, and creates the inner conflicts from which poetry comes. If this points to something in the nature of the literary imagination, we are bound to say that it will always lie a little beyond our understanding." And again, in writing of Longinus: "In . . . D. H. Lawrence we get both extremes of pride: the attack on the intellect in behalf of instinct, instinct itself hardening into a core of abstraction which operates as intellectual pride, as thesis; not as realized form." And still again: "Our belief in the inferiority of our own age to the past is due to the palsied irresponsibility of the Ivory Tower. But this belief is the fundamental groundwork of all poetry at all times. It is the instinctive counter-attack of the intelligence against the dogma of future perfection for persons and societies. It is in this sense, perhaps, that poetry is most profoundly the criticism of life." There is passage after passage of the same substance, and it is the substance upon which he stands in a kind of violence of uncertainty and conviction, deeply entangled in his beliefs and absurdly outside them. One more will perhaps do for the whole host pressing upon him. "The shadowy political philosophy of modern literature, from Proust to Faulkner, is, in its moral origins, Jansenist: we are disciples of Pascal, the merits of whose Redeemer were privately available but could not affect the operation of the power-state. While the politician, in his cynical innocence, uses society, the man of letters disdainfully, or perhaps even absentmindedly, withdraws from it: a withdrawal that few persons any longer observe, since withdrawal has become the social convention of the literary man, in which society, so far as it is aware of him, expects him to conduct himself."

If I may be permitted to exaggerate in the cause of contrast, I would say that this withdrawal is one Tate has never made; and the above sentences were written as a *cri de coeur*, an acknowledgment of a horror yet to come. To think of Jansenism as the separation from and submission to the state is only a figure of that horror. Where Tate adopts this he makes an insight into a mood—an anti-Cartesian mode of the mind: the mood of fierce withdrawal with existential understanding of the cats and rats which made Pascal think his reason unhinged. It is characteristic of the human that he cannot always be so; as the tiger burns sometimes brightly as a lamb, the human plays hyena. Pascal saw ordure in the hollow heart, and rejected humanity; thus he cut himself away from common things, except to see in them what he could not abide. Pascal is not a great man *manqué;* he is a great man, and also *manqué.* I think Tate only cries out with Pascal.

This he had reason to do. To those of old and perennial hopes it will seem that within the century government, which was balance, has become administration, which is manipulation, and this effects a dilution rather than a concentration of intelligence. Put another way, politics has become in general practice a machine—which gives enormous power to the persons who interrupt or alter where the machine goes. Yet the polity continues to exist in all the reality which goes with the contemplation of necessity: the area where chance and choice cross; and this polity is sometimes affected, and always guarded —if only in the enclave or the diaspora—by individuals, alone and in shifting groups, whose impersonal occupation is to bring out of contemplation, and engagement, force of mind. Force of mind, as it concentrates, is itself major human action, and attracts or compels other action. Words are a form of such action, and the man of letters has in his charge that form. He operates, in this aspect of his role, between the chance of history and the choice of vocabulary; and it is how we call our chances, and what we call them, that gives body to our conduct and articulation to our belief. It is this notion that is debased and disfigured when severe conflicts of interest are labeled or dismissed as problems of semantics, for semantics almost always makes wrong generalizations as to conduct and belief, since it omits consideration of the mystery in the element of choice and battens upon the confusion in the element of chance and is agreeable to the surrender of intelligence involved in doing so. The man of letters is he who is, or ought to be, unwilling to surrender his intelligence or his sense of the human condition as its chief regular informing agent. It is the intolerable task that makes life tolerable, it is, if you like, the drudgery of the soul and the soul of words.

Montaigne understood this very well, but people do not read that man of letters with much memory nowadays. "Je propose une vie basse et sans lustre, c'est tout un. On attache aussi bien toute la philosophie morale à une vie populaire et privée que à une vie de plus riche estoffe; chaque homme porte la forme entière de l'humaine condition." The man of letters will do as well with Emma Bovary or Hans Castorp as with the fall of Cromwell or the assassination of Lincoln, but he had better, so far as his intelligence is informed, attend the human condition in both. Montaigne found in Socrates his last overwhelming model, and when not Socrates, himself. Every life is "populaire et privée" when looked at by a man of letters, and so also are all human relations. It is this, and not Pascal's reasons, that keep us all outside and against the government, and why, too, we wish to run it with our earned prejudice. In his last essay, "On Experience," Montaigne reminds us that "He who remembers the evils he has undergone, and those that have threatened him, and the slight occasions that have caused a change in his lot, is thereby prepared for future mutations and for the understanding of his own condition. Caesar's life has no more examples for us than our own; and whether it be the life of an emperor or of a common man, it is still a life subject to all human accidents. Let us but give ear to it, and we tell ourselves everything of which we chiefly stand in need." I use Zeitlin's translation; in the last sentence the French is a tone stronger in the opening imperative: "Escoutons y seulement"; just let us hear this. It is precisely this the man of letters must hear first and always, whatever else he hears also and besides, which will be everything he can that lifts him or strikes him down. But he must do so, if he is to do so in a way worthy of the inner action we call reading, in the tone of the last sentences of the essay. "The fairest lives, in my opinion, are those which conform to the common or human model, with order, but without miracle and without extravagance. Now old age stands in need of being treated a little more tenderly. Let us commend it to that god who is the protector of health and wisdom, but a gay and sociable wisdom." The god is Apollo, who is also Lord of the Light's Edge, and Leader of the Muses.

It is in this spirit, because I think he deserves it of us, that I wish to put into series certain of the notions concentrated in single words and phrases in the essays of Allen Tate; and I still keep as my text, to go with the words of Montaigne, the name of the old church in the Abruzzi: San Giovanni in Venere.

For Tate, in his later essays, the curse of dissociated thought, and unrelated meditation, has been given the name of Angelic thought or imagination; which is thought freed from the senses, as if original, and freed from *Common things;* and is thus the opposite of Dante who saw agape with eros as a common thing in Beatrice's eyes—an *Incarnation* with which Tate has been increasingly concerned almost as if it were a *Logic* of the life of the senses, as what he learned at school gave to the mind a vital *Order.* These between them make available to the grasping sensibility *Experience.* In all this he sees the need for incubation and preparation by *Prejudice,* which is but the idiosyncratic leaning one captures and inherits from the *Historical Imagination,* where fate and purpose are seen to mingle and impose their *Will.* From these, taken all but the first in their order, he sees communication become *Communion.* Thus in the center is Experience that in the end may be understood by *Love,* for through the Love of God we learn to love our mortal neighbors. This is the Discovery the man of letters makes, when he thinks of San Giovanni in Venere.

This is Diplomacy on the high scale: how we learn to live with the sons of bitches, which is the Human Condition so much at the bottom of what we accept and damn and bless, in practical Wisdom—gay and sociable, with Apollo presiding.

(1959)

Part Three

AMERICAN
WITNESSES

10

In the Country of the Blue

WE ARE NOW about to assay the deep bias, the controlling, characteristic tension in the fiction of Henry James as it erupts in those tales where the theme is that of the artist in conflict with society. To erupt is to break out irresistibly from some deep compulsion, whether of disease or disorder, into a major reaction; and that is exactly what happens to James when in the first full maturity of his fifties he began to meditate, to feel borne in upon him, the actual predicament of the artist as a man of integrity in a democratic society. He broke out, he erupted from the very center of his being, and with such violence that to save himself he had need of both that imagination which represents the actual and that which shapes the possible. James made of the theme of the artist a focus for the ultimate theme of human integrity, how it is conceived, how it is destroyed, and how, ideally, it may be regained. For James, imagination was the will of things, and as the will was inescapably moral, so the imagination could not help creating—could not fail rather to re-create—out of the evil of the artist's actual predicament the good of his possible invoked vision. As the artist is only a special case of the man, so his vision is only an emphatic image of the general human vision; that James could make so much of the special case and the emphatic image of the artist comes about because, more than any other novelist of his scope, he was himself completely the artist. By which I mean that he was free to dramatize the artist precisely because he was himself so utterly given up to his profession that he was free of the predicament of the artist the moment he began to write. He felt none of that difficulty about conviction or principle or aim in his work which troubles a lesser writer; both his experience and his values came straight and clear and unquestionable, so much so that he seems to inhabit another world, that other world which has as substance what for us is merely hoped for. James, as an artist, was above all a man of faith. As he said of one of his characters in another connection, he was copious with faith.

But there is a disadvantage in too complete a faith, as well for an artist as for a saint. Complete faith runs to fanaticism or narrowness. The act of faith tends to substitute for understanding of the thing believed in. If your values come to you unquestioned, you risk taking them on principle and of course. Only the steady supplication of doubt, the constant resolution of infirmity, can exercise your values and your principles enough to give them, together, that stretch and scope which is their life. If you dismiss doubt and ignore infirmity, you will restrict the scope that goes with the equivocal and reduce the vitality that goes with richness of texture. So it was with Henry James. His very faith in his powers kept him from using them to their utmost and caused him to emphasize only his chosen, his convicted view. That is why he is not of the very greatest writers, though he is one of the indubitably great artists, and especially in our present focus, the portrait of the artist. That is why, too, as his faith increased he came less and less to make *fictions* of people and more and more to make *fables,* to draw parables, for the ulterior purposes of his faith. He came less and less to tell and more and more to merely say. But—and this is what saves him to us for reading—the habit of the novelist was so pervasive in him that he could no more than breathing help dramatizing his fables or actualizing, to the possible limit of his frame, the story of his parables. Indeed, in his old age, which for him constituted a continuing rebirth, he made of the frame of his fables a new frame for the novel or tale only less than the greatest frames. I refer to *The Ambassadors, The Wings of the Dove, The Golden Bowl,* perhaps to *The Sense of the Past* and *The Ivory Tower,* and certainly to the tales in *The Finer Grain;* for in these works the form of the fable, the point of the parable, are brought to extreme use precisely by being embedded in the sensibility of fiction. These take rise I think in *The Sacred Fount,* which, not a novel at all but a vast shadowy disintegrating parable, disturbing distressing distrait, indeed distraught, remains in the degree of its fascination quite ineluctable. It is the nightmare nexus, in James's literary life, between the struggle to portray the integrity of the artist and the struggle to portray, to discover, the integrity of the self.

This is another way of saying that the tales which exhibit the artist occupy an intermediate position in James's work; and we shall see that they look both ways, to the social novels that preceded them and to the fiction of fate that came after them. They look back to the conditions of life in general and forward to the prophecy of life beyond and under, or at any rate in spite of, the mutilating conditions. I think of Isabelle Archer, in *The Portrait of a Lady,* how the conditions of life, particularly the conditions of money and marriage and their miring in manners, slowly dawned on her. You feel that if Isabelle can only acknowledge the conditions, if she can see for once what life is like, she will be free to go on, where to go on means to meet more and more conditions. We know that in the process of going on she will lose—indeed she has already lost them—the freshness and promise and candor of youth, which are taken as the ordinary expenses laid out for the general look, whether dimmed or sharpened always somehow maimed and marked, of maturity. So for Isabelle Archer and most of the early fiction. On the other hand I think of Milly Theale in *The Wings of the Dove,* whom we see actually killed by the conditions of life, acknowledge them how she will, but who yet so transcends them that her image—the image of the lost dead—brings to Kate Croy and Merton Densher, who had betrayed her in life, an unalterable unutterable knowledge of what life is under its mutilated likeness. Things could, as Kate told Merton at the end, never again be the same between them; all because of the freshness and candor which had not perished but been discovered in the death of Milly Theale, and the unbroken, unbreakable promise of life which merely for *them,* as they had failed Milly, could not be kept but was to hover over them unavailingly ever afterwards. Milly had her triumph in death; but in *The Ambassadors,* Lambert Strether had his triumph in life, and so Maggie Verver in *The Golden Bowl,* both triumphing precisely over the most mutilating conditions of life that could well have come their way. So again, perhaps with the most beautiful lucidity of all, there is the shabby little bookseller Herbert Dodd in "The Bench of Desolation," whom we see deprived of the last resource of outward dignity —as a character he is all scar-tissue—till he has nothing left but his lonely hours upon his seaside bench of desolation. The bench of desolation is where you sit still with your fate—that of which you cannot be deprived. For Herbert Dodd that bench has these many years turned out to be enough, when the return of the lost love of his youth, whom he thought had betrayed him, makes it a bench of triumph as well. The triumph consists for him, as for the others, in the gradual inward mastery of the outward experience, a poetic mastery which makes of the experience conviction.

Between the earlier persons who master life by submitting to its conditions and the later persons who master what lies under the conditions by achieving a conviction of the self—for surely a man's convictions may be said to be the very shape of his self—comes the little, the slightly anomalous race of artists. Why they come between, rather than either as a culmination or a beginning, is plain when we look at their characteristic fate. The man who is completely an artist is incompletely a man, though in his art he may envisage man completely. The meaning of the artist in history, that is in life as he lives it, in the conditions under which he works, is like the meaning of history itself. History, as Niebuhr says, is meaningful, but the meaning is not yet. The history of the artist is prophetic, but the meaning of the prophecy cannot now be known. What happens to the artist, apart from his meaning, is common enough knowledge. If we look at the fables Henry James offers us, we see at once that all these artists are doomed men, as doomed as the characters in Hemingway, but not as in Hemingway by the coming common death. They are doomed either because they cannot meet the conditions of life imposed upon them by society or because society will have none of them no matter how hard they try. That, for James, was the drama of the artist, and he put it in the simple white and black terms of the fable and the fairy story. The artist either gave in to the evil and corruption of society, or society refused a living to the good and incorruptible artist. But let us ask why James chose the artist for the living focus of his drama, when it might as well have been the queen or the kitchen maid as in the fairy tales, or the men and women next door who provide us, unadulterated with any self-interest, such excellent views of our selves. Why, that is, did not James begin with the persons he came to?

We may say that he did not know enough, that he had not matured enough, and perhaps it would be better so to beg the question. But there is a kind of logic which we can apply after the event, which is where logic works best. The artist is *given* as in death-struggle with society, as much so as the thief or the murderer but with the advantage of heroism and nobility as a luminous character in the mere murk of the struggle. That every man and woman, and perhaps more so every child, is also engaged in a death-struggle with society, or at least with his neighbor's society, is not so clear; you would not think of *your-self* as struggling with society, but the artist and his critics have, I regret to say, vied with each other at every opportunity to see which could say so louder, especially since the spread of literacy and education has multiplied artists of all sorts at the same time that changing institutions took away the function of the artist in society. The artist became thus a natural puppet, ready-made, completely understandable, to represent the great central struggle of man as an individual, which is not often, when you consider the stakes, an understandable struggle at all, and to make a drama of which the novelist has to work from the ground up. It is no wonder then that James should consider the struggle of the artist as one of the great primary themes, especially when you add to the picture that he might incidentally dramatize himself a little—a temptation not beyond the purest artist—and do his trade a good turn.

But the evidence is not limited to the writings of artists and critics. There comes particularly pat to the kind of artist of whom James wrote a passage in de Tocqueville's classic work on The Republic of The United States of America. It was not quite going to be, he foresaw long before Henry James began writing novels, a model republic of letters. There is a little chapter in the first book of the second part called "The Trade of Literature" from which I extract the following passage. "Democracy not only infuses a taste for letters among the trading classes, but introduces a trading spirit into literature. . . . Among democratic nations, a writer may flatter himself that he will obtain at a cheap rate a meager reputation and a large fortune. For this purpose he need not be admired, it is enough that he is liked. . . . In democratic periods the public frequently treat authors as kings do their courtiers; they enrich and they despise them. . . . Democratic literature is always infested by a tribe of writers who look upon letters as a mere trade; and for some few great authors who adorn it, you may reckon thousands of idea-mongers." The picture is fresh enough for our own day, and we take it with the more authority because it was frankly prophetic on the part of a man more than generously disposed towards democracy. It is a description that James could have made for himself, and which in fact he did largely make, both in his life of Hawthorne and in the fiction which we are about to engage. De Tocqueville only reminds us of what James well knew, that an author can expect his readers to know that the race of literary artists is itself composed of good and bad, of very black and very white practitioners; so that the nobility of the good writer will go as granted once it is mentioned, as will the flunkeyism of the bad writer. Thus the author of a fiction about an artist has all the advantages of coarse melodrama without losing any of the advantages of high tragedy. He can merely impute unto his chosen character what virtues or vices he likes without being under any necessity to show them. In fiction, the stated intent of goodness, of high seriousness, is worthless in every realm of life except that of artist; elsewhere the character must be shown as actual, in the artist the stated intention is enough. We shall see that James fully availed himself of this freedom, redeeming himself only by the eloquence of his statement and the lesson of his parable. These, the eloquence and the lesson, will be what we bring away with us. For it goes without saying that James was never taken in, in his created characters, by the meretricious, and was always deliberately sold by the high serious. In this respect, as perhaps nowhere else in James, the reader always knows exactly where he is at. What happened to the literary personages will vary with the incident and the conditions recorded; but nothing can happen to their chances once they are stated, for their characters are articulated ready-made as soon after their first appearance as possible, like puppets or like gods as you may choose to think.

This is no accident nor any part of James's idiosyncrasy; it is a limiting condition of the artist as a character in fiction to the extent that he is represented in the role of artist. If he drops the role, anything within the power of the author to represent may happen to him as a person; as artist he is only a shrunken and empty simulacrum of himself in his other roles; he may know the meaning, but he cannot share the motion.

185

This is one of the lessons that, if James's fables are taken literally, they best attest; and literally is very near how James meant his lessons to be taken. But we do not need to stick to James. The character of Stephen Dedalus, both in *The Portrait of the Artist as a Young Man* and in *Ulysses,* certainly works of the greatest richness and scope, comes to us very fully as a young man, but as an artist he comes to us only by the eloquence of Joyce's mere statement. The poem he writes and the diary he keeps, the lecture he gives on Hamlet, come to us quite independent of the created figure of Stephen. Even the great declaration that ends the earlier book, where Stephen resolves that he will "forge in the smithy of [his] soul the uncreated conscience of [his] race," must be taken either as a free lyric spoken by an actor, where something else might have done as well, or as an image in which the whole boy shrinks suddenly into an agonized intention that can never be realized in life or act but only in art itself. It is much the same thing with Herr Aschenbach, the old novelist in Thomas Mann's *Death in Venice,* who is never given to us as a novelist except by imputation. The role of artist is indeed called on for other purposes, to give quickly a background against which the reader will find credible and dramatic the image of old Aschenbach, the famous and dignified novelist, as an outsider, a figure so isolated by his profession of artist that he fairly aches to corrupt himself, to debase himself, both as a man and as an artist. It might almost be put that to the degree that he had become an artist he had ceased existing—as it were, ceased living—so that the desire for life becomes identified with the temptation to corruption. And so it turns out. The only possible resumption of life for him is tainted with corruption, with effeminate infatuation, with deliberate indignity and self-humiliation. But it is too late in the season, the season of his life and the season in Venice, both of which are struck down by pestilence. His adored and beautiful Tadzio is taken away to safety, and Herr Aschenbach resumes his profession, in the act of dying, by in his delirium re-enacting the Phaedo of Plato. Aschenbach the artist could have no life except in that terrible privation of life which is art.

It is only the obverse of the same coin that André Gide shows us in *The Counterfeiters,* where the novelist reaches life only by a driven and deliberate corruption, a personal disintegration as great as the formal disintegration of the work of art in which it is represented. That Mann and Gide show us corruption as the necessary predilection of the artist, where James and Joyce show us art—that is, integrity of spirit—as the redemption of life, is perhaps due to the seeming fact that neither the German nor the Frenchman have as full and fanatic a conviction of their profession of artists as that suffered at an equal maximum by both James and Joyce.

To get back a little nearer to our particular problem of the portrait of the artist in Henry James—though indeed we have never been far from it—there is another way of expressing the predicament of the artist as a character in fiction. He comes to life only as he ceases to be an artist; he comes to life, in a word, only as he *fails* to be an artist, and he fails when the conditions of life overcome him at the expense of his art. This becomes a very pretty problem indeed when the novelist reflects that all this amounts to saying that the actual source of art, the life of which it is the meaning, is the artist's undoing. Gide solves the problem, and so does Mann, by disintegrating the art as well as the life. Joyce, with no greater honesty but with greater moral insight, represents the struggle of the man *in society,* not as an outsider but as one very much at the heart of things, to become an artist. It was not for nothing that Joyce defined the sentimentalist as one who "is unwilling to incur the enormous responsibility for a thing done." Stephen Dedalus is shown to us in the very process of realizing, for the sake of his art, responsibility for every deed of his life. In Joyce, the artist, like God, dies every day. He dies into man and is reborn; the death is necessary to the birth. Henry James had neither the catholicism of Joyce, the bitter protestantism of Gide, nor the faustian spirit of Mann at his back; he had rather—and only—his unquestioned faith in the adequacy of the free intelligence in life and the freed imagination in art. He had thus less equipment, or at any rate a less articulated philosophy, than the

others, and it is perhaps for that reason that he produced his
ideal artists who failed only in life and succeeded only in art,
and his other artists, equally ideal, who failed in art only because they insisted on success, financial or social success, in life.
The realm of the ideal is often nearest to those who have nearest to no philosophy; but so is the realm of the actual, which is
the artist's realm, and James may have been nearer right in
what he did with his facts than the others.

At least we have James's own abundantly eloquent answer
to the charge that he ought never to have exhibited in art creatures who never existed in life. I give part of the answer as he
made it in the preface to *The Lesson of the Master.* "What
does your contention of non-existent conscious *exposures,* in
the midst of all the stupidity and vulgarity and hypocrisy, imply but that we have been, nationally, so to speak, graced with
no instance of recorded sensibility fine enough to react against
these things?—an admission too distressing. What one would
accordingly fain do is to baffle any such calamity, to *create*
the record, in default of any other enjoyment of it; to imagine,
in a word, the honorable, the producible case. What better
example than this of the high and helpful public and, as it
were, civic use of the imagination?—a faculty for the possible
fine employments of which in the interest of morality my es-
teem grows every hour that I live. How can one consent to
make a picture of the preponderant futilities and vulgarities
and miseries of life without the impulse to exhibit as well from
time to time, in its place, some fine example of the reaction,
the opposition or the escape?"

In this passage, and in the whole preface from which it is
taken, I think James reaches the pinnacle of principle to which
he was able to expose the idealism with which he worked; and
I have planted my quotations here in the center of this discussion of the portrait of the artist because they raise—especially
just after our references to the practice of Joyce and Gide and
Mann—considerations of great importance not only to the criticism, the appreciation, of James's fictions but also to the
whole general theory of fiction itself—if you like, to the whole

theory of art. There are several theories of the value of art which are tenable until you begin to apply them in the interpretation of particular works of art, when as a rule the value of the art shrinks at once to nothing and there is *nothing but* moral value left. No artist and hardly any user of art whose eyes are open can take the slightest interest in any *nothing but* theory of art's value. James's theory is very tempting because, if adopted, it shows how moral value gets into a work of art without leaving you to shudder for the fate of the art. The artist, he says with all the rush and eloquence of immediate experience, the artist *creates* the moral value out of the same material and by the same means with which he creates his other values—out of the actual and by means of imagination. The values are, though distinguishable, inextricable. Some works may show aesthetic values without moral values, and other works very clearly have no aesthetic values and yet shriek to heaven with their moral values, but where you have both orders of value as they are created, together, so they must be felt together, at least so long as the work being enjoyed is enjoyed as art.

Among the consequences which flow from James's statement, if I understand it right, there are two which deserve emphasis for the freedom and the privation they impose on the artist. One has to do with the inclusive nature of moral value in art. As the experience in art must be somehow of the actual and as the record must be somehow of the imaginative, then the artist is free to create evil as well as good without risk of police interference. It is not that his vision of evil may overcome his vision of good, but that, if he is to be an artist of any scope, he must create both, and if the emphasis is on the one in a given work it must have the other as its under or supporting side. It is truly the devil who minds God's business as it is God who gives the devil something to do. But, and this is the second consequence kept for emphasis from James's statement, to have validity whether moral or aesthetic, whatever the artist *creates* (though not what he merely puts in by the way) must show its source in the actual; for it is otherwise either immoral or vapid, and likely both. If the architecture of even the noblest cathedral were not based on the actual it would fall apart, but without a vision beyond the actual it could have never been built at all. Art, on this view, tends toward the ideal but without ever quite transcending the actual from which it sprang. The ideal, in fact, in this restricted sense of the word, is what the artist creates; but the ideal, to have any significant worth, must approach the actual, with the striking effect which needs every meditation we can give it, that the nearer it approaches the actual the more greatly ideal the creation will seem. There is the force of Dante's ideal hell, that it approaches so close to the actual of this life; and there is the relative weakness of James's tales of the literary life, and despite his plea of moral necessity, that though they spring from hints in the actual world the "super-subtle fry" of his authors do not approach near enough to the actual. The fable is always frailer than the image, however more cogent. Thus Joyce's Dubliners who translated the initials IHS of *In Hoc Signo* over the cross, as I Have Suffered, were not blasphemers but better believers for so doing.

The examples are endless; but to our present interest it is the principle that counts, and its relation to the artist, and if we turn to our chosen tales of Henry James we shall find that though as dramas they do not show us very much of the actual, as fables they illuminate the principles by which James was later to anchor his most difficult and precarious ideals safe and firm—poetically valid—in flesh and blood. That is, as these tales occupy an intermediate position in the general development of James as works of art, so they represent for us an intermediate state of knowledge, that critical and fascinating state when principles fairly itch for action but have not yet run down into the skill of the hand that acts, that in this case writes. As stories they are stories about stories, and the most fascinating kind of stories, those that for both aesthetic and moral reasons can never quite be written. All the moral value is in the possibility not lived up to, and all the aesthetic value is in the possibility not lived down to. It is the same possibility, looking either way, the possibility of the really superior artist triumphing over society by cutting himself off from every aspect of it except the expressive, or the possibility of this same superior fellow—and I hardly know which version is more tragic—coming to failure and ruin, expressive failure and personal ruin, by hands whose caresses are their most brutalizing blows, the hands of society itself, the society that, in de Tocqueville's phrases, would like an author rather than admire him, or, worse, would enrich and despise him.

The possibilities are indeed wonderful, and furnish half the conversation at literary parties, where the most enriched authors always turn out the most despised, very often justly. James does not deal with the literary party, whether because the institution had not grown much in his day or because it was open only to satire, which was not his purpose. He deals rather with the English house party and the English dinner party where there is a reputable author present for demolition. The effect is not too different, and affords the advantages of an outwardly more decorous set of conventions and even for a welcome shift of scenes from lawn to church, dinner-table to parlor, or parlor to smoking room, smoking room to bedroom; which taken together, as even a novice at fiction should know, makes the problem of moving people from place to place and so of setting up new relations or modifying old ones, relatively easy. So it is that all but one of the fables we are dealing with make use of the machinery of entertainment for the mechanics of the plot. That is, the artifices that in actual society do most to prevent communication and obscure situations, James uses to promote intimacy and to clarify situations. He mastered the means which because of his life—in one London year he dined out three hundred times—were almost alone at his disposal; the lesson of which may be that it explains why so many of James's people are never able to meet each other openly and yet contrive to put everything between them that is necessary.

That is exactly the situation in "The Figure in the Carpet," where I think we may put it that we know what the puzzle is precisely to the extent we realize it is insoluble, like the breath of life. The narrator who is himself a writer and nameless (the narrators of all these tales are writers and most of them are nameless) reviews the latest novel of Hugh Vereker in a magazine called *The Middle,* and shortly afterwards attends a houseparty where Vereker is a guest, as is his book, both unopened by any of the company, though both are the principal subjects of attention. Someone shows Vereker the review and Vereker says it is very bad; he had not realized the reviewer is present. When he does so, he apologizes to the narrator but insists that, nevertheless, like everybody else, he has missed the Figure in the Carpet: the general intention, the string to his pearls, the passion of his passion. The narrator tries his best to make up, both by reading Vereker's works and by tackling him personally. On his failure he passes the puzzle along to his friend George Corvick, who shares the problem with his fiancée. They in their turn grow futile and frenzied—so frenzied that their marriage comes to hang upon their success. Corvick goes off to Bombay as a correspondent, and while there wires: Eureka. The narrator and Corvick's fiancée, Gwendolyn Erme, try to guess what it must be. Corvick stops off on Vereker at Rapallo during his return journey, and writes that Vereker has verified his discovery. Gwendolyn marries George on condition that he reveal his secret; he dies on his honeymoon before writing it down. Gwen refuses to tell the narrator what it is, because, says she, it is her life. Vereker dies. Then Gwen, who has remarried to Drayton Deane, a critic, herself dies on the birth of a second child. After a decent but excruciated interval —for in James decency most of all is subject to excruciation— the narrator does his best to discover from Deane what the secret of Vereker's work had been. But Gwendolyn had never told him; and the Figure in the Carpet is safe. Nobody knows or can know what it can be. What then was the puzzle? It may be that there was none, or none except to those who wrote—or read—for the passion of the passion; which was certainly not how the narrator, nor any of his friends, either wrote or read. A frenzied curiosity is not passion. Or it may be that the Figure in the Carpet is necessarily ineluctable. Perhaps it only ought to be there; that much, acuteness can discover. In his prefatory remarks, James does nothing to help; but says only that "the question that accordingly comes up, the issue of the affair, can be but whether the very secret of perception hasn't been lost. That is the situation, and 'The Figure in the Carpet' exhibits a small group of well-meaning persons engaged in a test." We can only note that well-meaning persons are notoriously unperceptive, and add that the secret of perception in readers comes very near the secret of creation in artists.

"The Figure in the Carpet" is perhaps a tea-time and tepid whiskey fable, for it is over these beverages that it largely occurs; and so represents, I think, no more than at most can be made out of obsessed gossip. James may have meant more for it—his preface suggests that he did—but it would seem actually, as written, to mean no more than that there is a figure in the carpet if you can imagine it for yourself; it is not there to discover. It is rather like Kafka, manqué, the exasperation of the mystery without the presence of the mystery, or a troubled conscience without any evidence of guilt.

Rather similar but carried further, further for actuality, by the very conventionality of its fantasy—its *glaring* incredibility —is the fable of "The Private Life." Here again the narrator is a writer unnamed, this time on vacation in the Alps in a house full of people connected with the arts. Among the guests are Clare Vawdrey, a writer of genius but a second-rate man; Lord Mellfont, a magnificent public figure but nothing much when not in public; and Blanche Adney, a great actress, for whom Vawdrey is writing a play, and who is quite friendly with the narrator. The second-rateness of Vawdrey and the magnificent public presence of Mellfont gradually become suspect to Blanche and the narrator. Pursuing their curiosity, the narrator sneaks into Vawdrey's room in the evening, while Vawdrey is outside talking to Blanche; there the narrator discovers Vawdrey's other self writing industriously in the dark. Later, by plan, Blanche gets her chance, and while the narrator keeps Vawdrey outside herself makes the acquaintance of the other or "ghost" self and falls in love with him. Meantime the narrator finds the outer self even duller than he had thought: "the world," he reflects, "was vulgar and stupid, and the real man would have been a fool to come out for it when he could gossip and dine by deputy." Lord Mellfont, on the other hand, must be himself an apparition, called into being by a public relation only; by himself he must be nothing, literally nothing. Blanche and the narrator go looking for him on that assumption, and of necessity he appears in front of them; if they had not looked for him, he would have been unable to materialize. "He was all public and had no corresponding private life, just as Clare Vawdrey was all private and had no corresponding public." Of this little piece what does one say but that the ghost story is the most plausible form of the fairy tale; it makes psychological penetration ominous because not verifiable. Who would care to verify a ghost, especially two ghosts who have the unity only of opposites? Life, the actuality, lies somewhere between; and it is a relief to think that your dull man of genius keeps a brilliant ghost in his work-room, just as it is a malicious delight to figure that your brilliant public man is utterly resourceless without a public.

"The Private Life" is a fantastic statement, so far as it has a serious side, of the inviolable privacy of the man of genius. "The Death of the Lion" makes a plea for the protection of that privacy, and for much more, on the ground that if you successfully violate it your genius, if he have no deputy self to gossip and dine, perishes from exposure. The narrator, again a young, detached writer and journalist with a strong sense of allegiance to the great, is sent to write up Neil Paraday at the moment he achieves, at the age of fifty, after a long illness, with his new book, the public success of being made a subject of a leader in *The Empire*. An interviewer for thirty-seven syndicated papers arrives just after Paraday has read the narrator the manuscript plan—a plan finished and perfect in itself—of his next and greatest book. The narrator takes over the interviewer, and goes on to take over as much protective custody of Paraday as possible. But Paraday, with his success, is nevertheless taken up by the unreading, by those who hate literature in the guise of adoring writers, especially by a Mrs. Wimbush who has the fortune of a great brewery. Paraday a little excuses his not throwing Mrs. Wimbush out of doors on the ground that he can get material for his writing out of her. The narrator, however, has a single success in keeping off an American girl with an autograph album to fill, but who really loves Paraday's work, understands that reading is greater than personality, and agrees to seek the author, as the narrator tells her to, "in his works even as God in Nature." Neil Paraday had been made, as the narrator says, a contemporary. "That was what had happened: the poor man was to be squeezed into his horrible age. I felt as if he had been overtaken on the crest of the hill and brought back to the city. A little more and he would have dipped down the short cut to posterity and escaped." To be a contemporary was to be a lion and lions of the contemporary necessarily die soon. Thus Paraday soon *wants* to become ill again; he knew what was happening to him, but he could not help surrendering to it. "He filled his lungs, for the most part, with the comedy of his queer fate: the tragedy was in the spectacles through which I chose to look. He was conscious of inconvenience, and above all of a great renouncement; but how could he have heard a mere dirge in the bells of his accession?"

What happens is inevitable from the title and from what has already been said. Paraday is seduced into going to a house party at Mrs. Wimbush's country place which is called Prestidge—a surface quality obtained, if you remember your etymology, by sleight of hand. There is to be a great foreign Princess there, and many others, all to hear him read his precious manuscript plan. He falls sick and, dying, instructs the narrator to print it as his last work, small but perfect. However, Mrs. Wimbush has lent it to a guest who in turn has lent it to another, and so on, none of them by any chance reading it; so that it is lost. Before our lion actually dies, he has become a burden, for the next two in Mrs. Wimbush's series of lions come before he is out of the way; and it is in the identity of the new beasts that we see the true estimation in which Mrs. Wimbush—in which society—holds literature. The new beasts are two popular successes, Guy Walsingham, who is a woman, and Dora Forbes, who is a man with red mustaches. Their publishers think it necessary that they take opposite sexes in their pen names. But the narrator says rather that they are writers of some third sex: the success-sex, no doubt, which can alone cope with the assaults of an adulating society.

Here we see the figure of a great writer preyed upon; the lion is brought down by the brutality of a society which could have no use for him except as quarry. In "The Next Time" we have the contrary fable, that of the writer who struggles desperately to make society his prey, but fails because he cannot help remaining the harmless, the isolated monarch of his extreme imaginative ardent self. Society, seen as his prey, has no trouble at all in keeping out of his way. Ray Limbert's only successful step was the initial step of a "bad" marriage to a good wife, who has a mother and bears children who require support. He has a sister-in-law who is a successful popular novelist, where he himself is incontestably a great writer. He gave the narrator (again a literary man) "one of the rarest emotions of the literary life, the sense of an activity in which I could critically rest." However, it was necessary for him to earn his living, and after failing at journalism, the narrator gets him the post of editor with a year's contract at complete liberty. As an editor, Ray Limbert resolves to contribute serially a deliberately bad novel in the hope of achieving success, and requires of his friends that they do not read the installments for shame. His difficulty there was that he was one of those "people who can't be vulgar for trying." He loses his post as editor, partly because of the authors whom he had printed but mostly because of his own novel, which so far from being popular or obvious was "charming with all his charm and powerful with all his power: it was an unscrupulous, an unsparing, a shameless merciless masterpiece. . . . The perversity of the effort, even though heroic, had been frustrated by the purity of the gift." As the narrator finished his reading he looked out the window for a sight of the summer dawn, his eyes "compassionately and admiringly filled. The eastern sky, over the London housetops, had a wonderful tragic crimson. That was the colour of his magnificent mistake." It was a mistake which Ray Limbert—by the terms of the fable—repeated, always believing that the next time he would do the trick. All the narrator could say was "that genius was a fatal disturber or that the unhappy man had no effectual *flair*. When he went abroad to gather garlic he came home with heliotrope." Finally he forgot "the next time." "He had merely waked up one morning again in the country of the blue and had stayed there with a good conscience and a great idea," and died, writing.

"In the country of the blue" is a very lonely place to be, for it is very nearly empty except for the self, and is gained only by something like a religious retreat, by an approximation of birth or death or birth-in-death. James tried for it in fiction I think but once, in "The Great Good Place," here mentioned but in passing, where there is an adumbration rather than an account given of the retreat of the author George Doane, made for the recovery of genius, "which he had been in danger of losing"; he had returned to himself after eight hours to find his room "disencumbered, different, twice as large. It was all right." Yet there was some constant recourse for James to the country of the blue; it was where he would have had his projected great authors live, and it was where, as we shall see he reported, he sometimes lived himself.

But before we look at that sight, let us look at the tale which of all that James wrote best prepares us for it, "The Lesson of the Master." This is probably the finest, surely the clearest, most brilliant, and most eloquent of all James's pleading fables of the literary life. It has greater scope than the others, itself rings with greatness, and is more nearly dramatic in character, more nearly joins the issue of the ideal and the actual. Unlike the other tales in our present list it is related in the third person from the point of view of the most implicated person in it, Paul Overt. The relations between that distinguished young talent and the Master, Henry St. George, who has for years done less than his best work, are exhibited in terms of Marian Fancourt, of an interest and an intelligence in the arts hardly less than her beauty, as a nexus for the conflict of loyalties between the master and the disciple. All three meet for the first time on a country weekend at Summersoft. Both men are taken with Marian Fancourt. Overt respects St. George vastly, and when St. George tells him that he is good and must be better, referring to his own inadequacy, he responds by a kind of preliminary submission. In London Overt falls in love with Marian, St. George more or less making way for him. For each the two others are the poles of attraction. Overt visits St. George in his study after a party, and for most of thirteen pages St. George exhorts him magnificently to give up everything, marriage, money, children, social position—all the things to which St. George himself had succumbed—for the sake of his art. Overt takes the master pretty much at his word and goes abroad for two years writing his best thing yet under great privation of all personal life. While he is abroad St. George's wife dies, and Overt returns to find St. George and Marian on the verge of marriage, and so feels brutally cheated. It turns out that St. George has married Marian partly to save Overt from succumbing to the false gods, to save him from having everything but the great thing.

The great thing is "The sense of having done the best—the sense which is the real life of the artist and the absence of which is his death, of having drawn from his intellectual instrument the finest music that nature had hidden in it, of having played it as it should be played." When Overt complains that he is not to be allowed the common passions and affections of men, St. George answers that art is passion enough. When the whole ascetic position is explained—for it is no less than ascetic in that it draws the artist as mostly not a man—Overt sums it up by crying that it leaves the artist condemned to be "a mere disfranchised monk" who "can produce his effect only by giving up personal happiness. What an arraignment of art!" And St. George takes him up: "Ah, you don't imagine that I'm defending art? 'Arraignment'—I should think so! Happy the societies in which it hasn't made its appearance, for from the moment it comes they have a consuming ache, they have an uncurable corruption, in their breast. Most assuredly is the artist in a false position! But I thought we were taking him for granted." It was when Overt found Marian married to St. George that he realized *what* he had been taking for granted. One *hardly* knows whether society or the artist is worse flayed here; but one knows, and there is only the need one feels for a grace note in James's concluding remark that "the Master was essentially right and that Nature had dedicated him to intellectual, not to personal passion."

The portrait of the artist in Henry James is now almost complete: the man fully an artist is the man, short of the saint, most wholly deprived. This is the picture natural to the man still in revolt, to the man who still identifies the central struggle of life in society as the mere struggle of that aspect of his life of which he makes his profession, and who has not yet realized, but is on the verge of doing so, that all the professions possible in life are mutually inclusive. One's own profession is but the looking glass and the image of the others; and the artist is he who being by nature best fitted to see the image clear is damned only if he does not. If he sees, his vision disappears in his work, which is the country of the blue. That is why the only possible portrait to paint of the artist will be a portrait of him as a failure. Otherwise there will be only the portrait of the man. That is why James portrayed the artist chiefly during his intermediate dubious period, and why in his full maturity, like St. George, but in a different richer sense, took the artist for granted and portrayed men and women bent, not on a privation but a fullness of being.

There remains still to record only James's portrait of himself as the artist in the man mature, and for that there are two passages to quote, of which one is from a letter written at the age of seventy to Henry Adams urging him to cultivate the interest of his consciousness. "You see I still, in presence of life (or of what you deny to be such), have reactions—as many as possible—and the book I sent you is proof of them. It's, I suppose, because I am that queer monster, the artist, an obstinate finality, an inexhaustible sensibility. Hence the reactions—appearances, memories, many things, go on playing upon it with consequences that I note and 'enjoy' (grim word!) noting. It all takes doing—and I *do*. I believe I shall do yet again—it is still an act of life."

That is the man in life as artist. The other passage, with which we end the chapter, is taken from some penciled notes written some time in his last years on a New Year's eve, near midnight, during a time of inspiration. Lubbock prints the whole of the notes in the Introduction to his edition of the Letters, saying that "There is no moment of all his days in which it is now possible to approach him more clearly." I quote only the last paragraph. The shape, the life, the being of a novel having shown itself clear, the exaltation is so great that James is left once again with just the story of a story to tell, this time of himself.

Thus just these first little wavings of the oh so tremulously passionate little old wand (now!) make for me, I feel, a sort of promise of richness and beauty and variety; a sort of portent of the happy presence of the elements. The good days of last August and even my broken September and my better October come back to me with their gage of divine possibilities, and I welcome these to my arms, I press them with unutterable tenderness. I seem to emerge from these recent bad days—the fruit of blind accident—and the prospect clears and flushes, and my poor blest old Genius pats me so admirably and lovingly on the back that I turn, I screw round, and bend my lips to passionately, in my gratitude, kiss its hands.

The feeling in this passage is not uncommon; most of us have been terrified at its counterpart; but the ability to surrender to the expression of it is rare, and is what brought James himself, for the moment of expression, into the blue.

(*1943*)

11

The Novels of Henry Adams

Adams' two novels, *Democracy* and *Esther*, unlike those of a professional novelist, do not show their full significance except in connection with his life. In the case of *Democracy*, the first of the pair, the connection will be obvious when once set up, for it had to do with that part of his life which had been absorbed in the effort to make a career of politics. That is to say, it focused, and judged, an objective ambition. With *Esther*, it is a very different matter, which it will not be easy to make clear, and upon which different opinions are possible; for in *Esther* Adams made his first attempt to express what was to most of his contemporaries an outer lack as an inner and inaccessible need. Where *Democracy* dealt with man in his relation to society in terms of existing institutions which, whether they controlled or failed to control political power, at

least represented it, *Esther* reached out to seize, to bring to
rebirth, the spiritual power which the existing church, as
Adams saw it in 1883, represented only by a kind of betrayal in
terms of Pilate's question. Adams was no Pilate, as who would
wish to be, but he could not help asking his question in the
form peculiar to his generation just as he could not help repeating it later, in his two great books, in forms which seem in
their vitality to have transcended those of his generation.

Adams was a lover of Matthew Arnold's poetry, not as he
loved Swinburne for intoxication and lyric escape, but because
Arnold expressed for him, as the two novels show, his own dilemma. Arnold spoke for Adams more deeply than he could
then speak for himself and with the blessed objectiveness of a
medium alien to him, and indeed made for him a touchstone
of his own fate, that fate which he felt by anticipation during
the years when he wrote his novels, and which he felt had actually overtaken him after the death of his wife in 1885. Adams
was above all one of those for whom Arnold spoke in his famous lines, as

> Wandering between two worlds, one dead
> The other powerless to be born.

That the dead world had a singular tenacity and assiduity as a
haunt and that the coming world had an overwhelming, if uncertain, necessity as a conception, made the distress of such an
image the more severe. If a man cannot act upon his dilemma,
or escape it in blind action, he will sometimes attempt to make
symbols or fables of what would otherwise drive him to action;
and it is as such symbols, such fables, that Adams' two novels
best clarify themselves. It is I think to a considerable extent
how he meant them, and it is certainly how we may best use
them for ourselves. They show what were to become twenty
years later his major themes slowly, rather lamely, and with
many concessions of a superfluous sort to the "exigencies" of the
popular novel, taking their first imaginative form, the one as
judgment and the other as the beginning of prophecy. It is
only by accident that we see them as novels at all.

Perhaps a man wandering between two worlds could not be expected to show much competence as a novelist, for if one thing is certain it is that the novel in the nineteenth century had to pay maximum attention either to one world or another and usually had to pay attention in terms of a story with either a satisfactory or a desirable ending. Adams did no such thing. He borrowed what he wished from the outsides of the popular novels of his day, and not from the best popular novels either or the newest, but from Lytton and Disraeli, from a romancer and a fabulist. His practical conception of what a novelist could do with difficult or interesting or obsessive material (and his material *did* obsess him) was not keen; and he lacked the native gift of the storyteller and the native necessity of the imagination that is able to create character. Thus he mixed in random proportions a love story, social comedy, social satire, and, for *Democracy,* the drama of politics or, for *Esther,* the drama of faith; and among these elements he set his chosen puppets to play and be played upon through arbitrary actions and dialogue either rootlessly brilliant or desperately conventional. Only when the author's intellect takes hold do the scenes come alive in the sense that the reader participates in them, and what the author's intellect takes hold of was what he knew when he began to write and not what the process of writing—of dramatizing—discovered for him. In short, if the novels were not by Henry Adams they would hardly be read today except to satisfy an omnivorous taste in the detritus of the third quarter of nineteenth-century American fiction.

But they were by Adams; and that fact provides us with enough good will so that we can take them, not as the third-rate novels they seem, but with the maximum significance that can be extracted from them in terms of Adams' life and work. To examine the stages by which an idea or an image or a major attitude gained its final expression is often to get rid of the idea, image, or attitude in an orderly rubbish pile, but it may sometimes be, altogether to the contrary, the most actual and the most dramatic means possible of understanding them. The idea or attitude in *Democracy* became in *The Education of*

Henry Adams the idea or attitude by which Adams envisaged intelligence as playing the supreme role in American political life, but in the novel *Democracy* that same intelligence is shown as defeated by the very inertia which Adams later showed as its source. In *Democracy* American politics is shown as failing by the accident of corruption, as it were by the inattentiveness of human intelligence. In the *Education,* political life is shown, not as failing but as in abeyance; and the question is put: whether human intelligence is, or is not, adequate to controlling the vast forces which had shaped its forms. The difference is between the mere corruption of public life and the question whether public life will, or will not, cohere.

The two problems are of course the same in the sense that the second is the deeper expression of the first. Corruption in public life comes about through a misuse of the intelligence, and political intelligence becomes adequate when, other things being equal, it is able to control its evident misuses. The labor of the man who exposes political corruption must always be first of all to expose it as wastefully unintelligent, and secondly to drive from power those who have given in to the easier forms of corruption. It is only the third and distant step that can envisage the application of active intelligence to an actual situation. The first labors are of debate, and the last is of imagination. Adams, writing *Democracy* in the winter of 1878–79, worked still in the toils of debate, but the beginning of imagination was in sight, or he would have tried his purpose in some other form than that of the novel: say the essay, the pamphlet, the broadside, forms of which indeed his novel provides running examples.

For his purpose was direct and immediate as well as remote and conceptual. A man knowing himself of great potential parts, he had reached that time of life when he realized that his early force was spent and knew that he could no longer regard all things as possible. But he had not yet discovered what was possible. There was a tension in him on the surface level as well as at the deep level. Active politics still pulled in him, had pulled him to Washington from Harvard, and pulled at least as hard as history; but at the same time it pulled, it repelled. As Henry James said of him as of that time, though he was not in politics, politics was much in him. The corrupt theft of the election of 1876 could not be accepted in despair but in hope, and the hope must still be in the establishment of an independent party of the center—the project which he had worked, with his friends, so hard upon for nearly ten years. The chief obstacles to such a party remained the party caucus, the party central committee, and the system of party spoils—all calculated to pervert public responsibility to one form or another of party irresponsibility, and all certain to transform the duty or ambition of power into a lust for power which could be gratified only in individuals, never in policies. And all the life of party lay concentrated, for Adams, in the single figure of James G. Blaine, who had twice prevented the nomination of his father, and who had only just escaped the nomination himself by a political trick of his enemies. Blaine was clearly the most powerful man in the Republican party and was the almost certain nominee for 1880. The tarnish of his corruption had somehow made his star shine more brightly. It must be made to fall. *Democracy* had as its immediate object to strike Blaine a mortal blow to which he could not retaliate; and if Blaine fell, it might signal the fall of the caucus system itself. The prospect was not good, so poor indeed that Blaine had to be turned into an ogre powerful in evil instead of a mere man intolerably weak at the center. As history would eventually judge, so art might immediately clarify the extremes. There must be an angel to contend with the ogre.

The frame Adams set up for the struggle was as simple and conventional as *Pilgrim's Progress*. Madeleine Lee, a widow of thirty with twenty-odd thousand a year, attractive, intelligent, well-connected, but with a degree of naïveté, comes to Washington with her younger sister Sybil, because she is bored with New York and Boston and social Europe. She wants to see how the country is run, and not only to feel its pulse, but to sit in the seat of power. Her interest, as Adams tells us, was in POWER spelt big, but it focused rather more upon the engineer than upon the force that drove the engine. In Washington she forms a relationship with her cousin Senator Clinton of New York, who represents the height of senatorial purity, and with Guy Carrington, a distant connection of her dead husband, a Virginian who had been by accident a rebel soldier, and now struggled with genuine honesty to make his living as a lawyer without office in Washington. Carrington falls deeply but ineffectually in love with her. He is, however, successful as her courier, running errands, bringing friends, taking her about as guide and instructor, and altogether furnishing her with the groundwork for an independent point of view. Senator Clinton serves to introduce her to official life. Between them she very shortly knows all Washington; she is a welcome guest and a sought-for hostess. Almost at once, she singles out Senator Ratcliffe of Illinois, and quite rightly, as the central agent of power, and when she meets him, she at once snares him for her own, quite without thinking, by comparing the speech she has just heard him deliver to Webster at his best. Ratcliffe, for his part, sets himself to catch her. From then on, Ratcliffe's shadow lies over the book, blotting out light after light.

But the other lights are necessary, and must be estimated, if the obliterative strength of the shadow is to be understood. There is Mr. Gore, the literary man and historian from Massachusetts, who vainly hopes for a foreign ministry to close his career, and who is presented to us as the man of integrity vitiated, like Sumner, by his egoism. There is French from Connecticut, the vulgar, conceited, but well-intentioned reformer: he is honesty shown as ineffectual because he does not understand the powers with which he must deal. There is Schneidekoupon, the protectionist coupon-clipper, who is rather more successful than French because he not only understands the men with whom he must deal but also has a community of interest with them. There is Lord Skye, the British Minister, who shows the foil of disinterested but sympathetic candor. Rather different, there is Baron Jacobi, who is Minister from Bulgaria, with no purpose in Washington but to drive barbs into the hide of American complacency and hypocrisy. Besides these official lights, there is also a small gallery of figures introduced either for social illumination or to promote the mechanical motion of the plot. There is Lord Dunbeg, the Irish peer, who furnishes the love interest on a low scale, and who is coupled with Victoria Dare, a young lady of great pertness, a gift for stuttering at opportune moments, and a fortune which she is willing to exchange for a coronet. There is Sybil Ross, who is sometimes coupled with Count Popoff, an attaché to a legation, and sometimes used as a foil with Carrington. Lastly, there is a Mrs. Baker, blonde and vulgar, the widow of Sam Baker the lobbyist, and it is through her that evidence of Ratcliffe's corruption is secured. Minor characters in addition are introduced as occasion offers, and dismissed when done with.

But there are lights which are not so much characters as they are scenes: incidents in Madeleine Lee's telescoped education. The story opens not long before the inauguration of the new President, the unknown "Stone-cutter from the Wabash," and Madeleine is sent to the outgoing President's first formal reception of the season at the White House, where she is shocked with horror and sees the futility of political ambition when she found herself "before two seemingly mechanical figures, which might be of wood or wax, for any sign they showed of life. These two figures were the President and his wife; they stood stiff and awkward by the door, both their faces stripped of every sign of intelligence, while the right hands of both extended themselves to the column of visitors with the mechanical action of toy dolls. Mrs. Lee for a moment began to laugh, but the laugh died on her lips. To the President and his wife this was clearly no laughing matter. There they stood, automata, representatives of the society which streamed past them." Afterwards she falls into conversation with Lord Skye, who will not answer her when she asks why he looks so melancholy, but coolly looks around the room then back into her face. But Madeleine insisted.

'I must have this riddle answered. It suffocates me. I should not be sad at seeing these same people at work or at play, if they ever do play; or in a church or a lecture-room. Why do they weigh on me like at horrid phantom here?'

'I see no riddle, Mrs. Lee. You have answered your own question; they are neither at work nor at play.'

What Lord Skye hinted at, and what Madeleine half saw, was that dead drive, that undercurrent of energy in the American people, which refuses to assert itself in intelligent or intelligible form, and which therefore can be employed by the first hand clever enough or greedy enough to seize it. If the President and his wife were automata, no doubt there was some hidden crew who pulled the strings that made them move. That was the image, and such was the suggestion, that should have printed itself on Madeleine's mind. But her naïveté had not yet affixed to itself a principle of illumination; for as Henry James said, the value of naïveté is like that of zero, it depends on what figure you attach to it, and Madeleine had none.

In another scene, however, the integer began to appear and the value to become prospectively certain. On a balmy day in late February, very nearly the whole cast of characters venture down the river to Mount Vernon. There is a good deal of talk about the character and achievement of George Washington, with each man giving his characteristic view. Mr. Gore sees him in history, Senator Ratcliffe vulgarizes him, and Carrington humanizes him. To Madeleine, with the Capitol fresh at her back and the White House in her eye, it seemed that the first President turned in his sleep. She "insisted that the tomb, as it stood, was the only restless spot about the quiet landscape, and that it contradicted all her ideas about repose in the grave." And when the party steamed away, she began to wonder whether she had not become tainted with the life about her. "Why was it, she said bitterly to herself, that everything Washington touched, he purified, even down to the associations of his house? and why is it that everything we touch seems soiled? Why do I feel unclean when I look at Mount Vernon?

In spite of Mr. Ratcliffe, is it not better to be a child and to cry for the moon and stars?"

What these scenes, and others like them, have as their function is to prepare Madeleine, by setting up values symbolically which at last she will be able to articulate dramatically. They put something at her back upon which, if she does not consider them herself, the reader can meditate for her, and perhaps apply to the actually meager words that she finally uses to rid herself of the political scene forever. Indeed, had the book been composed of such scenes alone, it might have done as a mystery play about the political Tree of Knowledge in 1879, and so been a pure enacted fable. But Adams had not that talent, not till long afterwards when he recounted the affair of the Virgin and the Dynamo or made a second telling of the affair of Héloïse and Abelard. He rather chose to set his scenes in a frame of action half that of a Grimm fairy tale and half that of an Oscar Wilde comedy.

As Madeleine begins visibly to associate herself with Senator Ratcliffe, others of her friends, especially Carrington and Baron Jacobi, begin to work against the Senator, partly because they like Madeleine but as much more out of their accumulated animus against Ratcliffe. Madeleine of course resists; the temptation of power is greater than the scruple of conscience, and she even accepts Ratcliffe's own account of how he held back the ballots of the northern counties of his state till he found how many were needed to save the election for the party; she accepts it as a patriotic necessity, to be forgiven as murder is in a soldier. Ratcliffe maneuvers himself into the new Cabinet as Secretary of the Treasury. Gradually it seems to her friends that she is lost to the Secretary, and Carrington resolves to betray a secret about Ratcliffe which he has learned in his professional capacity as executor for Samuel Baker, the lobbyist. He therefore prepares a letter describing how Ratcliffe had accepted a hundred thousand dollars from a steamship company to ensure the passage of a bill subsidizing the company. Ratcliffe has suspected something of the sort and attempts to buy him off with the job of Solicitor to the Treasury

Department, which he offers through Madeleine. Carrington refuses. Ratcliffe gets round him, however, by having the State Department offer him a job as Claims Agent in Mexico, and Carrington, unsuspecting of its origin, accepts. Before leaving he makes a bid for Madeleine's hand, and failing that, leaves his letter establishing Ratcliffe's corruption in the hands of Madeleine's sister Sybil with instructions that she give it to Madeleine only if it should seem likely that she was about to become engaged to Ratcliffe. Sybil agrees, and after seeing her sister and the Secretary of the Treasury in close and eloquent conversation at a great ball, taxes her with the question. Madeleine says she has not answered Ratcliffe but intends to in the affirmative. Then Madeleine is given the letter; she reads it, clears the house for action, and awaits her suitor with an as yet unclarified negative stout in her mind. The ensuing interview ends the book, and we shall see in a moment in what terms it reached conclusion.

But it would be unfair to the terms and would vitiate the conclusion if we did not first weigh for ourselves some of the preliminary matters which Adams has exhibited for us as pressing upon his young heroine—his woman almost of the world—to give her declarative energy. All the shallowness, weakness, and ignorance which Baron Jacobi had underlined and the others had marked with their various verbal weapons must then have risen in memory to help her, just as she must have refreshed herself with whatever traces remained in her mind of the single image she had herself made, not then for Ratcliffe but which now fitted him as if by design. It had been after she had reflected upon the conversation of certain unnamed "intelligent" Congressmen whom French, the Connecticut reformer, had brought to her house. "Underneath the scum floating on the surface of politics, Madeleine felt that there was a sort of healthy ocean current of honest purpose, which swept the scum before it, and kept the mass pure." Then she had employed her image to reconcile her to the Ratcliffian morals; he represented for her a kind of necessary double standard of morality, and she could not bring herself to stand in judgment. She had thought of him as helping, by whatever means, as foul as necessary, to sweep the scum away; now she perhaps could not help seeing him as the scum to be himself swept away, for he seemed as rotten inside as the material he handled. There was now too a truth of plain actuality rather than the flash of ungrateful wit in the attribution to Ratcliffe, which she must have heard though she might have forgotten it, of the following sentiment as the basis for his manipulation of the new President. "The issue now involved was not one of principle but of power. The fate of that noble party to which they all belonged, and which had a record that could never be forgotten, depended on their letting principle alone. Their principle must be the want of principle." She saw now clearly as she only thought she saw then how idle had been her adjuration to him to act for the public good. There was no public good at all in "this maze of personal intrigue, this wilderness of stunted natures where no straight road was to be found, but only the tortuous and aimless tracks of beasts and things that crawl." She saw now how he had played on her, when then she thought he had pled for her help; for, as her author had observed, "he had divined her character and read it as he read the faces and tones of thousands from day to day." Again, there was the observation that "Ratcliffe, too, had a curious instinct for human weaknesses. No magnetic needle was ever truer than his finger when he touched the vulnerable spot in an opponent's mind." This was when Ratcliffe had begun appealing, not to her ambition or her affection, but to her duty, to her sense of abnegation. The power in him, which showed as the eloquence of an actor, must now seem what it ought to have seemed then, the power to corrupt goodness in others by obviating it in the self. Whether she recast her unconscious experience after this fashion or not—and a better novelist would have shown how she did—surely she could not now fail to remember the words which Mr. Gore of Massachusetts had spoken so earnestly to her in her own drawing room under the charge of secrecy, after she had asked him point-blank what he himself believed in. He had with some preamble replied, and it may be observed that his language was Adams' as well as his own.

"I believe in democracy," he said. "I accept it. I will faithfully serve and defend it. I believe in it because it appears to me the inevitable consequence of what has gone before it. Democracy asserts the fact that the masses are now raised to a higher intelligence than formerly. All our civilization aims at this mark. We want to do what we can to help it. I myself want to see the result. I grant it is an experiment, but it is the only direction society can take that is worth its taking; the only conception of its duty large enough to satisfy its instincts; the only result that is worth an effort or a risk. Every other possible step is backward, and I do not care to repeat the past. I am glad to see society grapple with issues in which no one can afford to be neutral."

When Mrs. Lee asks him what if the experiment should fail, he suggests she visit the observatory and watch a fixed star burning up; but that was a gesture with a meaning, if at all, beyond words, and neither of them took it very seriously. No one ever takes the idea of a really fundamental change seriously, least of all in themselves, and if change does occur that cannot be ignored, they quote the French proverb and insist that it is all the same thing; and perhaps that is why we can now look at the last scene in Adams' novel of the corrupt politics of the seventies and see in it a fable for our own time.

When the Secretary of the Treasury came in to learn his fate in a Sunday call, Madeleine came up at once with a clear refusal, which she made, she thought, with the sole object of protecting herself. Her mistake was in not realizing that she had already surrendered a part of herself to him, so that she had not only to protect but also in a degree to save herself. In the degree lay the meaning of the fable. When he rejects her refusal and asks her reasons, she says merely that they lead divergent lives. "Show me," says he, "a single example of such divergence, and I will accept your decision without another word." At that she shows him Carrington's letter retailing the $100,-

ooo bribe. He reads it and attempts to explain it away by first admitting its substantial truth and then arguing that he had got no personal benefit from the money, but that he had done it all for the sake of the party. To this she answered nothing, but "she felt as though she had got to the heart of politics, so that she could, like a physician with his stethoscope, measure the organic disease. Now at last she knew why the pulse beat with such unhealthy irregularity, and why men felt an anxiety which they could not or would not explain." She was sure "that his courage was mere moral paralysis, and that he talked about virtue and vice as a man who is colour-blind talks about red and green; he did not see them as she saw them; if left to choose for himself he would have nothing to guide him." That is why he had the strength to continue his argument with a sincere sense of the justice of his cause, and that is why, too, the more eloquently and justly he pled the more she had to repel him. So long as he could see no divergence between them, so long as he saw their apparent differences as mere matters of accidental and superficial necessity, the more intolerable his declared identity of purpose. If he could say, as he did with every evidence of sincerity, that he wanted what she wanted, and half a minute later say with equal vehemence that if there were many people who persisted in her opinion there would be no government of the United States, then he was right in telling her that "she led a mere death in life" and resembled a saint on a solitary column, and there was nothing more she could say except the repetition of a blanker refusal. The Secretary then tries the new tack of offering to give up politics, but that was to pass the time. She, however, takes him seriously and says that she is not to be bought, to which he responds in fury that, as Mrs. Clinton had told him, she is a heartless coquette.

" 'A heartless coquette!' he repeated, still more harshly than before; 'she said you would do just this! that you meant to deceive me! that you lived on flattery! that you could never be anything but a coquette, and that if you married me, I should repent it all my life. I believe her now!' "

There was then of course nothing for Madeleine to do but to

remind him that he should be in a State prison. "Understand, once for all, that there is an impassable gulf between your life and mine. I do not doubt that you will make yourself President, but whatever or wherever you are, never speak to me or recognise me again!"

These are the last sentiments the Secretary and the lady exchanged; and it may be wondered whether Adams realized to what degree the balance of truth fell to the Secretary's side of the fulcrum rather than to the lady's. Madeleine herself perhaps realized it, for her last words in the book were that she would like to "live in the Great Pyramid and look out for ever at the polar star!" When the intelligence plays the coquette with corruption she is as sullied in her person as is the woman in whose guise she plays it. But what if there is no role for the intelligence to play in corrupt politics but that of coquette? How shall it be then? Shall she play no role at all?

Adams, hovering between his two worlds, had as yet no clear answer, no answer that he could stick to, nor have the liberals today. Pure intelligence still coquettes with the corruption which it fears, is still unwilling to cleanse necessity by performing it, but asks corruption rather to reform itself first, and then flees to its great pyramid and its pole star when corruption refuses the wooden nutmeg of reform. No wonder the *Nation*'s review of *Democracy* complained that the tale was too simplified and the characters too composite, on the one hand of evil and on the other of good, to be either representative or probable. The *Nation* had a stake in success at the polls, and at the moment when Adams wrote his book, he had begun to feel that he had no stake in the present and had not yet envisaged his stake in the future. He was not yet himself; and that, rather than the fear that his portraits might be recognized—for they *were* recognized, regardless—was the reason for his anonymity. So with Madeleine in her flight, for flight from the problems of the intelligence represents the desire of anonymity in the sense that it anticipates the refuge of lesser identity. That is the lesson of the fable of *Democracy*—perhaps in the way of life as well as the novel: it shows the intelligence which is willing to

THE NOVELS OF HENRY ADAMS

tamper with the actual without being willing to seize it, as properly humiliated and sent flying. If the failure of Madeleine lay deeper than that, it was perhaps that she never understood the principle that the intelligence must always act as if it were adequate to the problems it has aroused. That is, it must see the evils it attacks as the vivid forms of its own abused and debased self. Otherwise, it must give up.

But not to give up requires exactly a treasure in the self which Adams felt as deeply lacking. The intelligence, as he was fond of saying later in life, the intelligence is not enough; only faith goes beyond. Faith, in the '80's, came so cheap that for costly souls it was often not to be had. A long procession of men and their ideas—Darwin, Lyell, Maxwell, Huxley, Comte, Marx, and Herbert Spencer—had combined to remove Christian faith as a simple birthright and seemed to have substituted for it only a progressively expanding area of doubt as to even the provisional validity of any evolutionary faith unless you defined the fit as those who survive. Both what was roughly called "scientific" faith and Christian faith had come in one sense into a sort of precarious balance. Each had to be fought for, and constantly re-established, by the individual, unless you were willing to give up all the scruples of thought and procedure which had started the fight. Each presented a mystery. The Christian faith presented its mystery beforehand as the course of faith and ended with a mystery as well; the scientific faith ended in a mystery for which it seemed to have no foundation. The one was arrogant about its facts and the other was arrogant about its traditional source; neither could afford to be arrogant about its future, unless hope could be called arrogant. If you hung between the two positions, as intelligent people mostly did, the problem was the more painful in proportion to your intelligence, or to your responsiveness, intelligent or not. Only the poor were supposed to have solved the problem, for the intelligent supposed the poor to be stupid, and therefore had need of religion, though the fact was that the poor were not stupid but plentiful and therefore had greater need of religion; their facts they had for the asking. At any rate the intelligent man who tried to make his faith his own found himself in the desperate position of having to give up, at the critical moment, and no matter which faith he chose, intelligence itself. That perhaps was because, in that energetic age, he mistook faith for a superior form of energy, like coal power or water power or atomic power, rather than for a primitive—or fundamental—form of insight. The poor fellow wanted to transcend himself by calling upon a higher energy, when he ought rather to have tried to discover the faith of what he actually was. It was natural, therefore, that the dichotomy of religion and science should become artificially sharp, that the arrogance of doubt should set itself against the arrogance of dogma; the problem over which they fought was itself artificial and engaged greatly only the weakness of either side, hardly ever calling on either's strength.

Yet faith, whatever it was, and however misconceived, was what kept you going. What then was an intelligent person, exposed to both sides, to do? That was the question which Adams proposed to clarify in his fable called *Esther*.

How deeply he later regarded the book is seen in the two references to it in his published letters. To John Hay he wrote, 23 August 1886, from Japan, thanking him for his high opinion of it. "Now let it die! To admit the public to it would be almost unendurable to me. I will not pretend that the book is not precious to me, but its value has nothing to do with the public who could never understand that such a book might be written in one's heart's blood." To Elizabeth Cameron he wrote 13 February 1891, from Papeete, with reference to his history, then just wholly published. "It belongs to the *me* of 1870; a strangely different being from the *me* of 1890. There are not nine pages in the nine volumes that now express anything of my interests or my feelings; unless perhaps some of my disillusionments. So you must not blame me if I feel, or seem to feel, morbid on the subject of the history. I care more for one chapter, or any dozen pages of *Esther*, than for the whole history, including maps and indexes; so much more, indeed, that I would not let anyone read the story for fear the reader should profane it."

These sentences may make a mystery of what should be plain; perhaps Adams' distressed regard for the book was due to the change that had come over him since his wife's death in 1885, over a year after its publication, so that the book seemed to him a kind of posthumously reared symbol, like the monument at Rock Creek, for what their marriage had meant to him. Yet the publication itself had been made in curious circumstances. It was published not only anonymously, which might have attracted attention, but under a pseudonym, Frances Snow Compton. By Adams' instruction it was not advertised and was not offered for review. Search of the press shows only a single notice of it, and only some five hundred and twenty-seven copies seem to have been sold in America, with a few more in England. Henry Holt stated late in life that Adams had told him he wanted to see what the book would do on its own merits without promotion of any sort, and that it was to be published at his own risk. Rather than an act of publication, these circumstances seem to suggest an act of exorcism or objective suppression, as if Adams could not get rid of an inner burden except by printing it up and throwing it away, as one drives a pin into the wax image of the person whom one wishes to destroy.

A simpler explanation is that Adams had modeled Esther Dudley in the book after his own wife, and rather more closely than he had modeled the other characters after his friends La Farge and King, with perhaps a trace of himself in the character modeled after King. Certainly Adams' inability to create independent characters, and his regular tendency to copy his friends as though they were types, suggests that the unique freshness, warmth, and affection with which Esther is modeled, and his concentration upon her sensibility rather than upon her intellect as the measure of her growth and response, could not have been an exception, but rather represented the result of his cultivated and endeared meditation upon the image of Marian

Adams. If the figure of Ratcliffe in *Democracy* represents a combination in excess of the features of Blaine, perhaps the figure of Esther represents a combination in imaginative penetration upon the features of his wife, as if he wished to bridge that loneliness that lies only between the most intimately connected people. As Robert Spiller points out in his Introduction to the facsimile reprint of *Esther,* Esther Dudley is the first intimation of the woman all sensibility and imagination whom Adams symbolically enthroned in the heart of the medieval church, and whose energy, the double energy of sex and faith, he heard transformed in the Hall of Dynamos at the Paris Exposition of 1900. If that is so, then Adams wrote his Esther twice over in heart's blood, once from the heart of his love for his wife and again in the heart of the imagination which he created.

But the figure of Esther Dudley drew significance from another source as well, from the symbolism of Hawthorne's story of that name. Adams supplies the clue when he has one of his characters refer to the identity of name. Let us then rehearse Hawthorne's fable before seeing what Adams did with his version of it. It is the fourth of the *Legends of the Province House* and recounts how, when the last royal governor of Massachusetts fled before the revolutionaries, an aged lady named Esther Dudley, who had been for many years attached to the House, insisted on remaining until, as she firmly expected, the next royal governor came. Meanwhile she would keep the House protected and would hold the great key of entry. As time passes and no governor appears, she preserves what of the old ritual she can, placing lights in the windows on the King's birthday, giving gingerbread wafers with the royal crown stamped on them to the children, and calling up for herself and the children images of the departed worthies of the province. Thus she served, and maintained in hallucinated being, the full symbols of the old order which had else departed the Boston community. The people accepted her as a survival. When she celebrated the King's birthday they "laughed aloud, and would have thrown mud against the blazing transparency of the King's crown and initials, only that they pitied the poor old dame, who was so dismally triumphant amid the wreck and ruin of the system to which she appertained." At last, with the wars over, Governor Hancock appears and old Esther Dudley, mistaking him for a royal governor, meets him at the entrance with her saved key. When she realizes her mistake she asks death to come quickly, for she has herself let in a traitor. Governor Hancock does his best to soothe her in a formal address, reminding her that the day of her faith has long been done, and that there is a new race and a new faith come to take her place. " 'Ceasing to model ourselves on ancestral superstitions,' " he concludes, " ' it is our faith and principle to press onward, onward! Yet,' continued he, turning to his attendants, 'let us reverence, for the last time, the stately and gorgeous prejudices of the tottering Past!' "

It will be observed how easily Hawthorne's language transposes itself to the terms of a religious rather than a social faith, and indeed, till the nineteenth century, the two forms of faith had commonly been fused, and seldom did either exist independent of the other, but rather—to use John Donne's word—interanimated each other to make a common life. So, if Hawthorne's words be read in a chosen light, the two faiths, in the royal order and in the Christian order, disappeared from Province Court at about the same time. Never afterward did the authority of God show more than the authority of the King over the people of Boston; and the symbols that remained of both were hardly understood by those who used them, and if used, were used as branches of police power rather than as the substances of insight.

As, in a way, Adams showed us in *Democracy* a state where the only responsible power was the police power and other powers were held irresponsibly, so, in *Esther,* he shows us a religion where the only effective power wielded by the church was also a kind of police power, and the great problems of faith were either received in indifference or were left to those outside the congregation. He shows us the figure of Hawthorne's Esther Dudley, with a difference. She does not hold the faith in an alien world, but she waits in an indifferent world for someone to bring the faith to her. Her struggle, then, is not to reject the false comer, but to see if she can accept him when he comes, in the form, as it happens, of the new rector of the new Episcopal Church of St. John on Fifth Avenue. Esther Dudley is a young woman with a high taste in art and a high achievement in humanity, serious, with a conscience, an intelligence, and an infinitely malleable sensibility; she needs only a mastering faith to generate conviction and strength. She is first presented to us in the company of Professor George Strong at the first service to be held in the as yet unfinished church by the new rector, Stephen Hazard, an old classmate at Harvard of Strong's. The congregation is fashionable to an extreme, and to Esther there is no sense of spirituality or religion either in the new church or its worshipers. Hazard, when he mounts the pulpit, strikes her as all eyes and all arrogance, for he has one of those faces which at a distance show nothing but eyes, and his text was, "He that hath ears, let him hear," which involves the notion of mastery in the priest who speaks. She is therefore both repelled and a little disturbed, annoyed at the fashion and the dumb show, and innerly eager to hear.

As the story goes, she hears, but it is not the right word, and she continues to be repelled after having made a profound and exhausting effort to submit. Hazard, of course, falls in love with her, so that her conversion, if it took place, would amount to a marriage to the church itself, which is bad theology but in this case a sound trope. It is not only the question of her love for the man Hazard, but the much more difficult question whether she can create for herself a sense of profession within the spiritual edifice of the church.

Other influences are of course brought to play upon her. There is her father, William Dudley, who is enough of an agnostic to have, on the one hand a family pew, and on the other hand to distrust the church on earth as much as he distrusts kingdom come. There are her aunt and uncle, Sarah and John Murray. John Murray is on the type of Mr. Dudley, and his wife Sarah characterizes the police-power influence in the church; she sees that things are run in an orderly fashion, takes her religion with her ancestry, and contrives to make it as fashionable and as sensible as her address. Then there is George Strong the geologist, who believes in science, and who holds Esther up to his old friend Hazard as having nothing medieval about her. "If she belongs to any beside the present, it is to the next world which artists want to see, when paganism will come again and we can give a divinity to every waterfall." To complete the quadrangle of influence there is Wharton, the artist, who was evidently modeled on Adams' close friend John La Farge, and of whom Adams wrote in the *Education:* "One was never quite sure of his whole meaning until too late to respond, for he had no difficulty in carrying different shades of contradiction in his mind. As he said of his friend Okakura, his thought ran as a stream runs through grass, hidden perhaps but always there." In *Esther,* it is as a complete being rather than as a mind that Wharton serves best as a foil; for the others, with one exception, work upon the young woman's mind as fragmentary beings. The exception is Catharine Brooke, the fresh fledgling from the West, called the Sage Hen by her friends; the spirit of the wide places, the earth goddess of the mountains and prairies from which she came, all problems to her are but artificial forms of the simple problem of assent. She can assent to anything that strikes her as having meaning or character, without trouble of will or stress of spirit, for to her things are their own meaning, and you only deprive them of meaning by thinking about them.

All these characters work against the interests of Hazard in their different ways, not because they particularly wish to but because each has his own characteristic inability to accept what Hazard stands for. Here again, Catharine Brooke is an apparent exception, for she is as willing to accept him as any other natural phenomenon. But that, to Hazard, is fatal, for to him the act of choice is a matter of infinite importance, leading either to damnation or salvation. You are powerless if you choose against him, for all energies, to his mind, belong to the church; and if you choose for him, you have given yourself up, and what energy you thought was yours will be devoured by the church. To be saved, in his rule, was altogether to be absorbed.

The events which serve to frame out the theme are even simpler than those in *Democracy*. There is a church service or two, a tea party or two, an evening or two, and conversations on the scaffold in the church where both Esther and Catharine are employed to help Wharton paint saints on the walls; there is the death bed of Mr. Dudley; and three longish interviews between Hazard and Esther, the last of which takes place at Niagara Falls where Esther has flown to escape what has become the importunity and intolerableness of his love. There is no intrigue, except the quite adventitious affair of the return of Wharton's dissolute bohemian wife, which mars the unity of the book. It is in the serious talk that everything takes place, or is felt to have been touched on, adumbrated, or invoked.

Running through the midmost part of many of these conversations there is the image of Petrarch and his unlucky love of Laura and how Petrarch made his ill luck in love stand him in so great stead that he saw God. All three men, each in his way, are obsessed with Petrarch, Wharton because he had had such an unlucky love himself; Hazard because he was doomed to have such a love—only it was God who deprived him of his love rather than his love that led him to God; and Strong because he was doomed to have neither love nor sight of God; and all three managed to transfer something of their obsessions to Catharine and Esther. Catharine, as usual, assented to Petrarch as one more possibility; Esther made a new version, a new obsession, for herself by adding her own sense to that of the other three. She became both Esther and Laura; as if Adams had resurrected her so that she might play Laura's role, the forlorn and devastated role of the woman who has been impossibly loved.

For Petrarch, as Stephen Hazard was fond of remarking, had put Laura on the same footing as his deity, and when he had lost her he groaned over the time thrown away on her. The lines most repeated are those Adams translated for Hazard's mouth to speak:

> As sight of God is the eternal life,
> No more we ask, nor more to wish we dare,

but which return to the Italian in Esther's repetition,

> Siccome eterna vita è veder dio,
> Nè più si brama, nè bramar più lice.

She murmured them often to herself while working in the church, "and at such moments," Adams goes on, Hazard "began to think that he was himself Petrarch, and that to repeat to his Laura the next two verses had become the destiny of his life." But it was not, as Petrarch himself would have had the circle completed, until Hazard was about to lose Esther forever that he was able to make his repetition aloud, when, as he said, he felt for the first time their beauty:

> So, lady, sight of you, in my despair,
> Brings paradise to this brief life and frail.

Esther tells him to hush! there is nothing but friendship left for them. But Stephen Hazard, as his name would suggest—for Stephen was the first martyr; and there was a divine hazard which it was needful for a martyr to take—could not stop there any more than Petrarch. It is the last scene in the book. Hazard has pursued her in order to make his final plea for her love within sound and sight of Niagara Falls to which she has fled because she has finally made up her mind that she cannot accept both him and his church. His arguments are as good as such arguments can be, that atheism and religion are two forms of ignorance, the only difference being that his ignorance is joined with a faith and a hope. He reminds her that Strong, the scientist, as well as himself "must at last trust in some mysterious and humanly incomprehensible form of words." Esther could make no answer, she is able only to receive, to feel, and to re-create impressions. "She sat for some moments silent," Adams writes, "while he gazed into her face, and her eyes wandered out to the gloomy and cloud-covered cataract. She felt herself being swept over it. Whichever way she moved, she had to look down into an abyss, and leap."

Hazard drives her, and himself, further; he admits that the tyranny of his church is his own tyranny, and that at last wrings a pure cry from Esther: Be generous! "It is not my fault if you and your profession are one; and of all things on earth, to be half-married must be the worst torture."

In that cry I think was some of Adams' heart's blood; but there was more to come. Hazard goes on, risking everything by holding back nothing, and Esther goes on, for her part, holding back nothing of her disappointment and distrust and contempt for the worldliness of his church. Hazard's last plea, no less honest than his first, was fatal: he appealed to the "natural instincts of her sex," and to that Esther let go her second and last cry, to which there was no answer, since there was as yet in Adams no further imagination of energy whether of sex or of faith. Yet in giving Esther the words he did, he showed the fatal drained weakness in his own position.

"Why must the church always appeal to my weakness and never to my strength! I ask for spiritual life and you send me back to my flesh and blood as though I were a tigress you were sending back to her cubs."

Esther Dudley felt that for herself she had lost the romance in her life; she had played Laura to the full; but she had also played her ancestral part and had given up the key that would open no gate. Like Madeleine in *Democracy* she had been unable to use the strength within her and so had fled; and like Madeleine, too, she had been partly wrong in not realizing where her strength lay, just as Hazard was unaware of where the weakness in his position was. Yet it hovered; what was powerless to be born was nevertheless about to be delivered, precisely as it had never been dead, except in men's eyes. Sex was the energy that moved them both, and faith, if it had existed, would have clarified the energy. Twenty years later, Adams showed that he knew it, but in the 1880's it was the failure to realize his knowledge that spilled his heart's blood.

Neither of Adams' novels reached conclusions; they were rather fables of the inconclusive; complementary to each other, they represented the gropings of a maturing mind after its

final theme. Taken together they make the turning-point of a
mind which had constructed itself primarily for a life of political action into a new life which should be predominantly imaginative and prophetic. But the turning had not finally been
made. Adams lived still between two worlds.

(1943)

12

The Harmony of True Liberalism: Henry Adams' *Mont-Saint-Michel and Chartres*

To HENRY ADAMS the Virgin of the twelfth century made the world intelligible by divinity that took second thought; Americans tried atheism in the guise of free factions—for which, as Adams says, the Virgin's world was not ready. The great question is whether Americans are—or even were in a simpler context—ready either. Adams never outright asked this question; but, thinking of all "those others" who groveled in desperation of faith, he asked Why not me?—just as he asked whether the compass moved man or man moved the compass. No single man alone is ever capable either of deciding his relation to the forces which move him and which he moves, or of choosing which of the forces he greatly feels will suffice his allegiance. Thus Dante, writing after 1300, chose three—the Virgin, St. Bernard, and St. Thomas; and out of these three extremes of force developed the fullest imagined order any single mind in the history of Christendom has ever seen.

So it was with the whole age that preceded Dante. Neither to the twelfth nor the thirteenth century was the Virgin enough. The very extremity of her lodgment in the heart of mankind —the extremity of the waywardness with which she stood between man and God—required that men addict themselves also to other extremes: the extreme of intellect self-willed and anarchic as in Abelard, the extreme of the direct intuition of God as in Bernard who held the world in contempt, or as in Francis who loved all God's first creations, and the extreme of intellect architectural and hierarchic as in the reason of Thomas. So, in his last three chapters, Adams turned to the study, or rather to the dramatization, of these extremes in the astonishing relation by which, at least in perspective, they seem parts concerting into a whole. Irreconcilable if their positions were taken in reaction to each other, they yet had a common relation which kept them, for a time, in perilous balance; and that, in Adams' language, was their relation to the Virgin —or to the Church filled with the Virgin who, from each point of view taken separately, was not enough, but who, if all the points of view were to survive in harmony, was all the more necessary. The harmony was of true liberalism. "A church which embraced," wrote Adams, "with equal sympathy, and within a hundred years, the Virgin, Saint Bernard, William of Champeaux and the School of Saint-Victor, Peter the Venerable, Saint Francis of Assisi, Saint Dominic, Saint Thomas Aquinas, and Saint Bonaventure, was more liberal than any modern State can afford to be. Radical contradictions the State may perhaps tolerate, though hardly, but never embrace or profess. Such elasticity long ago vanished from human thought."

Adams could have added, to complete the full federation of faith, kings, dukes, and knights, the courts and communes— not to mention the dual empire—which, with whatever conflicts, the Church also embraced; but let us force attention simply on the individuals as Adams orders them. The sequence of dominant qualities attached to these names might be:—The Human; God as emotion; the intellect as machine; the humanistic; the love of God as creation; orthodox balance in the Church; intellect as architect; intellect as intuition. Society— the Church—did not force these contradictions, though it did those of the Albigensians; nor did it unite them; it tolerated and embraced them. So thinking, we may without serious risk ask whether so wide a unity of contradictions did not come about rather through some underlying movement of inertia than through any policy made by charity of understanding or by any deliberately kept sense of self-elasticity in the presiding mind. At any rate, consciousness turned soon enough to omnicompetence, and faith to *plenitudo potestatis* when the furies of fanaticism reigned everywhere. Becoming exclusively conscious, the age made the terrible mistake of trying to balance *only* congruous forces, seeking to destroy the incongruous forces which weight so much either side of any balance. Faith, to work, cannot be exacerbated; and yet, to work, faith seems always either to have persecuted the unfaithful or put them beyond the pale of faith's benefits. This was relatively true of the twelfth and thirteenth centuries; absolutely true of the following age; it is only on balance and on a chosen fulcrum of the impossible ideal that Adams could see his Church universal as housing and succoring a liberal society. It may be risked, thinking by choice only in admiration of Adams' chosen age, that the beautiful pang of great aspiration striking on great tolerance was possible because that age found itself merging in a *series* of commitments which only made a conviction when felt together. The unity was in the convergence of straight lines in the *general* mind and was most likely never unity at all in any single mind—unless in Saint Thomas'.

Certainly the commitments to which Abelard—Adams' first example of an extreme—lent himself, hardly reflected unity at all. That apostle of the Holy Ghost saw little comfort or grace in any mind but his own. His function was chiefly that of irritant, innovator, anarchist as rebel, and his power was that of the unaided intellect everywhere passionately equal to itself, everywhere calamitously unequal to the world in which it found itself. He was rather a John Randolph of the Schools: his ultimate weapon was temper; and the source of temper was much the same, for each felt, as the self-willed mind must, that official society cheated him of the use of half his talents. But the differences, once the type is recognized, are greater than the resemblances. Abelard was master of the common technique of the intellect of his time—the kind of dialectic formalized in the syllogism—and the trouble he got into came from the fact that he pushed his technique a century ahead of what his time was prepared to accept and did so, so to speak, entirely on his own authority; he made theology the creature of dialectics and made dialectics human. St. Thomas, a century later, made dialectics the servant of theology and made theology angelic—at least in presumed authority. Abelard made anarchic hash of official theology by introducing the human concept into the irreconcilable conflict between Realism and Nominalism: he knew that that was what men did in practice, or at least that it was the practice of his own mind. St. Thomas knew that the human concept was necessary if the official theology was to succeed and therefore built it syllogism by syllogism into the aspiring architecture of that theology. Abelard failed; Thomas perhaps succeeded—later, when he was canonized, officially and against all comers. But their enemies—those who were against the Schools, against dialectic, against the supremacy of any form of intellect—were differently disposed. Abelard ran into the emotion and pride and intemperateness of St. Bernard when Bernard was at the height of his power, having made a Pope and a King his own. St. Thomas ran into the emotion of the Franciscans after the death of St. Francis when his friars had become learned with a kind of school system of their own. Abelard was silenced, though imperfectly. Thomas, when he died, left his doctrine in living controversy in which it was at length changed so far as time could change it, and for purposes he could not have envisaged, made official. Abelard was the victim of political jobbery; he was promoted into positions of power in which he lost his freedom; but what else was he asking for when he invented, under the title of *Sic et Non,* the trick of setting up inconsistent or contradictory statements of the authorities in the obloquy of parallel columns? Perhaps St. Thomas, too, asked his own fate; for his great effort was to compromise objectively, not to sharpen subjectively, the irreconcilable problems of the mind, and that is the type of effort official society always looks on with interest and adapts to its own uses, with or without the aspiration which made the compromise a viable balance.

But it was not only the triangle of Realism, Nominalism, and Conceptualism that interested Adams in Abelard's mind. Despite or because of his celebrated affairs with Héloïse, which left her an Isolde and him much less than a Tristan, Abelard was a catholic-puritan prototype of those reformers who destroyed, among other things, the divinity of the Virgin. On the one hand an early workman on that version of the Great Chain of Being which by the eighteenth century left man dangling entirely free—or guyed only by threads of reason—on the other hand he attempted to replace man's actual relation to the Virgin with an intangible relation to the Holy Ghost. The temptation to do so had been by logical necessity always present in the frame of the Trinity, and it was perhaps chiefly the popular faith in the Virgin that had kept the temptation down. A Trinity of Father, Mother, and Child was natural, intelligible, and traditional: it was the infinite series of the human family and was by instinct felt as parallel to the family —to the mystery—of heaven. How otherwise could God show his Oneness as Diversity understandably to man, and yet keep the mystery of it actual, within the power of man to rehearse? Christianity had worked for some centuries on a tacit compromise between the Official Trinity and the Natural Trinity, and the bridge between had been in the shifting, multiple role of the Virgin. The Virgin, as the center of something like a separate religion, had so to speak triangulated the two versions of the Trinity; she was the access to the understanding of either without loss of mystery. Abelard, a philosopher who dealt with theology as if it were a part of the study of law, seems to have resented the human need for the Virgin and to have insisted that the Trinity could be explained in conceptual terms alone; castrated, he had become a lover of the abstract; the mystery disappeared because he could no longer feel it. But he had on his side the strength of future history—much stronger than the methods of logic and law—and even though the Church condemned him and compelled him to burn his book with his own hands, he was able with the support of the Abbé Suger to retire into the Church itself and built an oratory of reeds and thatch, dedicated to the Trinity but called Paraclete, to which his scholars followed him in great numbers, so that he became the chief contender with Bernard for leadership in popular intellectual opinion. Though Bernard won at the time, by political means, Abelard would seem to have won in the end; for certainly the concept, shorn of some of its scholastic logic, won over emotion, shorn of its faith. The novelty of what came to be called the Monastery of the Paraclete was only less shocking than the novelty, as applied to Scripture and theology, of the critical principle of parallel columns, and it was on the second novelty that he was sentenced to silence, than which, with the paranoiac energy of his mind, there could have been no judgment harsher.

But between intellect presumptuous and emotion presumptuous, what choice? Abelard made God logical and necessitarian, to be known in the abstract, and touched by the pointed arch of conceptual thought. Bernard felt God as mystery and emotion, to be known by revelation, and touched through the Virgin. Each was exemplary in his certainty of authority, where the arrogance of faith was no less than the arrogance of reason. Each thought that because the other led wrong he himself led right, and without alternative. Each therefore condemned the other without a hearing, the one from the depths of experience, the other from the heights of possibility. To those not caught up in the precarious grandeur of either position, there is no choice between them, only a perpetual stress of alternation.

How extreme the alternation is may perhaps be seen if we

plant between the figures of Abbot Bernard of Clairvaux and Abbot Abelard of Saint-Gildas the very different figure of Abbot Suger of Saint-Denis; for it is right, in this labor to understand the ideal force of the twelfth century, that we should see the humanist and patron of art set between the schoolman and the saint. Adams makes a dozen references to Suger, to his exquisite abbey church and to its glass for the Virgin in which the figure of Suger himself appears prostrate at Mary's feet, and to the political power by which he intervened between Bernard and Abelard, and Bernard and Queen Eleanor. Perhaps Adams' sharpest reference for our purpose is when he remarks that the flèche on the old tower at Chartres does not represent Bernard, who assumed leadership of the Second Crusade under it, but does represent Suger, Peter the Venerable of Cluny, and Abelard. With that reference in mind we can consult the portrait of Suger drawn by Erwin Panofsky in the introduction to his translation of Suger's essays *On the Abbey Church of St. Denis and its Art Treasures*. After observing that Suger was that Patron of Art who, alone among patrons, described his intentions, Professor Panofsky goes on:

As the head and reorganizer of an abbey that in political significance and territorial wealth surpassed most bishoprics, as the Regent of France during the Second Crusade, and as the "loyal adviser and friend" of two French kings at a time when the Crown began to reassert its power after a long period of great weakness, Suger (born 1081 and Abbot of St. Denis from 1122 until his death in 1151) is an outstanding figure in the history of France; not without reason has he been called the father of the French monarchy that was to culminate in the state of Louis XIV.

In short, Suger not only stood in the middle between the extreme of Bernard's emotion and Abelard's intellect, he stood also in the middle of what we now regard as society: in the middle of its art, politics, and economics. A good business man, ripe with the sense of practicable equity, and strong with the sense of his own rectitude, he secured a relation between the Crown and his abbey which was without conflict. Perhaps he

took advantage, in this relation, of the fact that his abbey har-
bored the relics of the "Apostle of all Gaul," and was therefore
a royal abbey, the tomb of kings; certainly he took advantage
of it as a means of uniting all France under the Oriflamme of
St. Denis against the threat of invasion by the Emperor Henry
V. The force of the abbey was the residual strength by which
he developed the prestige of the Crown and by which, also,
he made himself the "mediator and tie of peace" with local
counts, with England, and with the Empire. He abused his
power, as Adams might have said, only for legitimate ends: the
aggrandizement of the crown and the beautification of his
abbey according to his own lights and temperament.

Both lights and temperament were to Bernard's mind presumptuous, nor were they safe from the attentions of Abelard's
intellect. Bernard and Suger were at opposite poles as to the
conduct of religious life and perhaps as to its object as well. To
Bernard proper monasticism meant blind obedience and self-
denial, to Suger discipline and moderation. Bernard made a
cult of silence, Suger of conversation: one was glad of fasts, the
other delighted to find cause for feasts. Bernard would have
kept the people out of Clairvaux, Suger made more and more
room for the crowds at Saint-Denis. Bernard distrusted every
splendor of the senses. Suger thought nothing "would be a
graver sin of omission than to withhold from the service of God
and His saints what he had empowered nature to supply and
men to perfect: vessels of gold or precious stone adorned with
pearls and gems, golden candelabra and altar panels, sculpture
and stained glass, mosaic and enamel work, lustrous vestments
and tapestries": exactly what was to Bernard detestable. Yet
Suger represented perfectly a source or nexus of spiritual life
in the great fraction of men which Bernard did not understand
at all. As Professor Panofsky puts it: "If the spiritual pre-
eminence of St. Denis was Suger's conviction, its material em-
bellishment was his passion: the Holy Martyrs, whose 'sacred
ashes' could be carried only by the king and took precedence
over all other relics however much revered, had to have the
most beautiful church in France." Bernard left a treatise in

intense prose on the Steps of Humility, Suger left a record in elegant and Euphuistic Latin on the beauty and dignity of his abbey church. To Bernard art was a temporal snare—and a great risk to faith and spirit. Suger found in the philosophy of light transmitted from the Platonists to Christian terms by the Pseudo-Dionysius (whom he took to be the St. Denis of his own abbey) permission "to greet material beauty as a vehicle of spiritual beatitude instead of forcing him to flee from it as though from a temptation; and to conceive of the moral as well as the physical universe, not as a monochrome in black and white but as a harmony of many colors."

Suger was a proto-humanist, and no more a scholastic than he was a saint. Where he thought it prudent to make and keep friendly terms with Bernard, he also found himself generous enough to protect Abelard from Bernard and to tolerate, even when aimed against himself, the most irritating habits of Abelard's intellect. For when Abelard, after his mutilation, became a monk of Saint-Denis, he did a small piece of scholarly research which demonstrated that the patron saint of the abbey could not possibly be the Dionysius the Areopagite mentioned in Acts. This was treason to the Crown and Abelard was jailed; yet when he escaped, Suger seems to have made it possible for the affair to be overlooked providing Abelard kept out of monasteries. Later, when Abelard first got into trouble with Bernard, it was Suger who arranged the jobbery whereby Abelard's "punishment" was to be made abbot of Saint-Gildas. Protection of the independent and intransigent intellect against the authority of intransigent emotion could hardly have gone further. It was men like Suger and like John of Salisbury (himself a pupil of Abelard's, clerk to Thomas à Becket, and at the end of his life bishop of Chartres) who kept the extremes of twelfth-century intransigence in a relation of balance. Suger as well as John might have said, "I prefer to doubt, rather than rashly define what is hidden." But perhaps they spoke as statesmen and artists must, between good and evil; the one wanted beauty, the other charity; both wanted peace and order in the world they dealt with.

But they could only have it so, if at all, in terms of some extreme ideal or of some balance of extreme ideals—some Bernard and Abelard, some Francis and Thomas, some Pascal and Newton, each pair making extreme poles of emotion and intellect. One of the curiosities in studying such extremes is that the relation often becomes clearest in the art that lies between; for it is art that shows what happens to the extremes when actually experienced by minds otherwise ordinary. Art, in any fixed relation, is always the extreme of the ordinary. So Adams seems to have found; the emotions expressed by the artists, whether in architecture or poetry, gave him illustrations of what mystic and philosopher, what act and thought, must humanly have meant; the next step was inevitably to treat mystic and philosopher as themselves artists, only greater than the others—which was precisely how Adams had treated the Virgin; and the last step was by a little stretch of his nature to become himself an artist treating his own actual experience as material for his art. There was no other way Adams could master his material in detail or feel it together as unity; it was solely as artist that he could bring to his material what he had and take from it what he needed. He brought his feelings and experienced an emotion.

It is only with the sense that there was some such scheme in Adams' mind in the last three chapters of *Chartres* that we can understand what he is doing there or make any use of it for ourselves. How otherwise can we accept, as a preparation for considering St. Francis, an implied comparison of Bernard to Voltaire, and a positive comparison of Bernard to Bacon, the one having regard to a measure of skepticism, and the other having to do with contempt for schoolmasters. Voltaire distrusted those excesses of human reason which confounded human dignity, and Bacon repelled those which prevented direct response to direct experience. Both, together with Bernard, depended on revelation, insight, intuition, and on the observation of these. Each gave a path to human emotion and concentrated its force as an image of salvation; only in their sense of revelation did they differ fundamentally, and the nature of revelation was determined for each by the drift of his age—in their skepticism, which was governed by their faith in emotion, they were one. They were skeptical of what prevented access to reality. Each grasped reality directly, by authority. Authority, when used, is authorship, and the product of authorship is art—whatever else it may be at the same time. As if to forget whatever else it might be—as if to come on it plain— Adams inserts into his discussion of French mysticism text and translation of hymns from the school of Saint-Victor which if not pure authorship were pure emotion, and inserts also, just beside the hymns, what he calls the true Promethean lyric of Pascal, a passage put together from the *Pensées* expressing the pure emotion of a man who cannot tell whether to deny God or the validity of his own mind. The emotion of incertitude is put against the emotion of conviction. And what Adams says about each reaches into his own experience and becomes part of his autobiography. Let us put them side by side.

Of Pascal: "The mind that recoils from itself can only commit a sort of ecstatic suicide; it must absorb itself in God; and in the bankruptcy of twelfth-century science the western Christian seemed actually on the point of attainment; he, like Pascal, touched God behind the veil of skepticism." Adams had a closer relation to Pascal than is here apparent, and we shall come to it shortly, but can we not at this point assure ourselves that Adams was pointing to part of his own experience in the figure of Pascal? Ecstatic suicide is the recoil of a mind given, as Adams' mind in part was, to logic. Love is the recoil of the mind given, as another part of Adams' mind was, to faith and the poetry of faith, as in the Victorian hymns. "The art of this poetry of love and hope," writes Adams, "which marked the mystics, lay of course in the background of shadows which marked the cloister. 'Inter vania nihil vanius est homine.' Man is an imperceptible atom trying to become one with God." But he does not stop there; he adds as if in direct consequence to his image of mystical poetry a digression out of the concern of his own imagination. "If ever modern science achieves a definition of energy, possibly it may borrow the figure: Energy is the inherent effort of every multiplicity to become unity." It is no digression; it is the thing that was there all along, and in the personal sense it was to see it in terms of the twelfth and thirteenth centuries that Adams had made his whole study. It is such an apparent digression and true central stroke as this that makes us see how little Adams went to his Middle Age for escape and withdrawal and how much for backing and renewal. He had to read his need in another language to understand it in his own. Thus he writes of the French mystics: "The human soul was an atom that could unite with God only as a simple element"—the element of their own sinfulness, and then, to bring the idea back to himself, remarks that they "showed in their mysticism the same French reasonableness; the sense of measure, of logic, of science; the allegiance to form; the transparency of thought, which the French mind has always shown on its surface like a shell of nacre." The French saints were not extravagant; their aims were high, but not beyond reaching; and they expressed the paradox that the French mystics were not mystical, neither as mystics proper nor in philosophy, the arts, and religion. The drama was in balance, the climax in reserve, the substance in humanity. It was not Bernard and Abelard (nor Suger and John, at their easier levels) who could show the ultimate extravagance of the forces that were balanced, but rather Francis and Thomas, beside whom Bernard was practical and Abelard timid and their quarrels trivial; yet it is in the dramatization of the extremes of emotion and intellect which Adams makes of Francis and Thomas that we can understand the unity he saw in the Virgin, and the kind of unity he hoped to create for himself and for his own world; not the unity of Thomas, but the unity of both with what had necessarily to come in between to make either tolerable. By this treatment, Adams seems to imply that the Virgin was a little nearer Francis than Thomas, but perhaps he meant only that Thomas stood in a little greater credit than Francis in the twentieth-century mind as he did in the thirteenth, so that Francis needed the extra support.

Certainly no man ever stood more fully on the strength and

purity and risk of his own emotion than Francis does in
Adams' portrait of him. He knew what he wanted and he knew
what was possible; precisely what was visionary and beyond
what had been hitherto possible. He wanted, in absolute poverty of self, to love equally every created thing, from the grass
and flowers, the birds and men, to fire and death, and to praise
what he loved without taint of desire, and so love God. This
the intensity of his faith not only allowed him to do; it also, for
a time, swept thousands after him; his example gave shape and
humanity to a great popular emotion by which the world
might be denied without loss but a rise in love for all that God
had created in it. The emotion did not last Francis' lifetime;
but as an ideal of essential Christianity, an ideal of a deep
recurrent state of the human heart, the example of Francis
has never disappeared. It persists in the feeling we have as to
what manner of man Francis must have been each time we re-
read the Sermon to the Birds and the Little Song of the Sun.

Francis inflamed the substance of religion with its spirit. For
when Francis denied the world he denied chiefly human pretensions—and particularly institutional pretensions—about the
world; and he did so in order joyously to affirm the world
and human life and all life at every level that had not reached
pretension. Francis was a troubadour, a finder and worker
at the great role of saint, or else a saint playing the role of
poet. To him poverty was the riches of freedom from the
pretensions of wealth; poverty alone had accompanied Jesus
on the cross and afterwards to His borrowed grave, and it was
therefore that he invoked our Lady of Poverty: "O poorest
Jesus, the grace I beg of Thee is to bestow on me the highest
poverty." As with poverty, so with chastity and obedience. To
him chastity was the riches of freedom from the pretensions of
lust; obedience was these riches with which he praised sister
fire as dancing and warmth and radiance; the birds as the carol
of creation; the flowers and grasses as creation itself; and sister
death as the angel of return to the creator. All creation, loved,
was its own meaning.

All this, to Francis, was science and philosophy as well as

religion. To him humility, simplicity, and poverty were true science and led to heaven. To him fire and air and trees and birds had rational beings as well as men; and man no more than a thrush needed a psalter to praise God, and no more than a brook did he need logic. One of his friars once answered a series of theological arguments, says Adams, by a tune on a rustic flute. Such attitudes were certainly heretical to the official church, very much like the attitudes of the Virgin as the architects and poets had seen her. Adams puts it that "the Virgin was human; Francis was elementary nature itself, like sun and air; he was Greek in his joy of life," and goes on to quote in proof the Sermon to the Birds, with which fresh in mind he is able to explain why the heresies were accepted. "The immense popular charm of Saint Francis, as of the Virgin, was precisely his heresies. Both were illogical and heretical by essence. . . . The charm of the twelfth-century Church was that it knew how to be illogical—no great moral authority ever knew it better—when God himself became illogical. . . . Both were human ideals too intensely realized to be resisted merely because they were illogical." Thus Francis was able, when asked to control his order more in conformity to the general rules for religious orders, to answer in a great public convention including St. Dominic and many schoolmen, that he had to reject all rules but his own, which God had "mercifully pointed out and granted" to him. Then he concluded: "And God said that he wanted me to be a pauper and an idiot—a great fool—in this world, and would not lead us by any other path of science than this. But by your science and syllogisms God will confound you, and I trust in God's warders, the devils, that through them God shall punish you, and you will yet come back to your proper station with shame, whether you will or no." The effect of these words, as reported in *The Mirror of Perfection,* was that "the Cardinal was utterly dumbfounded and answered nothing; and all the brothers were scared to death," to which Adams adds his own imagination: "For a single instant, in the flash of Francis' passion, the whole mass of five thousand monks in a state of semi-ecstasy recoiled before the impassable gulf that opened be-

tween them and the Church." It was to such an image Adams
had been leading up, and he at once made the best of it. "No
one was to blame—no one ever is to blame—because God
wanted contradictory things, and man tried to carry out, as he
saw them, God's trusts. The schoolmen saw their duty in one
direction; Francis saw his in another." Apparently both were
failures, since after five hundred years society could adopt neither, though neither has yet been finally judged, and no alternative has been proposed.

Adams exaggerates the gap between intellect and act; he
could not only afford to but was compelled to, just as the
Church could not afford to and was compelled, for its life and
the life of society, to try both paths and ignore the gap between. The stress of that effort was perhaps the stress of life
itself in the institution of the Church, so that it is no surprise
to note that the Church moved first one way, then the other.
But it is even less of a surprise that Francis should have felt
antipathy to that half of the Church represented by the schoolmen. "If 'nostra domina paupertas' had a mortal enemy, it was
not the pride beneath a scarlet robe, but that in a schoolmas-
ter's ferule." For the rest Francis accepted the Church without
qualms or question as necessary for the ministry of the sacra-
ments, though otherwise he did not make much use of it. That
is, Francis felt only the inevitable conflict of the Ideal of the
Gospel and the Actual of the Church. Just as Francis was the
extreme to which the Church (under Innocent III) was willing
to go toward the ideal gospel, so the Church was the institution
which made his gospel possible. The Church was faced with
spiritual and lay revolt; Francis needed both spiritual and institutional support. They needed each other, to purify hysteria
and to humble authority. Each was the extreme the other
could tolerate. But the toleration was precarious; shortly before his death, the Church refused his primitive rule and afterwards, though she canonized him, denied the validity of his
testament. The Church only recognized the fact that Francis'
order itself had split into various degrees of rigor and relaxation. The Church accepted Francis as she accepted the Virgin

—as effects of popular will which could not be controlled until they could be, first, institutionalized and, second, formalized. Where the Virgin and Francis gave vigor in actuality to the life of the Church, the Church responded by turning the vigor into machinery: mankind was incapable of so much actuality for more than a few years. The interim period of imperfect control —of unstable balance—was the high point of aspiration, and, more than that, the maximum reach of actuality in the history of the Christian Church.

But Adams is all the more right for being a little wrong in exaggerating the gap between Francis and the schoolmen. The Church was heritage and opportunity which alone made his energy take form and achieve more than exemplary significance. The lesson for modern institutions should be plain: that balance is better than control, that responsibility is better than rule, that risk is better than security, and that stability is death. But the stability and security here spoken of are not the opposites of anarchy and starvation; they are the opposites, rather, of flexibility and variousness. The institutions of society must be kept flexible and various enough to receive and react to new impressions. This perhaps is the lifetime argument Henry Adams makes, directly in *Gallatin,* implicitly in *Chartres,* and in the compositional process of the *Education;* if we can feel the arguments and follow the process we have learned Adams' lesson.

Just the same, there is little use in the lesson of the Unstable Balance as illustrated in Francis, unless we think of it in terms of something Adams was well aware of but which he hardly touched on in his book, namely the ferocious and single-minded brutality which was the complement of every aspiration in the balance. The brutalities balanced too: those done for God, for Church, for simple aggrandizement, or for their own sake were somehow of equal weight and pressure in the general turbulence of society. Man is most violent in asserting and imposing order when his society is least capable of receiving it. The instance that comes to mind here has to do with the persecution of the Albigensians, which ran from the beginning of the eleventh century through the fourteenth century, but which reached its height in the twenty years between 1209 and 1229, when under the name of Crusade great numbers of heretics and others were massacred and burned, the authority of the Church was perfected, the House of Capet absorbed the south of France, and the Provençal civilization was destroyed. If the Crusade began in 1209, also in that year Francis collected his first eleven disciples. To Innocent III the Crusade was necessary to the safety of the Church; having protected himself, he could afford, seven years later, to sanction another and milder form of the same heresy in the ragged barefoot friars minor of Francis. There remains a wonder. The Albigensians —hating the world—effected some reform in the Church—in the conduct and celibacy of the clergy—and were exterminated. Yet the Church digested, transformed, and relaxed to more nearly normal monastic practice, the Franciscans—who loved God's creatures—and did so before Francis' death, as preparation for his canonization. The wonder is in the double act of slaughter and sanction; in that double act is the dreadful balance of denial and assent on which human identity is perched, and on each arm of which hangs, seesawing, fruit of pure Eden line. It is against the background of such a double act that Adams justly quotes Francis' *Cantico del Sole* as "the last word in religion, as it was probably its first," and turns then to grapple with its alternative in St. Thomas Aquinas.

Adams does not argue precisely that Thomas was the last word of human intellect, but he certainly treats him as if he were the archetype for whatever that last word might turn out to be: some form of forms, some system, in which every need and interest of man, if he accepted the authority of the system, would find itself harmoniously at home. One of the great temptations of the mind is to accept such an authority for the sake of the harmony without regard to the mutilations and suppressions and violent frivolities thus imposed on what is harmonized; the only worse temptation, in this direction, is to accept the mutilated harmony for the sake of the authority. Thomas found himself in an age when both these temptations

242

were open and had been indeed succumbed to, in part, by a hard-set papacy and a series of rising national states. Political and cultural unity were gone; emotional and religious unity were shaken. Thomas, under the authority of reason, had to rearrange and balance the disparate forces; whether consciously or not, his work tries to make the new assertions of authority tolerable by the force of intellect alone. Like Francis, he remains as example and inspiration, until a different world arrives to make intellect alone an adequate force.

For Thomas' task the times were wrong, though he could not have known it; he came just after what Adams calls the moment of equilibrium in 1215, when his thought would have given additional strength to social movement rather than mere expressive perfection, had the equilibrium only endured; but not again till perhaps the middle of the nineteenth century did an equilibrium of conflicting forces capable of absorbing his thought recur in the form of a liberal, scientific, and determined society. All that was needed was translation of that thought to the terms of economics, biology, and physics. The Roman Church, in making Thomas official a little after the Franco-Prussian War, moved in the opposite direction and tried to translate modern society into the old terms. Adams, accepting the society so far as he could understand it, tried to see what St. Thomas would be like as an expressive part of it, with the result that he sees him putting into balance the laws of science and the needs of man. The appeal of Thomas was for Adams and the Church the same, that his decisions were miracles, logical conclusions in advance of knowledge, which self-evidently added to the fund of positive knowledge. The method of the syllogism was human (Bernard thought it was presumptuously so) but in Thomas' hands it obtained what seemed superhumanly authoritative results, with an ease, assurance, and absence of effort as remarkable as was the apparently methodless method of Francis. On the face of it, Thomas merely selected between disputed opinions and rendered decisions; what gave his decisions the effect of miracle was the early maturity and elegance of form now associated with mathematical thought. His thought did not need to be immediately implicated in experience because it built on what had been abstracted from previous experience by previous minds using earlier forms of his own method. In such a system, if the form were elegant enough, one thing *truly* led to another. Thus the power of decision was immensely energized, as in poetry or architecture, by the sequence of formal relations. Conviction was inescapable so long as the forms held.

"Beginning," Adams writes, "with the foundation which is God and God's active presence in His Church, Thomas next built God into the walls and towers of His Church, in the Trinity and its creation of mind and matter in time and space; then finally he filled the Church by uniting mind and matter in man, or man's soul, giving to humanity a free will that rose, like the flèche, to heaven." In such a structure God—the foundation—could not be taken for granted, but had to be proved a concrete thing by the senses: *nihil est in intellectu quin prius fuerit in sensu.* The simple assumption of realists like William of Champeaux would not do, any more than the even simpler assumptions of conceptual-minded nominalists like Abelard; the one led to pantheism, the other to materialism, neither to the God of the Church, who had to balance both. Adams presents Thomas' situation by comparing it to that of a modern mechanical physicist. Thomas saw motion and inferred motor: the mechanic saw motion and inferred energy everywhere at work. Thomas inferred at the end (going backwards to the beginning) an intelligent, fixed motor; the mechanic saw the possibility but held it incapable of proof. To Thomas the notion of form—elegance of articulation of thought—required unity, and that requirement was to him adequate proof. There the mechanic—though Adams does not say so—must have confessed himself as dumbfounded as the Cardinal to whom Francis addressed his plea for freedom from control by the schools.

At any rate to think so is one way of seeing the gap between Thomas and Francis, and the greater gap between both and the twentieth century Adams knew. Both the fullness and freshness of Francis' faith and the ageless authority of Thomas'

reason seem far from the center of twentieth-century movement—so far that they seem, as Thomas meant them to seem,
very close together. To Thomas faith was not personal, what
he believed he believed as a proposition; revelation was to him
new knowledge rather than new life, and he appealed to the
fount of natural knowledge through Aristotle and Plato. The
mysteries of faith and the truths of reason were distinct forms
of knowledge, the first taking priority over the second, but
both capable of being handled in much the same way. Theology and philosophy were two branches of the same subject,
capable, so to speak, of receiving the same form. Thus the real
question for him was always: How shall we reach a predetermined conclusion in which the forms of revelation and of
reason shall be united? The answer his work made was: By
architecture: the art in which stability of forms in their most
daring use was proof of truth and manifestation of intent or
need. One hardly knows whether it was the analogy to architecture or that to physical science in Thomas which appealed
to Adams most; the ideas of imagination and of law were
equally near his heart; and the envisaged results, in a liberal
state and a predetermined mind, left him equally at home.

Doubtless Adams made no choice; doubtless the essence of
Thomas' attractive force was that by the authority of his form
he composed the dualism of fate and freedom, mechanism and
vital purpose, anarchy and organization, order and chaos, in a
single assertion of unity. By in some sense assenting to both at
the same time he achieved the perilous balance of Christian
theology. God was the metamorphosing margin between pantheism and materialism: the transforming act which created
both law and contingent freedom of choice within the law: so
that a criminal might choose "between the guillotine and the
gallows, without infringing on the supremacy of the judge."
The solution fitted needs, not facts. The needs were in man's
nature. Man

insisted that the universe was a unit, but that he was a universe; that
energy was one, but that he was another energy; that God was

omnipotent, but that man was free. The contradiction had always existed, exists still, and must always exist, unless man either admits that he is a machine, or agrees that anarchy and chaos are the habit of nature, and law and order its accident. The agreement may become possible, but it was not possible in the thirteenth century nor is it now. Saint Thomas' settlement could not be a simple one, or final, except for practical use, but it served, and it holds good still.

The mystics, skeptical of themselves, doubted the worth of Thomas' man-god relation; as Adams says, the mystics got into the Church by breaking the windows and had no use for what was to them the lock-step of the syllogism. "But society at large accepted and retains Saint Thomas' man much as Saint Thomas delivered him to the Government; a two-sided being, free or unfree, responsible or irresponsible, an energy or a victim of energy, moved by choice or moved by compulsion, as the interests of society seemed for the moment to need."

Such a theology—such a philosophy—could not help becoming art and ending in aspiration, like the spire on a church. Conceiving God as having the merely original freedom to create out of nothing the intent of his own will, Thomas gave man the contingent freedom to be wicked or absurd, and thus gave him more than the State ever did—some choice, a place in the Church and in the life to come, and a sense of holding a seat at the center of the universe. That is, the square foundation-tower of God's Act of Creation, which was the normal energy of God, the façade of the Church, "suddenly, without show of effort, without break, without logical violence, became a many-sided, voluntary, vanishing human soul." As with the old flèche at Chartres the transition was perfect, "and neither Villard de Honnecourt nor Duns Scotus could distinguish where God's power ends and man's free will begins."

It will only strengthen our conviction that Thomas' system —whatever we think of it as philosophy or theology—was great art, the formal expression of man's actual needs and responses, if we try to assess the practical situation which it met. Thomas came just after an age—1115 to 1215—in which thought and emotion flowered in unusual balance, and at the beginning of an age when the dominant thought and the dominant emotion, being out of balance, became equally fanatic. Where the institutions of society had been relatively free, that is, in some sense mutually responsible, they seemed now drawn once again into the panacea of absolutism where claims of power were made without mutuality or intent of balance, as we would say today unilaterally. The horror more than the glory of human institutions began to become manifest. Thomas labored to give the old balance a new form on the old or inherited model, and so far as what was inherited was actually transmitted he succeeded, both for his own and later time. But the dominant powers of the time had hardly more than ancestral piety for the old model—as we can see in the degeneration of the Crusades and the rise of the commercial spirit, in the multiplication of heresy, and in the substitution throughout the political world of arbitrary for representative power. Here is a sentence written of the papacy of Thomas' time, which shows how far that institution had gone and why its new position, by inspiring both rebellion and imitation, precipitated insoluble conflicts. "In the Popes of the thirteenth century this *plenitudo potestatis*, legislative, administrative, financial, and almost doctrinal, was undenied; and in their omnicompetence, so long striven for, they had the opportunity of making their gravest errors." Beside that sentence, here are three more, comparing the attitude toward the papal power of Gregory VII, who began this part of the history of the papacy in the eleventh century, and Innocent III who brought the papal power to its zenith in the thirteenth. "His [Innocent III's] spirit was never dismayed by the gulf lying between the high Petrine theory of sovereignty and the historical and more limited practice of the Roman bishop. It could be bridged, if one went carefully enough. It never affected him as strongly as it had affected Gregory VII, with his finer intuition and darker sense of conflict."

In such a situation it is not surprising that Thomas should have failed of pervasive influence in his own time. His thought in part moved with the time, in that it attempted to balance the new assertions of power, but in part it moved against and ahead of the time in that it anticipated an intellectual rigor for which the time was not prepared. His contemporary influence was controversial, and his system became a question of university politics at Paris and Oxford. The Franciscans especially attacked it for its presumptuous Aristotelianism and its usurpation of rational access to authority. Adams' own school of Chartres (as it disappeared) was anti-Aquinan, as was Robert Grosseteste in England. Thomas was *the other and impossible thing* to many minds, for there remained still a strong anti-authoritarian flow in thirteenth-century thought. And there was besides widespread conservative distrust of Thomas' means of supporting the universality of the Church on the Creed by setting up another and parallel authority in reason. The actual triumph of Thomas came in the nineteenth century when he was used to supply the authority in reason which the Church needed to encompass modern science and the combination of popular and dictatorial (non-Christian and anti-clerical) nations into which western society was breaking apart. As art, Thomas' triumph was the greater in that the skill of his solution (of the problem of balancing Faith and Reason) did not transpire until his system was used against a worthy opponent.

But his system would have been art even less than truth if it had not also been made in response to a radical problem of his own time. Here is the judgment of W. H. V. Reade in *The Cambridge Medieval History:*

The heroic attempt of Aquinas to define a sphere for philosophy without detriment to the sovereign rights of theology was simply one expression of the whole medieval struggle so to adjust the temporal power to the spiritual as to create a dominion of political freedom within the higher sovereignty of the Church. The project, we may hold, was impossible. It is certain, at least, that it failed. . . . Yet this failure was the last and greatest achievement of medieval philosophy. . . . The air of finality that hangs over the weighty pages of Aquinas has a prophetic significance. For the work of Aquinas, consummate in its kind, had exhausted the materials then existing for the edifice of philosophy, though not the ingenious art of arranging them in new patterns. The great age of dialectic had vanished with the rebirth of Aristotle; the age of Aristotelianism was to perish in still greater revolutions. Alike in politics and in science more portentous questions were soon to be uttered: whether a society founded on an immutable gospel could find room for the modern State, and whether a *scientia experimentalis* beyond the dreams of Roger Bacon could be reconciled with an infallible Church.

The notion will not bear too much pushing, but judging by Adams' response to him, Thomas anticipated these questions; for they concerned any State not wholly theocratic but with a tendency to become so and any body of knowledge in peril of thinking itself complete, and it was Thomas' intent to keep Faith and Reason open except as to origin and conclusions. That he has been used otherwise does not invalidate the intent, any more than the misuse or amelioration of Francis' rule invalidates the *Cantico del Sole*. What the nineteenth-century Church saw (from an immutable Gospel and an infallible Church) was the need for an order which would "place" the parliamentary state and a body of inclusive, inconclusive knowledge in an over-all architecture of aspiration and authority. The twentieth-century Adams, from the *other* point of view, saw the need which an immutable state and an infallible knowledge had for a gospel and a church. Both saw the need expressed in Thomas. Where the Church saw authority, Adams saw art: as objective and conventional in the Summa as in the glass of the Prodigal Son, but also as personal and human as the Court of the Queen of Heaven.

Thomas, that is, did not stand alone. Like the cathedrals, Thomas was the result of two hundred years of experiment and discussion. The art and the science—the religion and theology—were one because they represented a complex balance of effort by many debating minds around what Adams calls "the despotic central idea" of organic unity. The system of St. Thomas and the great cathedrals was possible only to minds in which that organic unity was a vital dogma, minds, that is, in which it operated both as energy or will and as the unfailing

249

standard of criticism. That was how the truth of the universe looked to the thirteenth-century mind, as an organic unity to which all roads and all lines of work necessarily led. Truth was not a relation, as it tends to seem in the twentieth century, but the source of the relatedness of things; and the difference is the difference between two kinds of universe, that in which unity is grasped precariously by faith and that in which centralization is imposed by incessant, and always inadequate, measurement of relations. Adams seemed to feel that it was not man who had changed the universe, but that it was the universe, by showing a different aspect as it moved, which had changed man's mind. But he also seemed to feel that the consequent weakening of intensity in man's mind was relative rather than absolute, and that therefore the work was all to do over again under new and more difficult conditions. Some kind of organic unity was his own ideal, and he had come on it by having grasped it imaginatively, in its last apparition, at the height of the Middle Ages. *Mont-Saint-Michel and Chartres* is the record of the imagination.

(*1952*)

13

Henry Adams: Three Late Moments

1. Richard's Prison Song

WHEN HENRY ADAMS left South Lincoln, Massachusetts, for Washington in the late fall of 1912, he had recovered as much as he was likely to do from the apoplectic shock which had stricken him in the spring. But if he was to return to his own house, alone, partially disabled, and always liable to another shock, someone must be found to keep him company, keep him alive, and keep him supplied with such contacts with the outside world as he either could not or did not care to make for himself. The supply of nieces, however copious and regular, might yet show gaps; for even nieces had lives of their own. What was needed was a permanent niece in residence—which may be a very general and ambiguous title, but which represented a constantly heavy if widely variable duty. How much care and thought went into the search is immaterial; no search could have produced more satisfaction than the event showed. Miss Aileen Tone, a young and charming woman, and already a "niece" of sorts, not only performed the full function of niece in residence to perfection, but also by the accident of her private talent gave Adams' sensibility a new vent and his imagination a final and extraordinarily apt form of expression. She brought him what he had apparently not dreamed of, the music of the Light Ages. As music is the ultimate art, the purest or the most primitive, the most formally sophisticated and incredibly the least committed to any prejudice or experience except itself, so it provided Adams the only form of expression he ever found that could unite all his aspiration and all his interest without distrust and anguish and doubt. Despair itself, in music, and even at seventy-five, could be a Vita Nuova.

Miss Tone, tall, slender, dark-eyed, Catholic by faith and training, and of a robustious feminine vivacity, had besides the accomplishments of personality a trained and lovely voice and a taste for singing such few old French songs as she had come across. When she came to Adams' house from New York she felt instinctively that her singing days were over for the time. However, she brought her music with her, including a new anthology of old French songs. That was Adams' stroke of luck, coming late but all the more lucky for that. He apparently remembered that she sang and brought the subject up himself. Sing? he said to her. Why not? Open all the doors in the house, and sing! She showed him her new anthology and told him that there were a few songs in it of the twelfth century. He showed astonishment and doubt; it had not occurred to him that there might be music for the poetry he had loved and worked on for so many years; and when he actually heard the words sung he was tremendously excited—to what degree and extent is shown by the following letter to Ward Thoron, who was still in the south of France.

13 Dec. 1912
1603 H Street

Dear Ward

Your letter of Nov. 30 arrives this morning. Since my last I have dug deep in new 12th century holes which needs, as digging, much help.

The new vein was opened by Miss Tone, when she came to make me a visit a month ago. She brought music, and especially a publication by J. B. Wekerlin, "Echos du Temps Passé," Vol. I, quite lately published, which began with a Chanson of the Châtelain de Coucy, who (Wekerlin says) died in 1192 in battle with the Saracens, on Richard's Crusade. Wekerlin says he himself copied the musical notation from Ms. 63 *fonds Paulmy*. When I saw that—just calmly written and printed as though it were figs,—I had three more paralytic strokes in straight sequence. Can such things overcome us like a winter's cloud, I cried. No! it can't be! and I begged Miss Tone to sing it, which nothing loath, she did. To our delight, it was as good as the 12th century glass at Chartres,—but quite that! The Tree of Jesse, blues, greens, and all. It was a misericorde,—*Merci Clamans*, —in face of death. Quite exquisite! Full of 12th century style and feeling! and quiet and simple as Richard's Prison-song.

Then we turned the page and found a song of Thibaut, also charming; and references to 63 Chansons notées of Thibaut's. Then two lovely songs from Robin et Marion, with references to the *fonds Lavallière* and *fonds Cangé*. For years I have pined for *Robins m'aime, Robins m'a*, and there it was! I had more fits—many more!

I set to work, and wrote to everyone on this side to help; but of course I must get the work done in Paris, and everywhere. There is no reason why I may not find this music anywhere. No one has touched it, or only to print it for cursed modern ears. I must search all over Europe for the music of Richard's Prison-song, which I want above all. It was and is the greatest historical monument possible to discover. My only wish is to live long enough to discover it.

I want you to take up the job, and have every bit of 12th and 13th century music now to be found, photographed or copied for me as soon as possible. I have not a minute to spare. If able to do it, I shall come over to Paris in March to help, and bring Miss Tone. We shall set up a college of the 12th century. Meanwhile if you will help, give orders at once. You can start on fcs 5000 to begin with. We shall have to do much travel, and I am a mighty poor wreck to travel or work, far feebler than anyone knows; but this interest will keep me on. Looly will be in it, and I hope Elsie Adams, and later Mrs. Keep.

I write in a hurry to catch Saturday's steamer. If necessary use the telegraph. The printed books are no great good. They are chiefly

Tarbé, "Chansons de Châtelain de Coucy," and of Thibaut de Champagne, Francisque Michel, 1830 (musical arrangement by Perne). And Lieder des Castellanes von Coucy by F. Fath, Heidelberg, 1880.

Good luck! Yrs in haste

H. A.

I will send you my new edition or anything else you want.

Mr. Thoron went to work with such great success that by the fifth of February Adams had his copy of the Prison Song and had cabled as his first thanks the single word Beautiful.

Neither Adams' surprise that the music existed, his delight in it and excited further search, nor his special desire for the score of the Prison Song, should seem in the circumstances anything but natural. Almost nothing of twelfth-century music was known in 1912, and what little was known was either unreadable or misread; the notation was then commonly misunderstood; the monks of Solesmes were then at work on the Gregorian modes but nothing had been done at all for the secular music; one man's guess was hardly better than another man's gross mistake, and only the wrong people had done any extensive guessing. Yet the few songs Miss Tone brought with her, with the help they got in reading them from Father John La Farge, who was stationed that year near Washington, and from Jean Beck whom they brought on precisely to help them, showed at once the pure strength of grace and directness. It was a matter, for Adams, almost of instinctive taste; if the twelfth century had any music at all it was bound to be great music; and the more one got of it the better off one would be. To Adams, the passion of pursuit, and discrimination, was among his continuing pleasures.

The pursuit of the Prison Song of Richard Cœur de Lion was instilled with a deeper passion than pleasure, and amounted indeed to the expression of a consciously inherited bias on a parallel and personal plane. The pursuit, that is, was of pattern, almost of composition. That the element of pattern or composition in question was personal to Adams' sense of his own life, and in a way equivocal or ambiguous, should heighten its interest for analysis: it is the style of the man himself, the quality of his imagination outside his works, of which we grow aware, and so learn to feel the slow cumulus of its pressure holding the works together.

The evidence should tell the story, and fancy need only see where the fragments fit. John Quincy Adams made an entry in his Diary for November 7, 1830, from which the following sentences are extracted.

No one knows and few can conceive, the agony of mind that I have suffered from the time that I was made by circumstances, and not by my volition, a candidate for the Presidency till I was dismissed from that station by the failure of my re-election. They were feelings to be suppressed; and they were suppressed. No human being has ever heard me complain. Domestic calamity, far heavier than political disappointment or disaster can possibly be, overtook me immediately after my fall from power. . . . In the French opera of *Richard Cœur-de-Lion,* the minstrel, Blondel, sings under the walls of his prison a song, beginning:

O, Richard! O, mon Roi!
L'univers t'abandonne.

When I first heard this song, forty-five years ago, at one of the first representations of that delightful play, it made an indelible impression upon my memory, without imagining that I should ever feel its force so much closer home. In the year 1829 scarce a day passed that did not bring it to my thought.

It should be observed that this entry is made a year and a half after the time to which it refers, and that no entry in 1829 mentions Richard at all.

When Henry Adams first read his grandfather's Diary for 1829 is uncertain; his father began publishing it in 1873 and ended in 1877; and Henry referred to it in his *New England Federalism,* published in 1877. At any rate he refers to the passage again in a letter from Paris to Elizabeth Cameron, 29 December 1891.

I hurried off to the Opéra Comique [he wrote], to perform an act of piety to the memory of my revered grandfather. Some people might think it a queer place for the purpose, and the association of ideas may not be obvious even to you, but it is simple. . . . He was so

255

much attached to Grétry's music that when he was turned out of the Presidency he could think of nothing, for days together, but "Oh, Richard, oh, mon roy, l'univers t'abandonne"; and as I had never heard the opera, I thought I would see it now that it had been revived at the Opéra Comique. Nothing more delightfully rococo and simple could well be, than the music of Grétry. To think that it was fin de siècle too—and shows it in the words—and led directly to the French Revolution. . . . Unluckily the Opéra Comique, which used to be the cheerfullest place in Paris, is now to me the dreariest, and poor Richard howled mournfully as though time had troubled him.

Rococo and simple and *fin de siècle* were not enough for Adams—or only enough for piety; the sentiment was sound, the occasion dramatic, and the tone enduring—for King Richard, for John Quincy Adams, and for his grandson—but as it were incipiently, putatively, and far short of the great level of imaginative actuality that a king, a president, or a mere memory-ridden man deserved. King Richard's own words, when he found them, were "a true cry of the heart, such as no other king ever approached," and he inserted his paraphrase of them, together with the text, on page 222 of his *Chartres*. The reader who is curious, or who needs to be satisfied of the long pains Adams took on this poem, may be referred to three letters he wrote to Frederick Bliss Luquiens on the 5th, 15th, and 21st of March 1911, when he was preparing the 1912 edition of *Chartres*. They are included in "Seventeen Letters of Henry Adams," edited by Professor Luquiens in the *Yale Review* for October 1920. The poem doubtless remains what Adams called it, "one of the chief monuments of English literature," and its verses show "the direct energy, simplicity, and intensity of the Chanson of Roland." Here we are concerned primarily with the use Adams made of it as an objective and actualizing symbol of his own suffering—an element in the symbolic pattern of acceptance, rejection, and expression in which he could not help composing his sense of his own life. The reader may find the texts as easily in *Chartres* as elsewhere. Here the beginning, the end, and an emphasis on one or two facts should suffice.

> Ja nus hons pris ne dirat sa raison
> Adroitement s'ansi com dolans non;
> Mais par confort puet il faire chanson.
>
> . . . .
>
> Comtesse suer, vostre pris soverain
> Vos saut et gart cil a cui je me claim
> Et par cui je suix pris.
> Je n'ou di pas de celi de Chartain
> La meire Loweïs.

The translation:

> No prisoner can tell his honest thought
> Unless he speaks as one who suffers **wrong**;
> But for his comfort he may make a song.
>
> . . . .
>
> Countess sister! your sovereign fame
> May he preserve whose help I claim,
> Victim for whom am I!
> I say not this of Chartre's dame,
> Mother of Louis!

The paraphrase is rough and some of the words lose force because of the exigences of English rhyme; Adams' accomplish-
ment as a poet was not equal to his instinct; but it should help
the reader feel his way into the Old French and find something
of what absorbed Adams there. "Pris," for example, which is
the end word of every stanza except the last, where it is the
center-word, is a strong, almost a physical word for the condition of being a prisoner; for being confined, isolated, and, as it
may be emphasized here, *deprived*. For that is the meaning
that may best be associated with the following phrase, where
"adroitement" surely means more than with *finesse d'esprit*,
means surely something nearer its etymon sense of uprightness
and justice, so communicating to "dolans" the sense of a wrong
justly felt as grievous. So, if you like, John Quincy Adams, who
was certainly a deprived as well as an abandoned man, may
have been imagined by his grandson as feeling. John Quincy
turned to a Providence in whom his faith wavered and kept
on with his work; his grandson, deprived by a Providence in

whom he did not believe at all, turned like Richard, at least by indirection, to the half-human and wayward deity of Our Lady of Chartres, in whom he did not believe either, except imaginatively, and also kept on with his work.

The music, when it came, the translation from verbal sound with all its accidents and barriers of sense and commitments to place and person, to pure and uncommitted emotion, only heightened the actuality of the Prison Song as symbol. As sung sound it meant *all* that it meant, and nothing else; hence it could bear infinite repetition, as in the condition of poetry it could not, and Adams had it sung to him and his friends many times in his last years without ever having to explain to others or troubling himself as to its particular meanings. Perhaps he did not know them, except as music.

Possibly it is necessary to point out what ought to be obvious, that there is nothing peculiar and certainly nothing mystical about Adams' relation to the Prison Song. It is only the instance, the particular, that is limited to Adams; as human behavior it is universal—and as for the instance, it was only, as his friend Henry James would have said, an extraordinary case of the normal. The imagination gives itself to music as to nothing else, without awkwardness or embarrassment or any sense of violation. People sing hymns or love songs; dance in public to music; attend opera or symphony or chamber concerts; and by a great and decent convention share and express the most terrible or most fundamental emotions, and do it over and over again, without feeling or even considering the necessity of wearing any mask other than that the music provides—which is no mask at all, but a voice. Adams with his Prison Song did no more than his neighbors; only he may have done it more deliberately, as an act of art, than is usual among even sensitive men. It is only one more illustration of the difference between the nondescript imagination and the representative imagination. The first we may say administers its experience without altering it and almost without suffering it. The difference is not in vitality but in response; for the representative imagination is driven constantly to force its experience to the crisis of expression. By expression we mean the achievement of external or objective form, where as a rule the experience becomes impersonal in just the degree that it is expressed, however personal its origin. The first paradox is, as any age of faith will show, that in that objectivity is our only sight of unanimity; and the worse paradox is that in even the best—the most objective—expression of private emotion there is an arbitrary or willful element which makes the moment of crisis the verge of collapse or emptiness. Hence we turn as Adams turned in his Prison Song to the support of some existing form or convention of the general imagination, as if, merely by existing and because we share it, its own profoundly arbitrary character might virtually lose itself in the exacting actuality of form. All that we are truly capable of believing is in what we can put into our gesture, our buildings, our images, or our song; and we know best what it is that we believe, curiously, when we respond as well as act, sometimes when we do not act at all but only respond, when we participate as spectator or audience: which is to say when we take account of the infinite complexities in the simple guise of objective form, the flèche on a church, a bar in a song. So Adams took his Prison Song, as deliberate art, hardly veiled gesture, to focus his sense of life. So we may take Adams, and know him best, at the remove of those forms in which he found himself.

2. Henry Adams; Henry James: The War

WHEN THE LAST war broke out, Adams was caught summering with his music and his nieces at the Château Coubertin, not far from Paris. After a few days of difficult arrangement, they drove to Dieppe, equipped with special permissions and stopped every few miles, and found the hospitals already filled with wounded. They were just in time, for they caught the last boat for fleeing passengers across the channel, and went down to Stepleton in Dorset.

The war was then expected to be short in the sense that few could imagine it as long and those who did were greedy to think themselves wrong. There would be either a decisive battle, or money, or men, or both, would run out; embattled *nations* was a mere figure of speech, as when we say the heavens rain, meaning a few clouds. At any rate Adams waited, taking what proved to be only the first mild lesson in four years of exhausting strain. No situation could have made the lesson more tolerable than the Dorset countryside in late summer and early autumn. Their music they had brought with them; the landscape was there; and old friends could be imported.

Among these last was Henry James, who came over twice from Rye and talked with Adams late into the night. This was the final and perhaps an unusually full meeting of the two extreme—and therefore deeply related—types of American imagination. Report must be regrettably conjectural, but with an element of firm predictability on two counts—their past lives and the war.

There had been an exchange of letters the previous spring over James's *Notes of a Son and Brother* in which James had attempted to reimagine, or as he would himself have said, to revise, his own version of post-bellum America. Both men were concerned with experience as education, and to both the judgment of education called for a specialized form of autobiography in which the individual was suppressed in the act only to be caught in the style. Let us say here merely that James imagined human reality always through dramatizing the bristling sensual record of the instance—almost any instance that had a story in it—and let the pattern, the type, the vis a tergo, take care of itself, which under the stress of the imaginative process it commonly did. Adams, on the other hand, tended in a given case to depend on his feeling for human type and pattern—for history and lines of force—as the source of drama, and hence saw the individual as generalized *first:* so that whatever happened would fall into the pattern, if you only had the wit to see how—which Adams by the strength of his conceptual imagination did commonly see. To put it another way, Adams' set of intellectual instruments more or less *predicted* what he would discover; James resorted to instruments only to ascertain what his sensibility had *already* discovered. If we may quote T. S. Eliot's remark that Henry James had a mind—a sensibility—so fine that no mere idea could ever violate it, then we should say that Henry Adams had an intellect so fine —so energized—that no mere item of sensibility could ever violate that. To be inviolate in one respect fairly calls for penalties in another. Adams paid in a want of freshness, James in a want of restraint. Adams might run dry, James frequently ran off the track. The thinness in James comes from excess of feeling; in Adams thinness comes, not from the want of feeling, but from excess of consideration. To make a maxim of it, excess of sensibility sterilizes the significance of form; excess of intellect reduces form, and sometimes imagination itself, to formula: the tendency of excess in either direction is towards the disappearance of subject-matter. There is a kind of shrinkage of value that occurs under the stress of the general excess we call sophistication, which is one trait common to James and Adams.

It was the signs of that shrinkage that James and Adams felt in each other as the penalty for the extraordinary riches provided. In the following letter from James to Adams I think we may feel a struck balance of the weakness and strength of both men; of James directly, of Adams by implication: for both men were obstinately artists at bottom.

March 21, 1914

My dear Henry,

I have your melancholy outpouring of the 7th, and I know not how better to acknowledge it than by the full recognition of its unmitigated blackness. *Of course* we are the lone survivors, of course the past that was our lives is at the bottom of an abyss—if the abyss *has* any bottom; of course, too, there's no use talking unless one particularly *wants* to. But the purpose, almost, of my printed divagations was to show you that one *can*, strange to say, still want to—or at least can behave as if one did. Behold me therefore so behaving—and apparently capable of continuing to do so. I still find my consciousness

261

interesting—under *cultivation* of the interest. Cultivate it *with* me, dear Henry—that's what I hoped to make you do—to cultivate yours for all that it has in common with mine. *Why* mine yields an interest I don't know that I can tell you, but I don't challenge or quarrel with it—I encourage it with a ghastly grin. You see I still, in presence of life (or of what you deny to be such,) have reactions—as many as possible—and the book I sent you is a proof of them. It's, I suppose, because I am that queer monster, the artist, an obstinate finality, an inexhaustible sensibility. Hence the reactions—appearances, memories, many things, go on playing upon it with consequences that I note and "enjoy" (grim word!) noting. It all takes doing and I *do*. I believe I shall do yet again—it is still an act of life. But you perform them still yourself—and I don't know what keeps me from calling your letter a charming one! There we are, and it's a blessing that you understand—I admit indeed alone—your all-faithful

Henry James.

Neither man thought of the other in terms of his full work; certainly James had not digested Adams' privately printed work; and the evidence seems to suggest that Adams had read little of James since the 'eighties. Their relationship was personal; their knowledge of each other on the social rather than the imaginative plane; and their community of purpose only instinctively recognized. Yet they made the most valuable criticism of each other: in their work and in their personalities as seen side by side. They had both enough in common and enough in radical opposition to be complementary figures. Perhaps they talked their late hours out only on London in the 'seventies and Washington in the 'eighties; they had been members of a vanishing society and each had kept a sharp eye —astigmatic, selective, but preternaturally sharp—upon what vanished, including each other. It would be more artistically probable—more just—to think of the two men, at last, in their seventies, bald-headed, and precisely at the moment that their world did blow up, finding a common ground, each strengthening the other, in a common vision of all that had happened —of all that they had, exactly, by the power of imagination, actually survived.

However that may be, it is certain that they talked of the war; and there the listener would have gotten a contrast in response sharper than any other blow could have provided. The war assaulted each man with equal violence. For each it was a long, never-subsiding panic of emotion, felt physically as stress and queasiness. Under that stress James broke down, and Adams did not. James had nothing but his sensibility, which withstood nothing, but sucked up the horror like a vacuum; he thought it criminal to think of anything but the war, and in the end resorted to hatred and fury and utter surrender of his sensibility to every idea and device of the Allied cause. In James's letters of the war years we see the unsteady stages of the violation of a great sensibility. Adams, on the contrary, had a formed and provisional intellect which guided and controlled his sensibility without excess. He was partisan—even as partisan as James—but he kept what he had previously most to depend on, he kept his head. He knew the war was coming, it was the outward toppling of a collapse that had already occurred. Another world, or else a dead world, was coming, in which he would take no part. He was the morning star fading unnoticed in a thunderstorm at dawn. He wanted greatly to live the war through to see what would happen. Meanwhile he could bear the stress because it was only the critical accentuation of normal stress, and because he knew it would be criminal *not* to think of something else. He could write to W. R. Thayer on December 17, 1915, that he was sorry for the Germans and proceed to compare, jocularly, his own plight with theirs. He had an imaginative refuge, characteristically his own, ready for everything. He wrote to Professor Luquiens on the 29th of December, 1914, from Washington, that they had sung all the best of the chansons, and that the "charm of the pursuit has almost obliterated that of the other studies." "Throughout all the terrors and roars of German howitzers," he wrote at the end, "we have lived on 'Seigneurs Sachez' and 'A vous amants,' in France and England as here, and they alone have given us repose. Reims fell, but Thibaut rose."

263

It should be said that these songs are songs of the Crusades. Professor Luquiens thought Adams' words wonderfully beautiful because they referred to the songs "of men unafraid to die." Perhaps another perspective would be more illuminating. Certainly it is a perspective more appropriate to our own day when we have again the sense of waiting our own turn to share in a new catastrophe which is but an extension, or a contagion of the old, I mean that before the explosive spectacle of human failure in the form of "energy without direction"—which is how Adams characterized the war—what is better, what possible other refuge could there be for the assaulted imagination than an art that still lived, and still intimately witnessed perhaps the surest and straightest direction human energy ever took.

3. Here Is My Portrait

NO REFUGE WAS complete, or was meant to be. In Washington, with his old friend Spring Rice, now the British Ambassador, at one elbow, and the war itself in the form of newspapers at the other, Adams wrote to Ward Thoron, in the middle of December, that the war kept him awake nights. The world had ended; then let Thoron come home and help make a new one. Adams had always expected the worst and it had always been worse than he expected. Here was Christmas—Peace and Good Will—and he, Adams, reminded himself of St. Augustine correcting syntax before the Germans came. Just after the New Year he wrote succinctly to Louisa Hooper, who remained in Lausanne, that there was in Washington a curious odor of W. J. Bryan, Wilson, sixty-odd senators, and Beacon Street, and that he had said ten years ago all he had to say about war. To both he wrote also about the music. There was much still to explore; and the songs to the Virgin were best.

Here we may find ourselves striking once again the major theme of Adams' life. He was in an imaginative, wholly poetic

sense increasingly the Virgin's man, as he remained historically
an eighteenth-century republican, as he had become intellec-
tually a twentieth-century speculative skeptic, and as he was
also all along, and always committedly, a man of the world. In
his poem called "Buddha and Brahma," written in 1891 but
not printed until October 1915 in the *Yale Review*, Adams had
expressed the central aspect of the predicament in which so
complex an allegiance might find itself.

> But we, who cannot fly the world, must seek
> To live two separate lives; one, in the world
> Which we must ever seem to treat as real;
> The other in ourselves, behind a veil
> Not to be raised without disturbing both.

The right solution, or one right solution, might consist, since
one could not actively deny the world like Buddha, in imaginatively giving one's inner allegiance to the Virgin. In the
Chartres (page 267) Adams emphasizes the possibility by comparing Milton's "They also serve, who only stand and wait" to
the lines spoken by a thirteenth-century chevalier when repre-
hended by his squire for lingering at a Mass to the Virgin
when the tournament was about to begin.

> "Amis!" ce dist li chevalier,
> "Cil tournoie moult noblement
> Qui le servise dieu entent."

This is rendered:

> "Friend!" said to him the chevalier,
> "He tourneys very nobly too,
> Who only hears God's service through."

It remained, however, only a possibility, and as a practical formula never reached the condition of temptation. Neither the
Virgin nor Gautama Buddha could any longer be brought into
the world without destruction except as poetry, and even as
poetry, if the symbol was made too explicit, the risk was immi-
nent—both to one's sense of the world and to one's sense of
oneself. Yet the religious necessity was at times paramount; the

veil had to be raised—by a mere fatality of insight or shock or understanding, frequently enough to seem habitual, one again and again saw it tremble to the thinnest transparency; and both lives were profoundly disturbed. Recovery—repose—was either in silence or in a kind of symbolic dramatization where one both participated and looked on, hardly knowing which, or it might be, rarely, that recovery was found in expression, which might be serious or poetic as in the talk with Gabrielle Chanler, or might be mocking and cryptically different, or might be, too, a combination, a blending of both. We are concerned with the disturbance seen as recovery, and we fasten, for our signs, both on the strokes of character and the strokes of imagination, strokes where the pattern of a life shows like a luminous embroidery.

For the Catholic Church itself, Adams had in his last years as always the respect due to a great historical institution and the interest due to a philosophy which, admirable in itself, he could not share. With Catholics as individuals he felt, as he often told Miss Tone, more and more *en rapport*. They had by virtue of their faith a security and fullness of spiritual tenure, or seemed to have, which non-Catholics only got, if at all, precariously, and by the constant uncertain stress of the individual imagination. It was a matter for envy as well as admiration. The Catholic instincts were right; Catholic practice, for him, impossible. Rapport was not unanimity; rapport was dramatic understanding, provisional and poetic, at arm's length, altogether in parallel. One was oneself always something else again; something tough, resonant within and not easily played upon from without, always, at bottom, a little willfully independent. One might give up by final default, and confess failure; but one could not give in—however near one came to doing so—precisely because such a surrender, to a scrupulous and provisioned soul, would amount to the surrender of integrity, would seem indeed a plain giving out. This sentiment, if correctly drawn, is characteristic of the puritan protestant tradition, which Adams consciously inherited, as qualified by the *riches* of the skepticism of Montaigne—or say any skepticism which sets every movement of the mind upon a provisional and frankly questionable basis.

For the protestant, who lacked the intercessory human grace and imagination of the Virgin, there was always agony in the approach to God. As skepticism increased it either impaired the sensibility as in Huxley and Sam Butler, or with a certain sophistication and a brand-new excruciating agony, it added to and richened the texture of the imagination as in Emily Dickinson, Henry James, and Henry Adams. If Adams had known Emily Dickinson's line, Faith is the Experiment of our Lord, he would not only have approved it but have borrowed it and transformed it to his own purpose. For twenty years he had saturated himself in the great imaginative experiment of the Virgin which had brought the diverse ener- gies of the Light Ages to unified purpose, and now in his last years he was lost in her music, the ultimate—ethereal—form that the imagination took. But he knew, unrelentingly, that the faith was experimental, however necessary, and that the experiment was imaginative, however vital its sources. Once it had enlivened and humanized a church; now the church was a simulacrum, a set shell, a spent experiment, a formula of im- agination that no longer applied—though individuals might and did occasionally rehearse the old imagination by instinct rather than formula: when one sympathized, deeply, as with an anachronism, which one might not reach and which could not be efficacious, with the charm, the humanity, the frailty, and the personal aspiration that now alone replaced, almost fortuitously, what was once a faith past reason.

To the individual Catholics whom he knew he was sympa- thetic to the point where some thought he was at heart one of them. His niece Mabel La Farge seems to have thought so and gave her views at the end of her introduction to her *Letters to a Niece*. Certainly there were many Catholics at Adams' house in the late years. Mrs. La Farge and Aileen Tone were both Catholics. Father John La Farge, the youngest son of the artist, a Jesuit, was stationed at a missionary parish in Maryland from about 1912 to 1914. Pale, intellectual, of what some call an Oriental—a Buddhistic—demeanor, Father La Farge, by birth a family friend, frequently visited Adams' house at this time, both out of friendship and to help with the music. Father Fay, of the Catholic University, was a constant visitor from 1912 to the end. Round, jolly, worldly to a degree that only an ordained priest can attain without loss of spirituality, he was quite the opposite type to Father La Farge, and quite as useful. He, too, helped with the music. Besides the clergy, there were of course such Catholics as the Winthrop Chanlers, who came in whenever they were in Washington. It would be as true to say that Catholics were attracted to Adams as that Adams was attracted to Catholics. In either case there was a barrier when what seemed to either the proper scope of the imagination was overpassed. For example, in offering indirectly to send to Justine Ward—who in the zeal of conversion had become a sort of lay nun—copies of such chansons as she wanted, Adams differentiated himself from her as being emphatically "of the world." And to the contrary, he reports in the spring of 1914 that he had been accused of being too intimate with Our Lady.

On the worldly plane the whole matter is best given in a report Mrs. Winthrop Chanler gives in her *Roman Spring*. "I asked him once," she writes, "how it was he did not become a Catholic, seeing he assented so warmly to what we believed. 'Do you think, my child, that Rhadamanthus would be less severe?' He said this half solemnly with a defiant twinkle in his eye." That was all; it makes an ellipsis lucid precisely because it is tantalizing. Rhadamanthus, the son of Zeus by Europa, was, it will be remembered, translated to Elysium because of the ideal justice of his life and opinions. Rhadamanthus, for any church, would be better outside, and probably better off for himself, too. One would not wish to see one's sense of justice forced to operate as a sense of mockery.

On the plane of the rational, but driven, imagination, which was for Adams always behind the worldly plane and disturbing it, the predicament of the modern sensibility confronted with the religious problem is expressed in the following extraordinary letter, dated February 15, 1915, to Henry Osborn

Taylor. Taylor had sent Adams his *Medieval Mind* and this
was Adams' answer.

My dear Scholar and Master

As you know, I am poor and ignorant besides being a senile, rep-
tile, and in one respect also am morally bad, for I never loved or
taught facts, if I could help it, having that antipathy to facts which
only idiots and philosophers attain; but with these drawbacks perhaps you will allow me to thank you for your last volume. I have
read it with grateful attention.

I cannot criticise. The field is not mine. I am concerned in it only
as a spectator, and now a very blind one. I cannot correct or suggest,
but I can do what may be equally useful.—I can tell you what effect
your treatment has on me, and as I am probably an extreme case, you
may infer its effect on opposite natures.

Perhaps I ought to say first, that once, at the most trying crisis of
my life—and of his—our old teacher in wisdom, Gurney, said to me
that of all moral supports in trial only one was nearly sufficient.
That was the Stoic. I cannot say that I have found it so, except in
theory, but I am talking theory. Putting myself in that position I
read your book.

You see at once what must follow,—what did in fact follow. Of
course all that goes before is futile except as failure; all that follows
after is escape—flying the ring,—by assuming an unprovable other
world. Logically, the religious solution is inadmissible,—pure hypothesis. It discards reason. I do not object to it on that account: as a
working energy I prefer instinct to reason; but as you put it, the
Augustinian adjustment seems to be only the Stoic, with a supernat-
ural or hypothetical supplement nailed to it by violence. The reli-
gionist preached it, and called it Faith.

Therefore to me the effect is of ending there. The moral adjustment, as a story, ended with Marcus Aurelius. There you lead us with
kind and sympathetic hands; but there, over the door to the religious
labyrinth, you, like Lord Kelvin, write the word Failure. Faith, not
Reason, goes beyond.

What you intend, either as reason or faith, is another matter. I am
giving only the effect on one mind. At the present moment perhaps,
the moral is somewhat pointed,—to me decidedly peaked. If you are
writing Failure over one door and Lord Kelvin over another, and the
Germans over the third and last—that of energy without direction,

—I think I had better quit. I said so ten years ago, but I put it down to my personal equation then, and I cannot believe that you mean it now. Are we, then, to go back to Faith? If so, is it to be the early Christian or Stoic?

The early Christian I take to have been abandoned long ago by the failure of Christ to reappear and judge the world. Whatever faith is to save us, it cannot be that. Is it, then, the Stoic?

I do not ask these questions for answers,—only to show you what questions are roused by your book, in order that, if you like, you may in any case, insert some provision against misapprehension. Of course, had I been the author, I should perhaps have been drawn into giving different values to the solutions, and should very likely have laboured damnably over the Buddhists and the Stoics. Marcus Aurelius would have been my type of highest human attainment. Even as it is, I would give a new cent to have a really good book on the Stoics. If there is one, lend it me. I need badly to find one man in history to admire. I am in near peril of turning Christian, and rolling in the mud in an agony of human mortification. All these other fellows did it,—why not I?

Ever yrs
Henry Adams

Characteristically, Adams' answer set up an attitude different from Taylor's and raised questions that neither mind could answer except provisionally, speculatively, imaginatively. In the mind's conversations as in those of manners the great thing was, as Adams never tired of saying, to keep the ball rolling, to furnish the cue, to *donner la réplique*. Other comment would be superfluous, except this, that while the letter may seem to represent the whole of Adams' intelligence at the age of seventy-seven, it actually does nothing of the sort. Rhadamanthus is still there. Adams' unity was a product not a multiplier, and the product varied from time to time. The unity of such a mind is what happens when you experience all you can manage of its aspects together. Here we may go on, with two pertinent illustrations of aspects not touched on in the long letter above. One is from a letter to Taylor written a year later, April 17, 1916, which begins by sympathizing with Taylor's cold, and proceeds with the following fable.

Yesterday I walked in the spring woods, and met a fly. To that fly I said:—'Fly! do you want me to tell you the truth about yourself?' And that fly looked at me—carefully—and said:—'You be damned.'

They have told me that now, just seventy-eight times. They are not tired, but I am. If you happen on a copy of my Education, kindly burn it. I have no longer a wish to educate. I think that, as an insect, I know! that is, I don't care to know any more. So, I'll join the beetles. They were, I think, the first, the greatest, and most successful experiment of nature. Read Fabre! Talk to Aileen!

So much for the fable and its gloss. Then he continues.

We go to Lenox! Seek us there! You can be as futile there as in New York:—almost as futile as here. No! I hate extreme and violent expressions! No! not as futile as here!

And, serious again, he ends off:

Stick to Montaigne. Never mind the rest. I can't find the book on the stoics.

The fable is seminal form; because it can never be applied exactly, it can always be applied with unfailing freshness; which is why Adams indulged in the form—it caught meaning from the air as it flew. The beetles are another matter, an obsessional image for energy as instinct, but used by Adams to refresh the powers of imagination: if you *imagine* life as instinctive, then your experience of it will once again be equivalent to, or will declare its own meaning.

But the transition to our second illustration is neither in the fly nor the beetle but in the admonition, stick to Montaigne. Montaigne is the great master of ironic wisdom, of wisdom which by the poetry of its manners suggests another version of itself in the very act of finishing or polishing off its present expression. That is its irony, the riches of its skepticism, that in reconciling two points of view into one it manages to imply the possibility of a third and quite unadjusted point of view. It was this aspect of Montaigne that I think Adams would have meant Taylor and himself to stick to; certainly there is something of the ironic *and* poetic quality of Montaigne in the

271

following anecdote—both in itself and as it illuminates by contrast the letter, the fable, and the Rhadamanthine reserve.

One evening towards the end of his life the conversation turned on John Singer Sargent. It may have been in the fall of 1917, when Sargent was in Washington painting President Wilson. Someone asked Adams why Sargent had not done him, and Adams answered immediately and with force: "I never would let Sargent paint my portrait. I knew too well what he would do to me, and I was too much of a coward." He paused, then added in a different tone, "But there *is* a portrait of me, and I have it here"—he rose and went to a drawer—"a twelfth century portrait";—he came back—"I have it here." What he had was a postcard photograph of a sculptured panel of the Nativity from the rood-loft or choir of Chartres Cathedral. He had sometimes sent copies to friends, calling it his favorite poem, but it had not hitherto been called a portrait. It has been said that Adams himself discovered the panel lost in a cellar and had caused it to be restored. The scene is traditional but executed with more familiar and intimate grace than is usual. The Virgin is reclining, weary and delicate, her right hand holding her head, her left arm a long curve running down to two fingers tenderly at the throat of the baby's swaddling clothes as he lies in the manger. Joseph, unfortunately decapitated, leans over the Virgin looking down at the baby, and holding back a fold of the drapery of the Virgin's bed in his hands. At one end of the manger is a sheep and at the other a donkey, his nose in the manger. The unknown artists had been faithful to the point of imagination. Adams handed the card. "That is my portrait," he said patiently. "It is the donkey sniffing the straw."

The story is all there, Marcus Aurelius, Fly, Rhadamanthus, and all. This was as near as Adams ever came to the Virgin or her son; it happened some seven or eight centuries ago; very near in the direction of faith, but not very near in the direction of a church; exactly how near the reader will have to figure as his own imagination bids him. It was a poem as well as a portrait; in neither art should a meaning be too closely nailed down, for in time another meaning is sure to spring the nails.

Here, through the focus of Adams' relation to religion, all we have been saying comes to this: Increasingly as he grew older, Adams was able to feel his own complexity as unity only in the form of a fable or a riddle. He could no longer, if indeed he ever did, feel the complexity as resolvable into a single energy. Even wisdom had to become poetry to be efficacious, and the poetry, as like as not, was not one's own but just what was available or came to hand. But let us protect ourselves from a false emphasis on religion, or wisdom, or poetry. We have been dealing with a relation as if it were sudden, and a relation of old age, which was actually the relation and the damage of a lifetime and only transpired in old age. We could as well, for truth, turn imagination backwards, even as far back as the ganoid fish Pteraspis or the Civil War, and find in the seed, pressed and perfect but a little cramped for expression, the final flower. Our ends resort to their means; constantly the pattern, like character, of which it is the inert form, reasserts itself, until in the end nothing but pattern is left—and character only its last sophistication.

(1940)